HTML & XML

for beginners

MICHAEL MORRISON

Microsoft

PUBLISHED BY
Microsoft Press
A Division of Microsoft Corporation
One Microsoft Way
Redmond, Washington 98052-6399

Library of Congress Cataloging-in-Publication Data
Morrison, Michael, 1970-
        HTML and XML for Beginners / Michael Morrison.
            p. cm.
        Includes index.
        ISBN 0-7356-1189-0
        1. HTML (Document markup language)   2. XML (Document markup language) I.
    Title.

    QA76.76.H94 M68   2001
    005.7'2--dc21   2001030415

Printed and bound in the United States of America.

1 2 3 4 5 6 7 8 9   QWE   6 5 4 3 2 1

Distributed in Canada by Penguin Books Canada Limited.

A CIP catalogue record for this book is available from the British Library.

Microsoft Press books are available through booksellers and distributors worldwide. For further information about international editions, contact your local Microsoft Corporation office or contact Microsoft Press International directly at fax (425) 936-7329. Visit our Web site at mspress.microsoft.com. Send comments to *mspinput@microsoft.com*.

ClearType, FrontPage, JScript, Microsoft, the Microsoft Internet Explorer logo, Microsoft Press, the Office logo (puzzle design), Outlook, PhotoDraw, the Reader logo, Visual Basic, Windows, and Windows Media are either registered trademarks or trademarks of Microsoft Corporation in the United States and/or other countries. Other product and company names mentioned herein may be the trademarks of their respective owners.

Some of the example companies, organizations, products, domain names, e-mail addresses, logos, people, places, and events depicted herein are fictitious. No association with any real company, organization, product, domain name, e-mail address, logo, person, place, or event is intended or should be inferred.

Acquisitions Editor: Casey Doyle
Project Editor: Aileen Wrothwell
Technical Editor: James Johnson

Body Part No. X08-04475

*To Sonny West, who so generously allowed his son Rick and me
to play and learn on his Apple II computer
back when a mouse was still just a furry little animal.*

Contents

Part 1

Getting Started with HTML

Chapter 3
Dressing Up Pages with Images   **37**

Chapter 4
Connecting Pages with Hyperlinks   **51**

Part 2

Beyond the Basics

Chapter 5

Visual Navigation with Image Maps   64

Chapter 6

Organizing Pages with Tables   78

Part 4

Adding Interactivity to Your Pages

Chapter 16
Assessing the Capabilities of a Client   271

Part 5
Leveraging XML

Chapter 17
Understanding XML   282

Chapter 18
Styling XML with XSL   300

Chapter 19
XHTML: XML Meets HTML   314

Part 6

Appendixes

Acknowledgments

Thanks to Casey Doyle, Aileen Wrothwell, Sally Stickney, Jim Johnson, Rita Breedlove, and the rest of the Microsoft Press gang for trusting me with this project and maintaining such an unbelievable level of quality with the content of the book. An enormous thanks goes to my literary agent, Chris Van Buren, who keeps me in business. And finally, a special thanks goes to my wife, Masheed, my parents, and all of my wonderful friends and family who are responsible for keeping me sane when I'm not staring at a computer screen with a glazed look on my face.

Part 1

Getting Started with HTML

Chapter 1

HTML Essentials

Web fact for the day

A 1999 study of 25,500 words from a standard English-language dictionary found that 93 percent of them have been registered as dot-com addresses.

Even if you're not dreaming of creating the next big dot-com, you've more than likely realized that Web pages are in your future. Along with this insight, you've probably come to understand that HTML is an acronym that has much to do with Web pages. As you may already know, HTML is one of a long string of acronyms that litter the landscape of the Web. If it's one thing techies love, it's a good acronym—and the more letters, the better. Although many people would like to believe that HTML really stands for Help Transmit My Love, it doesn't. The real meaning of those magical letters is HyperText Markup Language, which is more accurate but has considerably less sizzle than the love version.

As the name implies, HTML is a computer language that is used to describe how information is presented on a Web page. You can think of HTML as the bare-knuckle approach to creating Web pages. It requires you to use special words and symbols to create effects such as bold text and bulleted lists.

Knowing this, you might wonder why you shouldn't just buy Microsoft FrontPage or some other Web design tool that allows you to blissfully create Web pages without learning HTML. The answer is that you certainly can buy such a tool and create Web pages without ever learning any HTML. There's even a good chance that you'll use one of these tools after you learn HTML. But creating Web pages without knowing HTML is like using autopilot and not knowing how to fly—it just isn't safe. Okay, I'm exaggerating a little, but you get the idea: it's important to understand HTML to be truly creative with Web pages.

The goal of this chapter is to begin to take the mystery out of HTML by showing you how simple it is to create your first Web page. The idea is to start now doing real things with HTML—whether that's building the next Amazon.com or simply a Web site to immortalize your salamander.

What Is HTML?

As you probably know, the Web is a vast sea of documents—Web pages—that are interconnected so that you can jump from one page to the next. The official language of Web pages is HTML. This means that Web pages are written in HTML, just as a letter you might write to a friend in Rome is written in Italian. The obvious difference is that HTML is a computer language understood by Web browsers, and Italian is a human language understood by people in Italy. HTML is required on the Web to format text and images, as well as to add character and personality. It gives you options that help you communicate the precise message you want to send.

HTML also provides the critical linking mechanism that allows pages to link to one another. Without HTML, the Web would be nothing more than a bunch of dull text documents with no interconnectivity—no formatting, no style, no images, and really no fun! The most significant feature of HTML is called *hyperlinking*, which is the ability to link pages together. A hyperlink is simply a reference from one page to a different page. Click the link, and you immediately jump to that page. Hyperlinks are commonly used in navigation bars for Web sites. For example, when you see a button or image on a Web page that says Products, there's a good chance that a hyperlink is being used to link you to the Products page of the Web site when you click the button or image.

If you think of the Web as a big book, then hyperlinks are the dog-eared pages that make it easier to find what you're looking for in the book. The Web is not a book, however. It contains tons of incredibly disorganized pages, making hyperlinks a necessity when it comes to navigating through pages in any meaningful way. You will learn much more about hyperlinks and how to code them in HTML in Chapter 4. For now, I just want to make the point that the hyperlink is the one feature of HTML that is responsible for making the Web possible. If HTML really stood for Help Transmit My Love, as I jokingly asserted earlier, then hyperlinks would be the love potion that brings people together.

Your Pen Pal, the Web Browser

If HTML is so important in making Web pages pretty and connecting them, why don't you see it when you're on the Web busily shopping for lava lamps or researching Bigfoot sightings? The answer is that no one but Web page designers and Web browsers speak the language of HTML. When you design a Web page in HTML, you are in effect writing a personal letter to a Web browser about what you'd like a page to look like. It might go something like this:

```
Dear Browser,

Please place the picture of my pet salamander, Ernest, in the upper left
corner of the screen, and write his name in bold just below the picture.
To the right of Ernest, please list his vital statistics including height,
weight, color, and sliminess. Below all of that, please include a link so
```

that my friends can e-mail their best wishes for Ernest's improved health. One more thing - please make the background of the page pink, Ernest's favorite color.

Yours Truly,
Michael

Although this narrative description of the conversation between Web designer and Web browser is obviously not valid HTML code, it does convey the information that is typically described using HTML. The problem is that computers aren't very smart. You must give them detailed instructions to get exactly what you want on a Web page. HTML is the language used to communicate the detailed instructions.

Putting on Your HTML X-Ray Glasses

You might be struggling to believe that all of the Web pages you've ever seen are constructed using HTML. To put your mind at ease, I want to teach you a little trick that allows you to view the actual HTML code for any Web page. Along with showing you that all pages have HTML under the hood, this trick will prove valuable later on in your HTML career, because it allows you to explore pages to see how other designers pulled off certain looks. To view the HTML code for a Web page, first visit one of your favorite Web sites. When the Web page opens in your Web browser, select View on the main menu, and then Source. A new window will immediately open, showing letters and symbols like you've never seen them before. That is the HTML code for the page.

Note

This description of how to view the HTML code for a Web page assumes that you're using Internet Explorer. In Netscape Navigator, the menu command is named Page Source. You'll find that other browsers also support this feature, although the specific menu commands vary to some degree.

As you progress through this book, you will come to view HTML code as meaningful information and realize that it can be your friend. By the way, the Web pages you create while reading this book won't look nearly as messy as those that you typically see on the Web. The HTML code for complex Web sites has a tendency to evolve into something far removed from a fast read. You will learn to create HTML code that is much cleaner and easier to understand.

Note

HTML isn't the only language being used on the Web to create Web pages. Web page designers are beginning to adopt a new standard for Web pages known as XHTML. XHTML is a more structured form of HTML. XHTML is based on XML, which you will learn about in Chapter 16, "Understanding XML." Many people expect the language XHTML to someday alleviate many of the inconsistencies associated with how browsers display HTML. You'll learn about XHTML in Chapter 19, "XHTML: XML Meets HTML." I told you techies love acronyms!

Why Do I Need to Know HTML?

As an engineering student, I constantly found myself asking the question "why do I need to know this?" The piles of information I had to learn were seemingly unrelated to anything I wanted to do in the real world. Although no one ever answered that question for me, I can help you out about HTML. Why do you need to know HTML? The answer is that you don't need to know HTML. With so many excellent Web development tools around, you can create some pretty interesting Web pages without having a clue about HTML. So what's the deal? Have you bought this book, only to learn in the first chapter that you don't need it? Of course not.

Although you may not need to know HTML to create Web pages, it's an immeasurable asset to know HTML when something doesn't work as you expected it to in a Web page, or when you're pushing the limit to do something unique. Keep in mind that whatever tool you use to create Web pages, the end result is always HTML. When you don't know HTML, you are at the mercy of the tool. Anyway, you may be the kind of person who likes complete control over a situation. Knowing HTML guarantees that you will have complete control over your Web pages.

Note

There are some Web design tools that don't generate HTML. For example, Macromedia Flash is one such tool. It generates special animation files that must be embedded in HTML so that they will work properly. Bottom line, Flash doesn't generate HTML code, and you must know HTML to place Flash animations in your Web pages unless you use an additional Web page design tool such as Macromedia Dreamweaver.

There is another reason you should know HTML. The Web is a community that is based largely on sharing. It is common for a technique used to get a desired effect on a Web page to appear later on someone else's page. I'll let you decide if "imitation is the highest form of flattery." But the reality is that you can learn to do incredible things by studying the HTML code of Web pages that you like. Understand that I'm not endorsing or recommending that you make a habit of borrowing ideas and HTML from others. In some cases it may be illegal, and in others just not cool. What I am saying is that if you see a page you like, take a look at the code and figure out how to make your own HTML magic.

Note

Similar to books and music, Web pages are considered intellectual property, and therefore have rights associated with them. What this means is that an author of a Web page automatically has rights over the original material in the Web page, which prevents others from using the material without permission. To learn more about intellectual property law as it applies to Web pages, please take a look at this Web site: *http://www.eff.org/pub/CAF/law/ip-primer*. It contains an article titled "An Intellectual Property Law Primer for Multimedia and Web Developers," which does a great job of explaining the basics of intellectual property law as it applies to the Web.

Inside a Web Page

The medical profession is generally quite good at diagnosing ailments and quickly recommending a course of action for nursing us back to health. But when doctors reach a consensus that they have no clue what is wrong, the scariest of all medical procedures, exploratory surgery, may be necessary. This is when a surgeon opens you up just to have a look around. Although exploratory surgery can be something to dread, it also can be a life saver. Likewise, making an incision right down the middle of a sample Web page can give new life to your own project.

If you recall from the previous section, I wrote a hypothetical letter to a Web browser explaining how to lay out a Web page for a salamander friend named Ernest. If you take a look at Figure 1-1, you'll see a real Ernest the Salamander Web page that was created based upon this letter.

Figure 1-1.
The Ernest the Salamander Web page is a good example of how to structure a simple page using HTML code.

Along with giving our friend Ernest a place on the Web, this page serves as a good example of how to write clean, concise HTML code. Although I don't expect you to understand the code yet, you should at least be able to pick out some of the elements on the page, such as the text. The following is the code for the Ernest the Salamander Web page:

```
<html>
<head>
  <title>Ernest the Salamander</title>
</head>

<body bgcolor="pink">
  <table>
```

```
<tr>
  <td align="center">
  <p>
  <img src="Ernest.jpg">
  <br>
  <h2>Ernest the Salamander</h2>
  </p>
  </td>

  <td>
  <p>
  <h3>Ernest's Vitals</h3>
  <ul>
  <li>Height - 0.375 inches</li>
  <li>Weight - 40 grams</li>
  <li>Color - Reddish pink</li>
  <li>Sliminess - 6.5 (on a scale of 1 to 10)</li>
  </ul>
  </p>
  </td>
</tr>
</table>
<p>
This is Ernest the salamander, my pet and close friend. Ernest and I
have been friends for quite some time. Ernest has been feeling a little
puny lately, so I'd appreciate it if you could send him some e-mail at
<a href=mailto:ernest@slimyfriends.com>ernest@slimyfriends.com</a> to
cheer him up.
</p>
</body>
</html>
```

That may seem like a lot of code for such a simple Web page, but the amount has to do with how the code is organized. The first thing you'll probably notice about this HTML code is all the angle brackets (<>). In HTML, angle brackets enclose special codes, called *tags*, which indicate the structure and format of the content on the page. HTML consists of many tags that do a variety of different formatting and organizational tasks. The most important tag in a Web page is the <html> tag, which identifies the page as an HTML document. Notice that this tag actually consists of two tags:

1. A *start tag* (<html>), which is located at the beginning of the page

2. An *end tag* (</html>), which, not surprisingly, is at the end of the page

All the content in an HTML document must appear within the two <html> tags.

Note

You hear the word *content* often in the Web design community. Content is simply the text and images that are displayed on a Web page. You use HTML to mark up content so that it is displayed in a certain way. For example, the words "Ernest the Salamander" are content, and the HTML tags <h2> and </h2> are used to format those words in a certain font size.

The other two tags most relevant to the overall structure of the Web page are the `<head>` and `<body>` tags. These tags are important because they describe the two major sections of all Web pages, the *head* and the *body*. The head of a Web page is placed near the beginning of the page, and describes general properties of the page such as the title. The body appears below the head, and contains the content of the Web page. Like the `<html>` tag, the `<head>` and `<body>` tags consist of both start and end tags that enclose the content appearing in each section. An end tag is simply the start tag plus a forward slash that immediately follows the opening angle bracket (`<`).

The Brains of a Web Page

In general, the head of a Web page contains information about the page that isn't displayed by a browser, and the body contains everything that you see when you view the page. In other words, the head of a Web page contains information about the page such as the page's title and keywords that are used to help search engines find the page, but none of the page's content. The most important piece of information stored in the head of a Web page is the *title*, which is identified by the `<title>` tag. In the salamander example page, the third line of HTML code contains the title:

```
<title>Ernest the Salamander</title>
```

Although the title of a Web page isn't considered part of the page's content, it is important because it serves to identify the page. When you bookmark a page or add it to your Favorites list, the browser uses the title of the page to identify it. If you were to bookmark the Ernest the Salamander page, you would see the page referred to as "Ernest the Salamander" in your Favorites list.

Jesse "The Body" Ventura and HTML

Along with sharing its name with the outspoken governor of Minnesota, the body of an HTML document contains the content that is displayed by a Web browser. When you create a Web page later in this chapter, you will spend the majority of your time in the body of the page because that's where all the content is. Figure 1-2 shows a diagram of the basic structure of an HTML document, including the head, the body, and the tags that identify each.

Note

You might have noticed that I use the terms Web page and HTML document interchangeably. You may not think of a Web page as a document, but strictly speaking it is, just as your resume is probably a Word document. I've tried hard to interchange the words only when it makes sense to do so, but don't forget that Web page and HTML document mean the same thing. In many ways "HTML document" is a more formal description of a "Web page" because a Web page is a document that is coded in HTML.

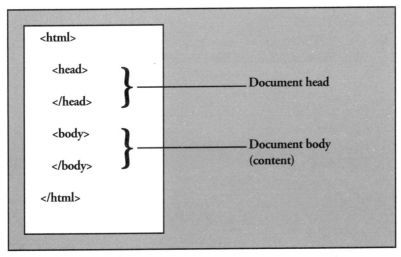

Figure 1-2.
Every Web page consists of a head and a body, identified by the `<head>` and `<body>` tags, which are enclosed within the `<html>` tags.

Common HTML Tags and Attributes

Now you know a little about HTML tags and how they're used to describe the different parts of an HTML document. It's time to take a closer look at tags and how they are used to describe content within a Web page. Although you've learned about a few tags already, let me warn you that HTML is loaded with tags that do all kinds of different things. Table 1-1 lists some of the most common HTML tags, which you will put to use in your first Web page in the next section of this chapter. Keep in mind that you'll continue to learn about additional tags as you progress through the book.

Although this is only a sampling of the tags used in HTML, you'll find yourself using these routinely in your Web pages.

Before you can begin putting these tags to use, it's important to learn about attributes, which play an important role when working with tags. An *attribute* is a customizable option for a tag. Sound complicated? Simply put, attributes are used to describe the properties of a tag. Take a look at this example:

```
<p align="left">
Let's sing a lament,
The world isn't round it's twisted and bent.
</p>
```

This is a paragraph of text, which consists of the `<p>` tag followed by text, followed by a `</p>` tag. Can you guess what the attribute is and for what it is used? The `align` attribute is part of the `<p>` tag, and it allows you to specify how text in a paragraph is arranged on the page: left-aligned, right-aligned, or centered. In this example, the `align` attribute is set to `left`, which results in the paragraph of text being left-aligned.

Table 1-1.   Commonly Used HTML Tags

Tag(s)	Usage
`<html></html>`	Identifies the document as an HTML document
`<head></head>`	Identifies the head of the HTML document
`<body></body>`	Identifies the body of the HTML document
`<title></title>`	Specifies the title of the HTML document
`<h1></h1>...<h6></h6>`	Sets the size of text to one of six preset sizes
`<p></p>`	Denotes a paragraph in the page
`<b></b>`	Bolds text
`<i></i>`	Italicizes text
`<u></u>`	Underlines text
`<img>`	Places an image on the page
`<a>`	Establishes a hyperlink (anchor)
` `	Creates a line-break, moving the insertion point to the next line
`<ul></ul>`	Denotes an unordered list of bulleted items
`<ol></ol>`	Denotes an ordered list of numbered items
`<li></li>`	Identifies an item within a list

Note

HTML is not a case-sensitive language, which means that you can enter tags and attributes in either uppercase or lowercase, or a mixture of the two. However, it is a good practice to use lowercase for tags and attributes, because it is a strict requirement of XHTML, which you will learn about in Chapter 19, "XHTML: XML Meets HTML." XHTML is a somewhat more finicky version of HTML. Because it represents the future of the Web, you might as well start thinking in terms of coding documents that meet its stricter guidelines. One of these guidelines is using lowercase for tags and attributes.

Attributes are used heavily in HTML to describe the specific properties of a tag. Not all tags support attributes, but it's important to familiarize yourself with the attributes for those tags that do. Attributes are always specified as part of a start tag, and always consist of the attribute name followed by an equal sign followed by the attribute value. This is another example of a tag with an attribute:

```
<body bgcolor="pink">
...
</body>
```

In this example, the bgcolor attribute is used to set the background color of the Web page to pink. If you are astute, you might recognize this code from the Ernest the Salamander Web page earlier in the chapter. The bgcolor attribute is part of the `<body>`

tag, and is capable of being set with various color values. Notice that the attribute is specified as part of the start tag, which is a strict requirement of HTML.

Note

A requirement that isn't so strict is enclosing attribute values in quotation marks. The only time you absolutely must enclose an attribute in quotation marks is when it contains spaces. Otherwise, you are free to specify it without quotes. On the other hand, as you learn later in the book, XHTML isn't quite so liberal, so you might want to get into the habit of using quotation marks.

Some HTML tags have *required attributes*, which are attributes for which you must supply values any time you use the tag. The idea is that required attributes contain information that is essential to the usage of the tag. A good example of a required attribute is the `href` attribute that is part of the anchor tag (`<a>`). The anchor tag is used to create hypertext links. A critical part of a hyperlink is the Web page to which you are linking, which is specified in the `href` attribute. That's why the `href` attribute is a required attribute. Following is an example of the `href` attribute at work:

```
<p>
Speaking of salamanders, you may want to visit my friend
<a href="http://www.slimyfriends.com/Ernest.html">Ernest</a>.
</p>
```

This example demonstrates how to link to a Web page using the `<a>` tag and the `href` attribute. The word "Ernest" in the paragraph serves as a hyperlink that points to the Web page located at *http://www.slimyfriends.com/Ernest.html*. The anchor tag (`<a>`) identifies the hyperlink, and the `href` attribute within the tag identifies the target of the link, which in this case is the Ernest the Salamander Web page.

Many tags support multiple attributes, and the attributes are listed one after the next in the start tag, separated by a space. You will learn a great deal more about attributes as you dig deeper into HTML tags.

Writing Your First Web Page in HTML

I'm generally the kind of person who likes to learn how to do something new by jumping in with both feet. Although I have plenty of scars to justify why this might not always be the best approach to learning all new activities— off-road skateboarding, for example— the learn-by-doing approach has served me well technically. For this reason, I want you to cut your teeth on HTML by creating a Web page for yourself. Relax though, I'm going to give you most of the code, and I'm going to give you all of the details to be sure that you understand what's going on.

Honor Thyself

Few of us can resist sharing with others our noblest interests and proudest moments. What better way to honor yourself and share a little with the world than by creating your own personal Web page? I encourage you to start out with a personal Web page as your first HTML project, because it deals with a subject you know better than any other—yourself! If you're worried about having to do research for this one, you may need to take time to reflect before continuing this chapter.

To get started on your personal page, create a text document using your text editor of choice. If you're using Windows, Notepad will suffice. Whatever editor you use, be sure to save your file as a text-format file, and use *.html* as the extension.

If you're on a different type of computer, then find a suitable program that will let you edit straight text files. The first code you need to enter is the skeletal template that describes the overall structure of the page:

```
<html>
<head>
</head>

<body>
</body>
</html>
```

This code establishes that you are indeed creating a Web page (HTML document) and that it has a head and a body, two important requirements of all Web pages. Now, name the page using the `<title>` tag:

```
<title>Sparky's Personal Page</title>
```

Do you remember where this line of code goes? A big celebratory ding if you said the head of the page! That's right, the title of a page is not considered part of the page's content, and must be placed between the `<head>` and `</head>` tags.

Adding a Splash of Color

Next on the agenda is to spice up the page with background and text colors. You use the `bgcolor` attribute of the `<body>` tag to specify the background color, and the `text` attribute to specify the text color. The `bgcolor` and `text` attributes are optional. By default, all Web pages are white with black text if you don't specify colors. The following are the predefined colors you can use as values for these attributes, one for each attribute: `white`, `black`, `silver`, `gray`, `maroon`, `red`, `green`, `lime`, `navy`, `blue`, `purple`, `fuchsia`, `olive`, `yellow`, `teal`, and `aqua`. Keep in mind that the text on your page must contrast with the background color in order to be seen. After selecting background and text colors, the `<body>` tag should look something like this:

```
<body bgcolor="silver" text="navy">
```

Note

If the text color of a Web page doesn't contrast with the background color, it will be very hard for people to read the text on the page. So, make sure that you choose colors carefully so that there is plenty of contrast. Black text on a white page provides the utmost contrast, which is why you see so many pages that are black on white. Even so, you can certainly find other color combinations that still provide reasonable contrast.

Tell Me Something About Yourself

Now, add a heading to the page so that everyone knows who you are. The `<h1>`, `<h2>`, `<h3>`, `<h4>`, `<h5>`, and `<h6>` tags allow you to format text at predefined sizes for headings. The `<h1>` tag creates the largest heading and should work great for displaying your name on the page:

```
<h1>Sparky the Clown</h1>
```

You're now ready to begin describing yourself, and what better way to do that than to display an image of yourself. The `<img>` tag embeds images in Web pages. If you don't have an image of yourself, feel free to find an interesting clip art image to use for the time being. A clip art image is an image that is made available as part of a collection of images, and once you've purchased the collection you can usually use the images as much as you want in your own Web pages. Microsoft offers a sizable collection of clip art on the Web that is completely free. Check out Microsoft's Design Gallery Live at *http://dgl.microsoft.com/* to access their clip art collection. Anyway, getting back to the `<img>` tag, the `src` attribute of the `<img>` tag is used to identify the file containing the image that you want to display. You can also control the alignment of the image with nearby text by using the `align` attribute. The following is an example of how you might embed an image of yourself in your personal page:

```
<img src="Sparky.jpg" align="top">
```

Note

Just in case you're worried that I'm glossing over some details, you will be learning a great deal more about images and how they are embedded in Chapter 3, "Dressing Up Pages with Images." For now, I just wanted to tell you enough about images that you could make your first Web page more interesting.

Keep in mind that most Web pages are organized into paragraphs. It's a good idea to start your personal page with an opening paragraph that includes the image you just coded as well as some introductory text. You might structure the paragraph this way:

```
<p>
<img src="Sparky.jpg" align="top">
This is the personal Web page of Sparky the Clown. Click
<a href="mailto:sparky@sillyclowns.com">here</a> to e-mail Sparky.
</p>
```

Notice that the `<img>` tag is placed within the paragraph just before the text. It is important to note that the setting of the `align` attribute forces the image to be aligned with the top of the text in this paragraph. Another interesting thing about this code is the usage of the `<a>` tag to provide an e-mail hyperlink. You use the `href` attribute of the `<a>` tag to set the target for the link, which in this case is the e-mail address for Sparky the Clown. Substitute your own e-mail address after the colon following `mailto`, and you're good to go.

Listing Your Activities

To wrap up your personal page, you might want to include a list of your favorite activities. These can be hobbies, sports, or anything else you enjoy that's legal. Because your activities list is logically separate from the introductory paragraph, you might include it in its own paragraph using the `<p>` tag. Taking things a step further, this is a great time to use the unordered list tag, `<ul>`, in conjunction with the list item tag, `<li>`. The idea behind these two tags is that you set up a bulleted list with the `<ul>` tag, and then identify each item within the list using `<li>` tags. This is an example of how your activities list might be structured:

```
<p>
These are some of Sparky's primary interests:
<ul>
<li>Jumping off balconies</li>
<li>Doing silly little backflips</li>
<li>Floating children with helium balloons</li>
</ul>
</p>
```

It's important for you to remember to close tags that come in pairs. For example, end the `<ul>` tag with `</ul>` and the `<li>` tag with `</li>`. Otherwise, a Web browser could get confused and do ugly things to the content of your page.

The Finished Page

While you've been busy doing a personal inventory of activities and carefully committing them to HTML code, you may not have realized that you've already written your first Web page in HTML! The following code contains the complete Sparky.html Web page, which should mirror your own personal page in structure and form.

```
<html>
<head>
  <title>Sparky's Personal Page</title>
</head>

<body bgcolor="silver" text="navy">
  <h1>Sparky the Clown</h1>
  <p>
  <img src="Sparky.jpg" align="top">
  This is the personal Web page of Sparky the Clown. Click
  <a href="mailto:sparky@sillyclowns.com">here</a> to e-mail Sparky.
  </p>
  <p>
  These are some of Sparky's primary interests:
  <ul>
  <li>Jumping off balconies</li>
  <li>Doing silly little backflips</li>
  <li>Floating children with helium balloons</li>
  </ul>
  </p>
  </body>
</html>
```

Before you began reading this chapter, you might have looked at this code and thought it was incomprehensible. Now, only a few pages later, you are speaking simple HTML. Figure 1-3 on the next page shows the finished Sparky the Clown Web page as viewed in Internet Explorer.

In case you're wondering how to view your new masterpiece, just fire up your Web browser. (You probably have an icon handy on your desktop). Once the browser window opens, perform these steps to open your page:

1.   Select File from the main menu, and click Open.

2.   Browse and select the HTML file on your hard drive.

3.   Click OK to open your page in the browser.

You may not have realized it until now, but you can view Web pages stored on your local hard drive as if they were located out on the Web. In fact, this is how you test all of your Web pages as you assemble them on your computer. If you have something against menus, another quick way to open a local Web page is to drag the Web page file onto the Web browser window. When you let go of the file after dragging it onto Internet Explorer, for example, Internet Explorer will open the file and display it just as if it was located on the Web.

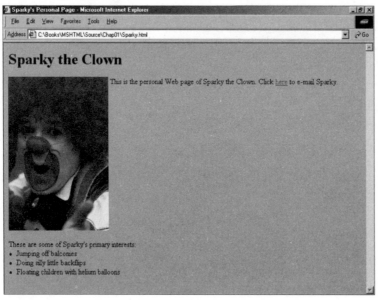

Figure 1-3.
The Sparky the Clown Web page should mirror your own personal Web page in structure and form.

Publishing Your First Web Page

Although it's certainly a thrill to view your first Web page in a browser and instantly see the results of your foray into HTML, the real reason you want to create Web pages is so you can share them with the world. To share Web pages with the world, you must publish them, which simply means that you will copy them to a special computer on the Internet. This computer, connected to the Web, was set up to store Web pages. Before I get into any more specifics about how a page is published, it's worth taking a moment to explain how the Web works in terms of accessing Web pages.

If you have any geeky friends, you may have heard your Web browser referred to as a Web client. These are probably the same friends who insist on describing every piece of electronic equipment they own as either analog or digital. Not to worry, the term Web client is quite straightforward and helps to explain how the Web works. When you view a Web page in a Web browser, the page is actually being delivered to the browser by a special program known as a *Web server*. Its only job is to receive requests for Web pages and serve them up for viewing. The Web browser, the client, asks a Web server to deliver a certain page, and the server obliges. This relationship between the Web browser and server is known as a client-server relationship, which is why browsers are referred to as *Web clients*. Figure 1-4 reveals the client/server relationship between Web browsers and servers.

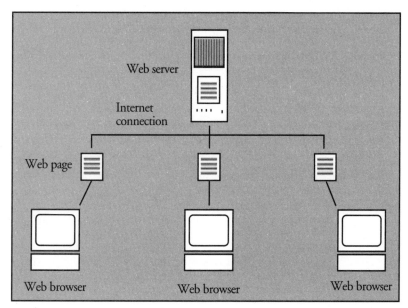

Figure 1-4.
Web browsers and Web servers have a client/server relationship in that Web pages are delivered from servers to browsers by request.

As a Web surfer, all you've had to concern yourself with was the client side of the equation because you interacted only with the browser. When you begin publishing Web pages, you will have to pay some attention to the server side of the equation. You must either install Web server software on a computer that's always connected to the Internet, or use a Web hosting service. Either way, the Web pages you create will be stored on the computer with the Web server, as opposed to your personal computer. You will still create the pages locally on your own computer and test them there. Once they are ready to go live, you must copy your pages to a Web server. Copying a Web page to a Web server is similar to copying a file on your hard drive. The difference is that you are copying the Web page file across the Internet. It sounds tricky, but special programs designed for this task make it almost as simple as copying files between folders on your own hard drive.

Note

Most visual Web development tools include a feature that automatically copies, or publishes, pages to a Web server via File Transfer Protocol (FTP), which alleviates the need to use a special FTP program. A visual Web development tool is a tool that uses a graphical user interface to allow you to practically point and click your way through the creation of Web pages.

I want to reiterate that you don't need access to a Web server of any kind to learn HTML and develop your own Web pages. Web servers come into play only when you want to publish pages for the whole world to view. So, if you want to create a family Web site that is only going to be viewed on your local computer and doesn't need to be on the Web, you can simply develop the pages on your computer and view them in a Web browser straight from the hard drive. Of course, you probably have plans of making your Web pages much more publicly accessible, in which case you must publish them to a Web server. When you are ready to publish pages, you might find that your existing Internet service includes Web hosting space as part of your deal. If this is the case, you can contact your Internet Service Provider (ISP). They'll tell you how to copy the pages to the appropriate Web server and publish them. You can also pay a monthly fee for a Web hosting service through an ISP.

If you're interested in having your own dot-com name, then you'll need to register the name and set up a Web hosting service. Visit *http://www.networksolutions.com/* to see if your name is available. This is the Web site of Network Solutions, which is the company that oversees domain name registrations, and that also offers hosting services for Web sites at relatively little cost. Also, if you are a member of America Online (AOL), there is Web space included with your service that you can use to host your pages. The Microsoft Network (MSN) also has Web hosting services for its members.

Note

If working through all this Web hosting information felt like being in the middle of a whirlwind, that's because it was. My intention in this section isn't to teach you everything there is to know about publishing Web pages. You learn all the ins and outs of Web page publication in Chapter 10, "Publishing Pages on the Web." For now, your first page is up and running. Bask in the limelight!

If you're using Windows, you have a built-in tool that allows you to quickly publish pages on the Web. I'm talking about the Microsoft Web Publishing Wizard, which you can run by following these steps:

1. Click the Start menu.
2. Select Programs, Accessories, and then Internet Tools.
3. Click Web Publishing Wizard to run the Web Publishing Wizard program.

Figure 1-5 shows the opening screen of the Web Publishing Wizard. To get started publishing your personal page, click Next. You will then be prompted to enter the name of the file or folder of the page you wish to publish (Figure 1-6). In this case, you are better off selecting the folder containing your page because there is also an image that you'd like to be published. When you select a folder, all of the files in the folder are automatically published. You can click Browse Folders to find the folder on your hard drive.

After selecting the folder containing your Web page, click Next to continue. You are then prompted to enter a descriptive name for the Web server to which you are copying the page (Figure 1-7). This name can be any name you want, but it's a good idea for it to describe the name of your Web hosting service (AOL, MSN, Network Solutions, Earthlink, or other service).

Figure 1-5.
The Web Publishing Wizard is a program that simplifies the process of publishing Web pages.

Figure 1-6.
The first step in the Web Publishing Wizard is to select the file or folder containing the Web page to be published.

Figure 1-7.
The second step in the Web Publishing Wizard is to enter a descriptive name for the Web server to which you are copying the page.

After entering the name of the Web server, click Next to continue. You are then prompted to enter the Internet address for the Web server (Figure 1-8). This is the location on the Internet where your Web page is to be copied. You must obtain this information from your Internet or Web hosting service, because it will be unique for you. Once you obtain this information, enter it in the Web Publishing Wizard.

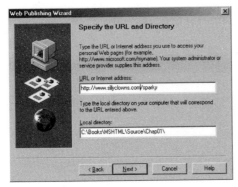

Figure 1-8.
The third step in the Web Publishing Wizard is to enter the Internet address for the Web server.

Note

An Internet address is like an online version of a mailing address. The technical term for an Internet address is URL, which stands for Uniform Resource Locator. All you need to know at this point is that an Internet address, or URL, uniquely identifies a Web page in the same way that your mailing address uniquely identifies your house.

After entering the address of the Web server, click Next to continue. You then move along to the final step of publishing your Web page, which is entering the user name and password (Figure 1-9) that your Internet or Web hosting service provider gave you.

Note

The user name and password that you use in the Web Publishing Wizard may or may not be the same ones used to connect to your e-mail. Be sure to check with your Internet or Web hosting service to confirm the user name and password for publishing Web pages.

After entering your user name and password, click OK to publish your Web page. It takes a few moments for the page to copy across the Internet, but once it's finished anyone can view your page. To view your page on the Web, enter its address in a Web browser. The address of your page is the Web server address, followed by the name of the Web page file. So, the URL of the Sparky the Clown Web server is *http://www.sillyclowns.com/sparky*, and the Web page file is Sparky.html. Put the two together for the complete address of the Web page:

```
http://www.sillyclowns.com/sparky/Sparky.html
```

Anyone with Web access anywhere around the world can now enter the same Web page address to view your newly published page!

Figure 1-9.
The final step in the Web Publishing Wizard is to enter the user name and password your Internet or Web hosting service provider gave you.

Conclusion

At this point you may be reeling from all the information in this opening chapter. The pace will ease up a bit as you continue through the book. This chapter is in some ways the most difficult because you started at ground zero and went all the way through creating your first Web page. That's a lot of territory to cover in so few pages. Of course, the upside is that you got a great deal done in a short amount of time. Many of the concepts you learned in this chapter will be reinforced and explained more thoroughly in upcoming chapters. The emphasis here was to expose you to as much HTML as possible without drowning you in too many specifics.

Let's quickly recap what you learned so that you can take some quiet time and reflect on your early successes with HTML (or dive into the next chapter). You began the chapter by covering the fundamentals of HTML and its relationship to the Web. You discovered that although you could probably get through life without knowing HTML, the basics certainly will give you much more freedom and flexibility in creating your own Web pages when you become fluent in HTML.

You then took a look at the HTML code for a Web page to get acquainted with how the code is laid out. From there, you tackled some of the most commonly used HTML tags and how they are used. Finally, the chapter concluded by guiding you through the creation and publication of your very first Web page—which, quite appropriately, pays homage to you.

Chapter 2
Formatting Text

Web fact for the day

In 1994, Jeff Bezos decided on "Cadabra" as the name for his new online book sales business. But Bezos' attorney worried that the name sounded too much like "cadaver," and convinced the entrepreneur to go with his second choice, "Amazon." You know the rest of the story.

Cadabra, cadaver, Amazon—what's the difference? They all make for clever marketing, right? In the real world there is a big difference between magic, a dead body, and a big river. And as strange as some Web business names are, who's to say whether Amazon.com would have become as successful as it did if it had been named Cadabra.com? Maybe Amazon's huge success had something to do with the way that the names of the books were formatted on the page.

Okay, that's probably not it either, but it serves to bridge into the topic of this chapter, text formatting. Granted, text formatting may not sound like the most exciting of topics associated with Web page development, but stick with me. This chapter shows you how to do some neat formatting with HTML.

As you learn how to use various HTML tags to format text in Web pages, you'll find that HTML provides you with a surprising amount of control over how text appears on a page. Yet, text formatting in HTML is not the same as text formatting within a word proc-essor or desktop publishing program. Where a word processor or desktop publishing program gives you exacting control over the size and placement of text on a printed page, HTML merely provides an approximation of how text will be displayed on a Web page. This may seem like a small distinction, but it does matter, especially if you have desktop publishing experience. If you don't have any experience with desktop publishing, lucky you. Your blissful ignorance will allow you to easily embrace HTML text formatting.

Organizing Text

A picture may be worth a thousand words, but I doubt you would go along with a federal initiative to do away with all the text in American newspapers and replace it with pictures. Fortunately, most members of Congress can read and they have initiated no such initiative, yet. The point is that although Web pages are a visual medium with a multitude of graphics, text still reigns as the preferred means of presenting information. Because of the importance of text to a Web page, organizing and formatting text so that it's easy to read is a critical part of constructing any Web page. Text formatting is therefore an important part of HTML.

Text and the Head of a Page

You learned in the previous chapter that a Web page is organized into two main sections, the head and the body. Although each of these sections may contain text, only the body houses text that shows up in the Web browser window. Before going into how text is organized in the body of a Web page, let's recap why you'll find text in the head section.

The `<title>` tag, nestled cozily between the start and end `<head>` tags, allows you to specify the title of a Web page. This title isn't displayed in the contents of a browser window, but it does appear in the title bar of the Web browser. For example, the following HTML code specifies the title of a Web page:

```
<head>
  <title>Ralph's Rock Collection</title>
</head>
```

Note

In addition to holding the title of a Web page, the head section can store scripting code. Scripting code, which is programming language that's triggered by tags within the body of the page, executes tasks such as calculating a mortgage payment or accessing information in a database associated with a Web page. You will learn much more about scripting in Chapter 14, "Dynamic HTML."

When viewed in a browser, the page shows up with the title in the bar at the top. This title is also the basis for naming favorites or bookmarks in a browser. For this reason, be sure to use `<title>` tags in the head section of all of your Web pages. And, choose descriptive names that give your pages names with meaning beyond the context of the individual page. For example, a page named "Table of Contents" could link to one of a jillion Web sites. On the other hand, you're sure to remember a favorite named "Ralph's Rock Collection: Table of Contents." Although certain other tags can be used within the `<head>` tag, the `<title>` tags are the only ones that should be placed in every Web page.

A Body Full of Text

The drama starts to unfold in the body section of a Web page. Recall that the body of a page is where you put the travelogue you wrote during your trip to the Amazon or the pictures of the antique fishing lures you want to sell. In other words, the material that appears on the page in the Web browser is located in the body. The `<body>` tags take on the responsibility of housing the content in the body of a page. You have two options when it comes to placing content in the body of a page. You can insert it directly in the body or within paragraphs in the body. It is usually better to break text into paragraphs, because they organize the content more efficiently than simply dropping text into the body.

Two particularly useful tags for organizing text within the body are the `<p>` and `<div>` tags. These tags define paragraphs and provide sectional divisions, respectively. The paragraph tag (`<p>`) is popular and separates paragraphs from one another. Unlike the old-fashioned typewriter, modern HTML doesn't normally observe carriage returns. It requires HTML code for *newlines*, and a new line is started for each paragraph tag.

Note

A *newline* is a special text character used to indicate that a new line is to start in a sequence of text. In a simple text processor, a newline is inserted in a document whenever you hit the Enter key. You press the Enter key to make the cursor go to a **new line**, hence the name "newline."

You can't insert an extra newline HTML code to start a new paragraph, because all extra white space (spaces, tabs, and newlines) is removed from the text when it is displayed. In practical terms, this means your beautifully spaced paragraphs probably will not be positioned on the page the way you intended.

If you don't want to go to the trouble of identifying paragraphs with the `<p>` tag, you can also use the `<br>` tag, which represents a line-break. When a Web browser encounters a `<br>` tag, it interprets it as a request for a new line and moves down a line and back to the left margin before displaying the next text in the document. Following is an example of how two sentences are separated using the `<br>` tag:

```
<body>
This sentence wants to be alone.
<br>
This sentence also wants a little space.
</body>
```

This approach works fairly well, but in some ways is considered poor usage of HTML. It doesn't provide enough logical organization for text content. The `<br>` tag tells the browser to move down and start a new line, and the `<p>` tag tells the browser that this is a paragraph. The `<p>` tag not only has an impact on the appearance of the text, but also adds meaning by declaring that this text is a complete paragraph. In other words, context is added when you specify paragraphs of text with the `<p>` tag, as opposed to specifying newlines with the `<br>` tag. Following is the same example, marked up using the `<p>` tag to identify the two separate paragraphs:

```
<body>
<p>
This sentence wants to be alone.
</p>
<p>
This sentence also wants a little space.
</p>
</body>
```

Unlike the `<br>` tag, the `<p>` tag includes start and end tags that must be placed around the paragraph, but you wouldn't know that by looking at the majority of Web pages. Web developers typically use the `<p>` tag in the same manner as the `<br>` tag, to establish a new line for text. This means that the `<p>` is often mistaken as a means of separating paragraphs, as opposed to its correct usage—enclosing paragraphs. Fortunately, Web browsers aren't too discerning when it comes to how the `<p>` tag is used, which explains why the incorrect technique works in all the popular browsers.

But the future of HTML is structure, and structure requires some discipline. I encourage you to use HTML tags as they were intended, regardless of what you might be able to get away with. Demonstrate your rebellion against the establishment by getting a tattoo or an elbow ring, instead of bending the rules with HTML.

Note

For the record, `<br>` tags are not evil. As in life, there is a time and place for everything in HTML. You legitimately need a simple newline in some situations, and the `<br>` tag is perfectly suited for the task. However, given the choice between using a tag that simply changes the way text looks versus using a tag that adds meaning to the text as well, always use the more meaningful tag.

The attributes of `<p>` tags include several that allow you to fine-tune the formatting of paragraphs. The most common is undoubtedly the `align` attribute, which can be set to the following values:

- `left`—aligns the paragraph text to the left
- `right`—aligns the paragraph text to the right
- `center`—centers the paragraph text

Note

The latest HTML version, HTML 4.0, phases out the `align` attribute of the `<p>` tag and encourages you to use style sheets, which are described in Chapters 11 through 13. Style sheets offer a more advanced means of formatting Web content. Unfortunately, style sheets are more difficult to use than most of the tags and attributes they are intended to replace. And the easier-to-use tags won't go away anytime soon. So, it's important to learn how to format text using the tags and attributes that are still prevalent in most Web pages.

Following is an example of how to center a line of text using the `align` attribute with the `<p>` tag:

```
<p align="center">
This text is centered on the page.
</p>
```

The `align` attribute brings up an interesting question regarding attribute values: what happens if you don't specify an attribute? Attributes have default values. In the case of the `align` attribute, the default value is `left`, which is why paragraph text is left-aligned if you don't ask for the alignment of your choice.

The `<div>` tag serves a function similar to the `<p>` tag, albeit somewhat more general. The `<div>` tag is used to divide an HTML document into sections, and plays more of an organizational role than the `<p>` tag. The `<p>` tag identifies a section of a document as specifically being a paragraph. The `<div>` tag merely provides a division between the section and the rest of the document, and it doesn't distinguish the section as being a paragraph of text. The `<div>` tag is often used to identify a section of a document for scripting purposes. You will learn much more about scripting in Chapter 14, "Dynamic HTML."

Basic Text Formatting: The Look or the Meaning?

Once you've organized text into paragraphs or sections, you can begin formatting it using various HTML formatting tags. HTML provides two different types of formatting tags: content-based tags and physical tags. Content-based formatting tags are used to add meaning, or context, to a piece of text, which in turn affects how the text is displayed. Physical tags, on the other hand, provide no meaning and deal directly with how text is displayed.

Consider the names of the infamous 1930s gangsters, "Baby Face" Nelson and Frank "The Enforcer" Nitti. Although the name Baby Face describes the juvenile appearance of this prohibition-era bank robber, it tells you nothing about him or what he did. Without knowing anything about the many people he killed, you might think he was just an average guy with a youthful appearance. The Enforcer, on the other hand, says all you need to know about Al Capone's favorite henchman. The name is both colorful and descriptive, leaving no doubt that this was a dangerous man. To put these names in terms of HTML formatting tags, Baby Face provides a physical description, and The Enforcer provides a content-based description.

Note

The reason for two different types of tags is that in some instances you care more about how a Web page looks than the content in a page. And vice versa. That creates a constant struggle in HTML coding between a desire to make a page look good and a desire to give its content more meaning. These two desires run contrary to each other because adding meaning to HTML content doesn't always result in a visually appealing Web page. Fortunately, there is no true right or wrong when it comes to this struggle. Throughout the book, I attempt to describe the ideal situation: adding meaning to the content while taking practicality and aesthetics into account.

The next couple of sections describe the content-based tags and physical tags used to format text in HTML. In addition to these tags, there are a few others that don't clearly fall into either category. These are heading tags, which identify sectional headings in an HTML document. These six heading tags describe headings of various sizes, in order of decreasing significance: <h1>, <h2>, <h3>, <h4>, <h5>, and <h6>. By decreasing significance, I mean that <h1> might be used to describe the title of a book, <h2> could be used for the chapter titles, and <h3> could be the chapter sub-sections. The heading tags affect the display of heading text because the size of the text increases with the significance of the tag. Figure 2-1 shows text formatted with the six different heading tags, as viewed in Internet Explorer.

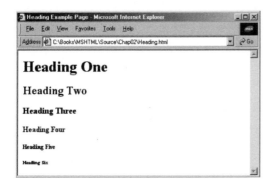

Figure 2-1.
The HTML heading tags allow you to format heading text, which is displayed in a font size related to the specific heading tag used.

The body content for the Web page shown in Figure 2-1 looks like this:

```
<body>
<h1>Heading One</h1>
<h2>Heading Two</h2>
<h3>Heading Three</h3>
<h4>Heading Four</h4>
<h5>Heading Five</h5>
<h6>Heading Six</h6>
</body>
```

Notice that each of the heading tags requires both a start and an end tag. The heading tags serve as a great way to identify headings in a Web page without getting into the display specifics of font sizes. Keep in mind, though, that the browser ultimately determines how the specific heading sizes are displayed. This is a perfect example of how HTML fails to give you complete control over text formatting. Instead of specifying an exact font size, a heading tag lets the browser determine the best way to display the text on the page.

Content-Based Text Formatting

Content-based text formatting involves using HTML tags to mark up text according to the meaning of the text, as opposed to how the text is displayed. The motivation for using content-based formatting is that text content may be viewed in a variety of different ways. For example, consider the possibility of Web browsers for the visually impaired who read Web page content aloud instead of displaying it on the screen. In this scenario, an emphasis (<em>) tag makes more sense than a bold (<b>) tag, because emphasis can be placed on the text as it is being read. But bold has no meaning outside of displaying text. Consequently, whenever possible you should use content-based tags over physical tags.

These are the HTML content-based formatting tags, along with brief descriptions of their usages:

- <cite>—identifies a bibliographic citation, such as a book or magazine article title
- <code>—identifies monospaced code, such as programming code
- <dfn>—indicates definitions, such as might appear in an online dictionary
- <em>—adds emphasis to text
- <kbd>—identifies text that is typed on a keyboard
- <samp>—identifies a sequence of literal characters
- <strong>—adds strong emphasis to text
- <var>—identifies variables in code, such as programming code

All of these tags enclose text content with both start and end tags. Following is an example of using the <em> and <strong> tags to mark up a sentence of text:

```
<p>
The collapse of the market came as an <em>enormous</em>
surprise to many, and delivered a <strong>crushing</strong>
blow to many individual portfolios.
</p>
```

Figure 2-2 shows the results of this code, illustrating how Internet Explorer displays <em> text in italics and <strong> text in bold.

Figure 2-2.
The HTML content-based formatting tags allow you to format text based upon its meaning, which indirectly impacts how it is displayed.

Note

Although I've referred to the content-based formatting tags as being useful for formatting text, you can use them to format images as well. Because the emphasis is on the meaning of content, you can mark up an image with the `<strong>` tag to indicate that the image has a strong meaning with respect to other content on a page. You will learn how to use images in Chapter 3, "Dressing Up Pages with Images."

Physical Text Formatting

Content-based formatting tags allow you to format text according to its meaning, and physical formatting tags define how to format text based on how you want it to appear in a Web browser. Physical formatting tags have served as the primary means of formatting text on the Web since its inception, which is why it isn't realistic to assume that content-based tags are going to take over any time soon. The convenience of physical tags is significant when it comes to clearly specifying how text is to be displayed.

In some cases, you'll find that browsers render a content-based tag the same as they render a physical tag. For example, the `<em>` content-based tag appears as italicized text in most browsers, but the same result is achieved with the `<i>` physical tag. The difference is that you aren't guaranteed italics with the `<em>` tag, because the tag doesn't directly address how text is displayed, whereas the `<i>` tag does. Here are the physical formatting tags, along with brief descriptions of their usages:

- `<b>`—Indicates bold text
- `<big>`—Increases the size of text
- `<blink>`—Indicates blinking text
- `<i>`—Indicates italicized text
- `<s>`—Indicates strikethrough text
- `<small>`—Decreases the font size of text
- `<sub>`—Indicates subscript text

- `<sup>`—Indicates superscript text
- `<tt>`—Indicates a monospaced font (all characters are the same width) for text
- `<u>`—Indicates underlined text

Similar to the content-based tags, these physical text-formatting tags are used to enclose text content, and must have both start and end tags. Following is an example using several of the mark-up tags:

```
<p>
When I was <small><small>smaller</small></small> than I am now,
I dreamed of being much <big><big>bigger</big></big>. As
<b>excited</b> as I was about the prospect, the amount of time
it would take to get there made me <i>sad</i>.
</p>
```

Figure 2-3 shows the formatted paragraph in Internet Explorer.

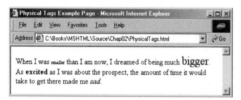

Figure 2-3.
The HTML physical formatting tags allow you to format text for specific display.

You may wonder why the `<small>` and `<big>` tags are used repeatedly. It's simple. Each occurrence of the `<small>` and `<big>` tags decrease or increase the size of text by a certain amount. The basic idea behind this approach is that the physical formatting tags acknowledge six font sizes. When you use one of the `<small>` or `<big>` tags, the enclosed text is decreased or increased one size. To further decrease or increase the font size, you must use the tags repeatedly, as in the example.

Note

Technically speaking, the `<blink>` tag was never part of the HTML standard. Instead, it is a Netscape extension that is still supported to this day. Many Web designers view the `<blink>` tag as the worst example of inconsistency among Web browsers, because Internet Explorer doesn't support its usage. Your best bet is to avoid using it when possible. Additionally, the `<u>` and `<s>` tags are both deprecated in HTML 4.0, but they are still commonly used in many Web pages.

VH-1 and The List

The popular VH-1 music show, <u>The List</u>, takes the novel approach of asking people to work together on a list of the best selections for a musical topic, such as Best Rock Anthem or Best Hair Band. Although I can't promise you celebrity appearances by Meatloaf or Kevin Bacon, I can open a new discussion surrounding a version of <u>The List</u> for HTML. I'm referring to HTML lists, which are used to break a sequence of text into an ordered or unordered list. Ordered lists, also known as numbered lists, typically outline the steps required to perform a process. An unordered list might be used to specify the ingredients for a recipe, for example. There are actually three types of lists supported in HTML:

- Ordered lists contain numbered items.
- Unordered lists contain bulleted items.
- Definition lists contain terms with corresponding definitions.

Different tags specify each type, and they are covered in the next few sections.

Unordered Lists

Unordered lists consist of items displayed with a bullet next to each one. The `<ul>` tag encloses an unordered list. Within the list, individual items are coded with the `<li>` tag. The following code demonstrates how to use these tags to create an unordered list:

```
<p>
Following are the sports in which I regularly participate:
<ul>
<li>Hockey</li>
<li>Cycling</li>
<li>Skateboarding</li>
<li>Wiffle Ball!</li>
</ul>
</p>
```

Note

Since the items in an unordered list are identified by bullets, as opposed to numbers or letters, they are considered "unordered." You learn about ordered lists in the next section.

Note

Although it isn't imperative to place each item on a line of its own in HTML, it makes the code easier to read and understand.

Figure 2-4 shows the formatted paragraph viewed in Internet Explorer.

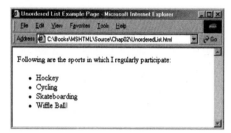

Figure 2-4.
The <ul> tag allows you to create unordered lists of items.

Notice that the <ul> tag consists of both start and end tags that enclose the entire list. The <li> tag identifies each item within the list, and also requires both a start and an end tag.

The <ul> tag supports a type attribute that allows you to change the type of bullet shown next to each item in the list. The following values are acceptable for use with the type attribute. Note that disc is the default bullet:

- The disc tag indicates a solid circle

- The circle tag indicates a hollow circle

- The square tag indicates a solid square

Note

The type attribute of <ul> isn't used too often, even in older Web pages.

Ordered Lists

Ordered lists are similar to unordered lists, with the exception that they are identified by numbers when displayed, instead of bullets. The numbering starts with "1" by default and increases by one for each value in the list. The <ol> tag is used to create ordered lists. Following is an example of a simple ordered list similar to the unordered list you previously examined:

```
<p>
Following are the sports I regularly participate in,
ranked in order from most favorite to just fun-to-do:
<ol>
<li>Skateboarding</li>
<li>Hockey</li>
<li>Cycling</li>
<li>Wiffle Ball!</li>
</ol>
</p>
```

Figure 2-5 shows the formatted paragraph viewed in Internet Explorer.

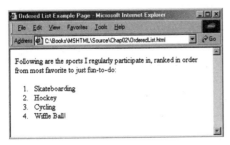

Figure 2-5.
The <ol> tag creates ordered lists of items.

Figure 2-5 illustrates how numbers are assigned to items in an ordered list, even though no numbering appears in the HTML code. You might be concerned about the potential limitations on ordered lists such as always beginning with an arabic "1" and proceeding from there. Fortunately, HTML permits you to change both the starting number and the type of numbering system. The start attribute allows you to specify the starting number for a list, and the type attribute specifies the type of numbering system. Here are the allowed values for the type attribute, along with an example of the associated numbering system:

- 1—1, 2, 3, 4, ... (default)
- A—A, B, C, D, ...
- a—a, b, c, d, ...
- I—I, II, III, IV, ...
- i—i, ii, iii, iv, ...

To change the numbering system for an ordered list, simply assign one of the above values to the type attribute. Next is an example of using both the start and type attributes to alter an ordered list:

```
<p>
Following are some of my favorite letters:
<ol type="A" start="5">
<li>The letter E!</li>
<li>The letter F!</li>
<li>The letter G!</li>
<li>The letter H!</li>
</ol>
</p>
```

In this example, the type of list is set to "A" to display capital letters next to the items. The starting number of the list is set to "5," which results in identifying the first item with the letter "E" to indicate the fifth letter of the alphabet.

Definition Lists

If Noah Webster had had access to HTML in 1806, he would have appreciated definition lists for marking up terms and their associated definitions. Webster published the first American dictionary, which evolved over the last two centuries into today's popular Merriam-Webster dictionary. Although you probably aren't putting together your own dictionary, you may still find definition lists useful.

Definition lists consist of terms and their associated definitions. A definition list is enclosed within <dl> start and end tags, and each term in the list is identified by the <dt> tag. Another tag, the <dd> tag, must follow the <dt> tag in a definition list to provide the definition of the preceding term. I realize that this sounds confusing, but I promise it's relatively simple. This example shows how these tags fit together to create a list of definitions:

```
<p>
Following are a few technologies related to Web page
development, along with a brief description of each:
<dl>
<dt>Java</dt>
<dd>A programming language designed to add interactivity to Web
pages through special programs called applets that run within
the context of a page.</dd>
<dt>JavaScript</dt>
<dd>A scripting language designed to add interactivity to Web
pages by embedding script code directly in HTML code.</dd>
<dt>VBScript</dt>
<dd>A scripting language that serves a similar role as
JavaScript, but that is loosely based upon Microsoft's popular
Visual Basic programming language.</dd>
</dl>
</p>
```

Figure 2-6 shows the formatted text viewed in Internet Explorer.

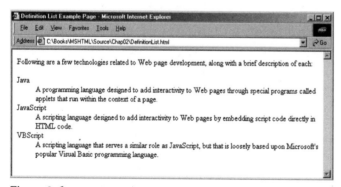

Figure 2-6.
The <dl> tag allows you to create definition lists containing terms and their definitions.

As you can see in the example, creating definition lists is straightforward; you enclose the entire list with the start and end `<dl>` tags, and then mark up the terms and definitions with the `<dt>` and `<dd>` tags.

Note

Regarding lists in general, the list tags are all designed to support nesting—which means that you can nest lists within other lists. Make sure that you match every start and end tag properly, especially when nesting lists within other lists.

One Last Comment

We all have one of those friends who has a comment about everything. As much as you may love to hear their musings on current events, too many comments annoy. Not so in HTML. HTML comments describe the code. More specifically, comments in HTML code identify information that isn't part of the document's content and isn't processed or displayed. Comments are marked up with the special comment delimiters, `<!--` and `-->`. Following is an example of a simple comment placed in HTML code:

```
<!-- Finish the following paragraph -->
<p>
It all began innocently enough in the fall of 1987...
</p>
```

In this example, the comment is used to describe work that needs to be done to the document. Comments can also be used to temporarily ignore lines of HTML code during testing. The most popular and important usage of comments is placing scripting code, such as code written in JavaScript or VBScript. Web browsers capable of interpreting such code will routinely scan comments in a document to see if there is any scripting code. In this way, comments can certainly do more than just contain information that won't be processed. However, from the perspective of pure HTML code, browsers simply ignore comments.

Note

Comments cannot be nested within another comment. When a Web browser encounters the `<!--` that signals the start of a comment, it continues ignoring everything until it finds the `-->` end delimiter, which signals the end of the comment. If you nested a comment about an image within another comment about a paragraph of text, the browser would end the comment at the first `-->` end delimiter for the image comment and not know what to do with the remainder of the paragraph comment. The moral of the story is that all comments must learn to fly on their own, or be booted from the nest.

Conclusion

One thing is certain at this point: you can't claim ignorance about text formatting in HTML! Although it may not be the most sizzling of Web design topics, text formatting forms the basis of Web page design. Imagine a Web with pages and pages of text all the same size, with no spacing or other formatting. You'll quickly realize why text formatting is such a big deal. You'll learn much more about getting the most out of text in your Web pages in the future. But that will wait until later. First, you need to firmly grasp the fundamental HTML techniques required to build Web pages before you tackle the more advanced topics such as style sheets. You will learn in Chapters 11 through 13 how to use style sheets to gain an incredible amount of control over text and how it is formatted.

In this chapter, you gained a thorough grounding in text formatting, using both physical and content-based HTML tags. Although these two classifications may have sounded complicated, you found that they're just a fancy way of distinguishing between marking up content for display only and associating meaning with the tags. Either way, the result of using text-formatting tags is that your words look different on the page depending upon how you use the tags. You examined the HTML list tags, and how they provide a means of organizing information into bulleted or numbered lists. You finished up the chapter with a quick look at comments, which allow you to add information that isn't processed or displayed by a Web browser, to the body of a Web page.

Chapter 3

Dressing Up Pages with Images

Web fact for the day

Wired adults will spend an average of 5.3 percent of the rest of their lives online, according to the research firm Cyber Dialogue. That adds up to a total of 23.5 months, or 17,500 hours.

If you are a Web addict, you can certainly relate to spending a significant portion of your waking hours online. No doubt you invest the vast majority of that time doing incredibly useful and important things—such as trolling eBay for tapes to complete your ABBA 8-track collection. But there is the off chance that a smidgen of that time is wasted. Regardless of how productive a Web surfer you are, you encounter your fair share of images (photographs, cartoons, logos, etc.) while tooling around the Web. And, that brings us to the topic of this most visual of chapters—images.

It's hard to go anywhere on the Web without encountering images of some sort. They convey meaning, share information, and serve as window dressing for the vast majority of Web pages in existence. Although it is certainly possible to misuse images from a graphic design perspective, almost anyone would argue that Web pages benefit from them. Images helped spur the Web's rapid acceptance, and will continue to draw attention to the Web as it evolves.

This chapter will show you how to display images using HTML. More specifically, you will learn about the single tag that embeds images in Web pages. You'll also get friendly with the basic types of images, along with the details about when to use them.

The Scoop on Images

I mentioned already that nerds like me love to throw around acronyms when discussing technology. If you've ever heard talk about images or scanned pictures, you've likely heard the terms JPEG and GIF. These two acronyms, which you will learn more about shortly, refer to the two most commonly used types of images on the Web. Before I get into the specifics of how the two image types differ—and why they are necessary—let me get to the heart of exactly what an image is.

An *image* is an arrangement of little colored squares known as picture elements, or pixels. A *pixel* is the smallest piece of graphical information capable of being displayed on a computer screen. It is actually a small single-colored rectangle. If the resolution of your monitor is set to 800x600, the picture on your screen has 800 pixels across and 600 pixels down. Although all images are ultimately displayed as a rectangular group of pixels, a number of different image formats have been developed, each offering some unique combination of image-file size and display quality. Two major formats, appropriate for different types of images, are in common use on the Web and both are supported by most Web browsers.

- The JPEG image format, named after the Joint Photographic Experts Group, helps photographs travel light, with a format especially designed for storing them efficiently. These image files typically have a .jpg or .jpeg file extension.

- The GIF image format, named for the Graphics Interchange Format, more efficiently stores images that are not photographs, such as illustrations and diagrams. These image files typically have a .gif file extension.

Note

A third image format now showing up on the Web is called PNG, which stands for Portable Network Graphic. The PNG image format is intended to replace the GIF format. It compresses image files even more than GIF, and avoids licensing problems associated with the technology underlying the GIF format. Although PNG images are likely to grow in popularity over the next few years, they're not likely to seriously challenge the popularity of GIFs for a while.

So, how do the two most popular image formats differ? Basically, both are designed to store certain types of images. By choosing the appropriate format for an image, you keep the size of the image file at a minimum while maintaining its quality. To summarize what this means to you: Store photographic images in the JPEG format. The GIF format works best for other images, such as illustrations.

You probably know from experience that images often take a noticeable amount of time to download over most Internet connections. Because keeping image sizes to a minimum is the most efficient way to speed things up, making the right format choice is critical in Web pages. Despite the growing number of users with high-speed Internet access, you can't count on the average Web surfer having such a connection in the near future. And even with high-speed Internet access, network congestion increases download time.

Note

High-speed Internet connections are often referred to as *broadband* connections. Examples of broadband Internet connections include cable and DSL modems, as well as direct corporate connections such as T1 and T3 lines. If you are using a traditional modem to dial an Internet service, you do not have a broadband connection.

The JPEG format is designed for photographic images with many shades of color, and it significantly reduces the size of the image file. It doesn't fare so well with illustrations, and it is not the ideal image format for them. For illustrations and virtually any image that isn't photorealistic, a GIF is your best choice. Photorealistic images are primarily photographic images that were either scanned from a photograph or taken as pictures using a digital camera. Non-photorealistic images include most hand-drawn artwork, as well as the majority of clip art that comes with popular desktop publishing tools such as Microsoft Publisher. The GIF image format provides flexibility that isn't available with a JPEG image: transparency and animation. These are popular features for Web page development.

Transparency lets you "see through" a region of a GIF image, allowing the background color of a Web page to show through. Think about the weather report on your local news broadcast; the reporter appears "in front of" the computer-generated weather map. The background around the reporter is transparent, allowing the weather map to be displayed as a backdrop.

Animation is a GIF feature specifying multiple frames of an image, which are displayed in succession to yield the effect of motion. Although animated GIF images can be annoying if overdone, they can be quite compelling when used properly. You will learn more about animated GIF images later in the chapter, in the section titled "Using Animated Images."

Note

In addition to how the size of images affects time and efficiency, take another aspect of image size into account when you're creating pages. It is important to create Web pages that aren't so large that people have to scroll the page.

Working with Images

Would it come as a big surprise if I told you that there are twelve different HTML tags involved in formatting and displaying images? Images are certainly powerful, and they offer a lot of bang for the buck in terms of Web page design. So it wouldn't be surprising if a large number of complex tags were involved. Interestingly though, only two HTML tags are necessary to put an image on a Web page: `<img>` and `<a>`. The difference between these tags has to do with how you tell the Web browser to display an image.

This brings up an important distinction between images and text. Unlike text, an image is stored outside of a Web page in an external file. An image file has to be referenced, or called, from HTML code to have the image displayed on the page.

So the actual image is always located in a separate file. What's the big deal? This changes the perspective. From an HTML perspective, you are dealing with a file other than the Web page. You must reference an image file in one of two ways:

- A reference to the file in which an *inline image* is stored displays the image directly on the Web page with the surrounding text and other images. The more common approach of the two, an inline image basically parallels the way traditional desktop publishing handles images.

- A reference to an *external image* is a link to the image file, which is displayed only when someone clicks the link. These external images work differently also in that they are not displayed directly on the Web page with the link.

The next two sections describe how to use each approach to incorporate images into Web pages.

Displaying Inline Images

A simple HTML `<img>` tag places inline an image—a photo of a scenic waterfall or a detailed schematic, for example—on the Web page. This tag has one required attribute, `src`, used to identify the address of the image to be displayed. Briefly mentioned in Chapter 1, such an address is also known as a URL, or Uniform Resource Locator. You will learn a great deal about URLs in the next chapter, but for now just keep in mind that they identify the location of files on the Internet. The image URL specified in the `src` attribute includes the image filename, along with any other path information. If you specify just the image filename, the Web browser assumes that the image is located in the same directory as the Web page's file. I realize this may seem confusing at this stage, but it's fairly simple when you see how it works. Look at this example of an `<img>` tag that displays an inline image:

```
<img src="Jump.jpg">
```

I told you it was simple! This example uses a *relative path* to identify the image file, looking for it where the Web page file itself is located. Following is a similar example that instead uses an absolute path to reference the image file:

```
<img src="http://www.thetribe.com/images/Jump.jpg">
```

This second one is a little more complicated, but it's not so confusing when you understand what is going on. In this example, the *absolute path* of the image file is specified, which means that the complete address of the image file is used. This is like using those four extra digits in your ZIP code. You must use an absolute path if you are displaying an image that isn't stored in the same directory with your Web page file. For example, you want to put a picture of your favorite arcade game on your personal Web page, so you refer to an image located on the Killer List Of Videogames (KLOV) Web site *http://www.klov.com*.

Note

A good way to think of the difference between relative and absolute paths is to consider how you give your phone number to people. If it's someone who lives in your city, you probably just give him or her the local seven-digit number. On the other hand, you tell someone out of state the entire ten-digit number, including the area code. In the local example, the seven-digit number is relative because the area code is assumed. In the national example, the ten-digit number is absolute, because it represents your complete phone number.

Another good example of heavily used absolute paths is eBay listings. If you list an item on eBay, you can't place the image of the item directly on eBay's Web servers. Instead, you must use an image hosting service or place the image on your own server. When you create the eBay listing, you enter the absolute path to the image so that it can be displayed with the listing. If you are clueless about eBay and don't have any idea what I'm talking about, put down this book and go to *http://www.ebay.com* to browse around.

Formatting Images

Like text, images are considered Web page content, so the `<img>` tag can be used anywhere text can appear. You can place images in the middle of paragraphs or even in headings. Images are also susceptible to many of the same formatting issues as text, such as using the `<br>` tag to move to the next line of a page, spacing images out vertically. You can also place images in paragraph tags, by themselves, to separate them from surrounding text. You will see some examples of how this is done in the next few pages.

In addition to the required `src` attribute, the `<img>` tag has another important attribute: `alt`. The `alt` attribute is used to assign text to an image—a succinct text label that describes the image, for example. This text is displayed in lieu of an image when the display of images has been disabled in a browser or when a Web browser doesn't support images. Alternate text is important because, if an image cannot be displayed, users of such Web browsers will see only a blank rectangle if no text appears where the image should be. Because most Web browsers can display images well these days, the text appearing in the `alt` tag now serves an additional purpose, the little text box that appears if you pause the mouse pointer over an image on a Web page. The words that appear in the box are specified by the `alt` attribute. Next is an example of using the `alt` attribute to provide information about an image:

```
<img src="Jump.jpg" alt= "Here I am catching a little air.">
```

To get a feel for how this image might fit into the context of a real Web page, take a look at the following code:

```
<html>
<head>
  <title>Mountain Biking at Tsali</title>
</head>

<body>
<h2>My Tsali Mountain Bike Trip</h2>
<p>
Tsali is a system of mountain bike trails in western North
Carolina on the edge of the Smoky Mountains. I recently took a
trip there with a couple of friends. Following is a picture
from the trip:
</p>
<img src="Jump.jpg" alt="Here I am catching a little air.">
</body>
</html>
```

Pausing with the mouse pointer over the image causes Internet Explorer to display a small text window containing the alternative text, as shown in Figure 3-1.

Figure 3-1.
The <img> tag allows you to place inline images adjacent to a paragraph of text, and can provide optional descriptive text for the image.

Tweaking the Size of Images

The <img> tag includes a couple of attributes that allow you to set the width and height of an image: width and height. Wait a minute, aren't the width and height of the image determined when you create it? Yes, but the width and height attributes of the <img> tag aren't used only to change the size of an image. Knowledgeable Web page designers often use width and height attributes to improve the efficiency of images on Web pages.

It works like this: When a Web page is first loaded, the browser must assess each image to determine its width and height. During this process, the browser resizes and relocates parts of the page to accommodate the images. If you specify the width and height of each image with the width and height attributes, the browser knows the measurements of the image. Consequently, it doesn't waste time figuring them out, and presto: happy Web surfers see the page displayed more quickly. For this reason, it's a good idea to specify the width and height for your Web page images—just make sure that they match up with the actual dimensions.

Or, if you like pushing the limits, you can change an image size by changing the width and height attributes. Specify a width and height that differs from the actual size of an image, and the browser will stretch or shrink the image to fit. Although this can be a problem if it is unintended, it is a benefit if you want to resize an image within a page. Using thumbnails of images is an example of where this is useful. Consider the scenario of displaying several images in the previous mountain bike Web page. If you displayed them all as large as the jump image, they would take up a lot of space on the page. A solution is to provide a series of thumbnail images that link to the external full-size images. Instead of creating smaller thumbnail images, you might want to use the width and height attributes of the <img> tag to decrease the size. On the other hand, there is a problem with this solution. Make a guess?

Note

Thumbnail images allow you to present a greater number of small images within a page; the viewer clicks on a thumbnail image to see the full-size image. You will learn how to use thumbnail images later in the chapter, in the section entitled "Linking to External Images."

The problem with resizing images using the <img> tag, as opposed to resizing the image file, is that the full-size image must still be downloaded to the Web browser. It takes longer to download the image than to display one you resized using an image editing tool. Don't forget that the main reason for using thumbnail images is that they take up less space and are faster to transfer. So, I don't recommend using the width and height attributes to decrease the size of an image; it is only useful if you want to increase the size of an image. In this case you have to pay careful attention to image distortion in the larger sized image.

Note

An image editing tool such as Microsoft PhotoDraw allows you to resize an image. When you resize an image with such a tool, the size of the image file changes to reflect the new image size. So, if you resize an image smaller using an image editing tool, the resulting image file will actually be smaller than the original file.

Giving Images Room to Breathe

Because images often appear alongside text and other content, you might wonder about the spacing of images with respect to other content. Fortunately, the <img> tag allows you to precisely control the space around an image, using the hspace and vspace attributes. For example, if you want two pixels of space on the top and bottom of an image, set the vspace attribute to "2". Likewise, the hspace attribute specifies the number of pixels on the left and right sides of an image. These attributes primarily come into play when you have text flowing around images, or images placed next to each other. In these situations, you want to provide some visual distance between each element.

Building Walls Around Images

If you've tried adding space around an image and you still doubt it's safe, you can go a step further and create a border for the image. A border is simply a colored line drawn around an image. Borders are made possible by the border attribute of the <img> tag, set to the width of the border, in pixels. To create a border that is 5 pixels in width around an image, use code similar to this:

```
<img src="Jump.jpg" border="5">
```

Figure 3-2 shows the image from Figure 3-1 surrounded by a 5 pixel border.

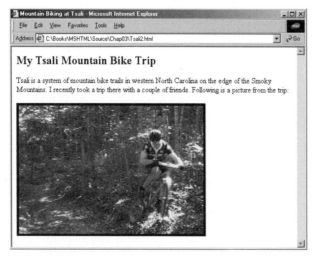

Figure 3-2.
The border attribute of the <img> tag allows you to place a border around an inline image.

If you choose to use both borders and spacing, the border is applied to each edge of the image, then the space is applied to the border.

Borders may occur with your images whether you want them to or not. When you use an image as a hyperlink—more on this in the next chapter—most Web browsers automatically display a border 2 pixels wide around the image. If you don't want a border around a linked image, use the border attribute and simply set it to zero.

Aligning Images

In the previous chapter you learned to control the alignment of text that appears within a paragraph. Although the technique you learned allows you to control the alignment of text within a paragraph, it doesn't do much to control the alignment of text near images. Keep in mind that images can be placed directly in a paragraph of text, which can present some problems in terms of aligning the image with surrounding text. Tricky. Fortunately, the <img> tag also provides the align attribute.

The `align` attribute controls the positioning of an image and the flow of text around it. Following are the possible values for the `align` attribute, and what they do:

- `left`—aligns the image along the left margin, flowing text around it to the right
- `right`—aligns the image along the right margin, flowing text around it to the left
- `top`—aligns the top of the image along the top edge of the current line of text, or the tallest image in the current line
- `texttop`—aligns the top of the image along the top edge of the current line of text
- `middle`—aligns the center of the image along the bottom of the current line of text, commonly referred to as the baseline of the text
- `absmiddle`—aligns the center of the image along the middle of the current line of text, or the tallest image in the current line
- `center`—aligns the center of the image along the middle of the current line of text, or the tallest image in the current line, which duplicates the effect of `absmiddle`
- `bottom`—aligns the bottom of the image along the bottom of the current line of text, which is usually the baseline of the text
- `baseline`—aligns the bottom of the image along the bottom of the current line of text, which is usually the baseline of the text. This duplicates the effect of `bottom`
- `absbottom`—aligns the bottom of the image along the bottom of the current line of text, or the bottom of the tallest image in the line

Note

The `border` and `align` attributes are more of those pesky deprecated parts of HTML, meaning that they will eventually be phased out and replaced with style sheets. But like most deprecated tags and attributes, the `border` and `align` attributes are still in use throughout the Web—and realistically, will be around for some time. It's worth pointing out that the `texttop`, `absmiddle`, `absbottom`, `baseline`, and `center` values for the `align` attribute were never a part of standard HTML. Nonetheless, they are supported by most browsers and have enjoyed wide usage.

Rather than go through exhaustive examples of how each of these alignment values affects the positioning of an image, let's look at a simple example. This HTML code illustrates how you can control the flow of text around an image using the `align` attribute:

```
<html>
<head>
  <title>Mountain Biking at Tsali</title>
</head>

<body>
<h2>My Tsali Mountain Bike Trip</h2>
<p>
Tsali is a system of mountain bike trails in western North
Carolina on the edge of the Smoky Mountains. I recently took a
```

```
trip there with a couple of friends. Following is a picture
from the trip:
</p>
<p>
<img src="Jump.jpg" alt="Here I am catching a little air."
hspace="10" align="left">
In this photo, I'm catching a little air off of a jump located
on the Right Loop of the Tsali trail. This jump was the last
in a series that provided a refreshing change of
pace from the fast descents and smooth climbing the trail had
to offer.
</p>
</body>
</html>
```

This is the mountain bike Web page mentioned earlier in the chapter, with some text added. Notice that the `hspace` attribute is set to 10, which provides 10 pixels of space on the left and right sides of the image. The `align` attribute is set to `left`, which aligns the image along the left margin of the page, forcing the text to flow around the picture on the right. Figure 3-3 shows this page viewed in Internet Explorer.

Figure 3-3.
The `hspace` and `align` attributes of the `<img>` tag were used to fine-tune the placement of the image.

Linking to External Images

Earlier in the chapter, I mentioned that external images are images that don't appear inline with other content on a Web page. Instead, they are referenced externally and viewed separately from the page where they are referenced. Sound confusing? All will soon be clear.

The main difference between an external image and an inline image is that an external image isn't displayed automatically. You must click a link to view it. External images are coded using the <a> tag, which establishes a hyperlink to the image. You will learn more about hyperlinks in the next chapter, "Connecting Pages with Hyperlinks." For now I'll cover enough to get you going with external images. The idea behind the <a> tag is to enclose content that will serve as a hyperlink to some other Web page or resource, or in this case an image. To reference an external image, you simply sandwich HTML content between <a> start and end tags, and reference the image using the href attribute. Following is an example:

```
<p>
Here is a <a href="Jump.jpg">picture</a> of me jumping.
</p>
```

Note

A *resource* is a general term that describes any piece of Web content, such as an image, audio clip, or another Web page.

In this example code, the word "picture" refers to the external image, Jump.jpg, displayed in most Web browsers when the viewer clicks the word. Notice that the href attribute is used to specify the URL of the external image, in this case the image filename, a relative path. Recall that thumbnail images are often used as a means of referencing external images. Following is an example of how you might use a small thumbnail image, SmJump.jpg, to reference a larger external image:

```
<a href="Jump.jpg"><img src="SmJump.jpg"></a>
```

This code looks a little more complex, so let's dissect it to see what's happening. The thumbnail image, SmJump.jpg, serves as the source of the hyperlink. It is displayed on the Web page with a border around it. When you click the thumbnail image, the larger external image, Jump.jpg, is displayed in the browser window. Following is additional code that uses this technique to add thumbnail images to the mountain bike Web page:

```
<p>
<a href="Jump.jpg"><img src="SmJump.jpg" alt="Here I am
catching a little air." hspace="10" align="left"></a>
<a href="Cruise.jpg"><img src="SmCruise.jpg" alt="Here I am
cruising by Fontana Lake." hspace="10" align="left"></a>
In these photos, I'm catching a little air off of a jump
located on the Right Loop of the Tsali trail, as well as
cruising by Fontana Lake on the Left Loop. The jump picture
shows the last in a series that provided a change
of pace from the fast descents and smooth climbs. The cruise
picture shows how the water in the lake was lowered due to dam
maintenance.
</p>
```

Figure 3-4 on the next page shows the results of adding this code and a bit more text to the mountain bike Web page.

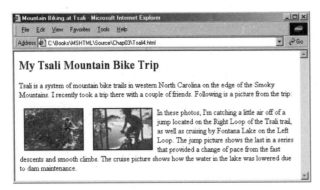

Figure 3-4.
Thumbnail images provide a convenient means of optimizing a Web page for arrangement and size by using the `<a>` tag, in conjunction with the `<img>` tag.

Notice that in the figure, by using thumbnails, you fit more content on the page, even allowing the page to be smaller. You can have more information on the page, and the page loads faster. You click on thumbnails you're interested in to see the full-size image. It's a win-win situation!

Using Background Images

You've no doubt seen Web pages with interesting backgrounds that often have a textured appearance. Admit it, you've lost sleep wondering how it's possible to display an image behind a Web page. This is known as a *background image.* And despite how restless you are over them, I'm here to tell you that they are simple to use and can dramatically improve a Web page or make it almost impossible to read. That's right, background images are both incredibly cool and dangerous at the same time. The positive side of background images is obvious, but the negative side is that a bold image lacking good contrast with the text on the page can render text illegible. Be careful when you choose background images for your Web pages.

Background images are used differently than the images you've encountered so far in this chapter. A background image isn't displayed by using the familiar `<img>` tag. The `<body>` tag has an attribute named `background` that specifies the background image. The following line of code demonstrates how to use this attribute:

```
<body background="DirtBack.gif">
```

Figure 3-5 shows how this code affects the mountain bike page that you saw earlier in Figure 3-3. Although it is somewhat difficult to see in a grayscale figure, the background image used in the example contains muted colors, which makes the black text clearly visible when it appears on top of the background. It is important to provide contrast between the color of the text on the page and the colors used in the background image. It is also important to ensure that the background image is designed so that it tiles appropriately. This means that the edges of the image line up with one another so that no seams are visible. The edges of the background image are a concern because background images are fairly small. The background is created by repeating the image multiple times across and down the page like the countertop tile in a kitchen. This is why background images are sometimes referred to as *tiled images*. Unless you are adept at using image editing tools to carefully manipulate images, you are better off not trying to create tiled images. Try looking for Web sites that offer free background images that tile seamlessly.

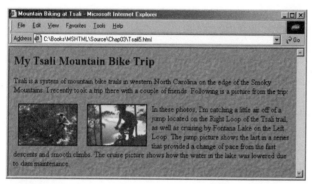

Figure 3-5.
The background *attribute of the* <body> *tag allows you to specify a background image for the Web page.*

Another topic related to the background of Web pages is the bgcolor attribute, which allows you to set the background color of a Web page instead of using a background image. You normally use either the bgcolor or background attribute, not both, because a background color will be hidden by a background image unless the image contains transparent areas. You specify colors in the bgcolor attribute by using the name of a predefined color or a special number that identifies a custom color. To learn how to specify custom colors in HTML, take a look at Appendix C, "Using Custom Colors." If you want to go with a predefined color, you can choose from the following list:

```
aqua      black     blue      fuchsia
gray      green     lime      maroon
navy      olive     purple    red
silver    teal      yellow    white
```

For example, setting the background of a Web page to a predefined color, olive, would look like this:

```
<body bgcolor="olive">
```

One other attribute of the <body> tag is the text attribute used to set the text color for the page. Although both the background and text attributes are now deprecated, they are prevalent in the HTML of existing Web pages. The text attribute finds more usage in pages where the background has been set to an image or a color other than white, the default color. When using the text attribute, the color value is specified as either one of the predefined colors previously listed, or as a special custom color number.

Using Animated Images

I mentioned earlier that the GIF image format supports animation, which makes it possible to display cartoons and animated effects. The interesting thing about animated GIFs is that all of the parameters of the animation are specified when creating the image. The image looks like any other from the perspective of HTML code. In other words, you don't have to do anything special when displaying animated images with the <img> tag.

To create animated GIFs, you must use a special graphics tool. Microsoft created a tool called GIF Animator, which is designed for creating animated GIF images. It was later integrated as a component of Microsoft Image Composer 1.5, a component of Microsoft FrontPage 98 and later versions. Several shareware image tools also create animated GIF images.

Note

Internet Explorer supports another type of animation known as marquee text animation. This animated text makes use of the <marquee> tag, an Internet Explorer extension to HTML that is not a part of standard HTML.

The main point is that there is nothing special required of animated GIFs from the perspective of HTML. You place an image on a Web page using the <img> tag, and the Web browser takes care of the rest. All of the real work with animated images takes place when the image is created.

Conclusion

Without images on the Web, you couldn't view weather maps, download clip art, or browse items for auction. You wouldn't even be able to create an online photo album of your vacation. And, because images play such an important role on the Web, they are an important part of HTML.

This chapter explained how images are used in HTML. It clarified the types of image formats that are used on the Web, along with when to use each type. You explored the different ways that images are referenced from Web pages, including both inline and external images. Toward the end of the chapter, you tackled background images, which dress up Web pages with an image that appears behind other content on a page. The chapter concluded with a quick look at animated images, which are used to display small, animated effects on Web pages.

Chapter 4

Connecting Pages with Hyperlinks

Web fact for the day

According to a NUKE InterNETWORK poll, 52 percent of Internet users have cut back on watching TV in order to spend more time online, and 12 percent have cut back on seeing friends.

Few people would doubt the importance of the Internet as a way to share information. Yet when people exchange lots of information on the Internet, they don't necessarily connect to other people. Don't get me wrong: the Internet was never intended for matchmaking or reacquainting long lost buddies. But you'd think that a global sharing of information would reinforce relationships between people. On the contrary, the experts say that 12 percent of Internet users are cutting back on seeing friends in order to stare for hours at a computer screen.

I can proudly say that thanks to e-mail messages, I've avoided many a phone call. I'm doing my part to put virtual relationships above real ones! Callers who don't get me on the phone can rest assured that I'm sitting here with a big grin, typing an e-mail message.

The point of this discussion about human relationships and the Internet is to introduce the idea of relationships between Web pages. Like people, Web pages benefit from good relationships. Of course, Web page interactions boil down to one page simply having a link to another page. This connectivity between Web pages is the true killer feature of the Web and the primary reason for its rapid integration into modern culture. The ability to link Web pages, with no regard for their physical location, makes for an unbelievably powerful system of sharing information. The impact of this system is so significant that it's redefining entire industries. The Web is changing the way we live—how we shop, how we learn, and how we communicate.

This chapter tackles the subject of linking Web documents together using hyperlinks. By linking documents, you effectively weave a web of your own documents within your Web site. As you'll also learn, other types of Web resources can be linked to documents with hyperlinks. Perhaps even more interesting is finding out how to create links to other documents and resources on the Web. In effect, you can incorporate the Internet-at-large into your own valuable resources.

What Is a Hyperlink?

As a Web user, you've no doubt heard the term *hyperlink* used in conjunction with Web pages. Let me clarify before you rush out for a self-help book on how to treat your "hyper" Web pages. Hyperlinks are an important part of virtually all Web pages, and they have nothing to do with hyperactivity. A *hyperlink* is a connection between an HTML element such as text, an image, or anything else on the page and another resource. That link might be to another Web page, an external image, or an e-mail address. Hyperlink text is usually displayed in a different font color to distinguish it from other text, and it is typically underlined as well. When you hover the mouse pointer over hyperlink text, the pointer changes—usually to a hand symbol—indicating that clicking the text takes you to linked material. Hyperlink images are also displayed a little differently than other images. They are shown with a 2-pixel-wide border surrounding them. Figure 4-1 shows how hyperlink text stands out in a paragraph.

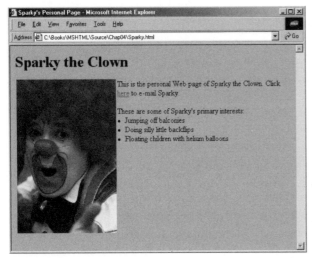

Figure 4-1.
Hyperlink text is generally displayed in a different color and with an underline to help distinguish it from the text.

Note

Chapter 3, "Dressing Up Pages with Images," shows how to remove the border that is automatically drawn around hyperlink images.

This figure should look somewhat familiar since it's based on the same file that was used in Chapter 1. I'm using it again because it contains a good example of a simple text hyperlink. The word *here* in the second sentence is a text hyperlink and provides an e-mail link so that you can e-mail your good friend Sparky the Clown. When you click the link, the Web browser will automatically launch the program that handles e-mail. It addresses a message to the recipient, who, in this case, is Sparky. Let's take a look at how an image can be used as a hyperlink. Figure 4-2 shows a Web page with a couple of familiar image hyperlinks.

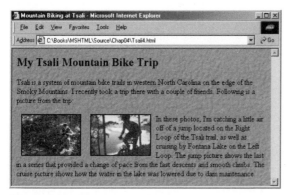

Figure 4-2.
Hyperlink images are displayed with a thin border to help distinguish them from other images.

Notice the 2-pixel-wide border around the thumbnail mountain bike images: both are hyperlinks. You'll learn how to analyze the code for both text and image hyperlinks shortly. First, though, take a moment to learn or review the basics on Uniform Resource Locators, which we know by the name URLs.

Understanding URLs

As you may already know, URLs identify Web pages and other resources such as images. You can type a URL in the address box near the top of your Web browser to open the Web page with that address. Similarly, hyperlinks rely on URLs to nail down the exact location of the linked resource on the Web. Given the importance of URLs to hyperlinks, it's worth spending a little time to better understand them.

Note

Minor debate continues over the correct pronunciation of "URL." I prefer saying the letters as if you were spelling a word: U-R-L, or "you are el." However, you'll also hear it pronounced as "earl," so that it rhymes with the word "pearl."

Host Names and URLs

Web resources ultimately reside on computers connected to the Internet, and each of those computers must be identifiable to get to the resources. To find an image that is located on the Web, you must first find out which computer (Web server) the image is stored on. Servers on the Internet are uniquely identified by *host names*. Every server connected to the Internet has its own unique host name that is used as a means of identification. Host names for servers connected to the Internet are similar to social security numbers for people, in that they provide a means of uniquely identifying every online server. Most URLs contain a host name that helps identify the location of a Web page or other resource.

If the term "host name" sounds somewhat arcane, allow me to calm your nerves by revealing that you're already quite comfortable with host names. I'd be willing to bet that you've memorized several host names and could list them right now. You see, the name of every Web site is in fact a host name. So, *www.amazon.com*, *www.ebay.com*, *www.yahoo.com*, *www.msn.com*, and my own *www.incthegame.com* are all host names.

Dissecting a URL

Host names may be clever or informative, or they may be both. But what do they have to do with URLs and hyperlinks? Keep in mind that Web browsers use URLs to navigate to specific pages on the Web. Here's an example of a complete URL:

```
http://www.incthegame.com/news.htm
```

This URL is the location of the news page for my board game Web site. A URL consists of a protocol, a host name, and a resource. Following are these three components of the URL *http://www.incthegame.com/news.htm*:

- `http`—the protocol for the resource (HTTP)
- `www.incthegame.com`—the host name of the computer where the resource is stored
- `news.htm`—the resource (a Web page in this case)

Note

The `http` portion of a URL specifies the protocol of the URL. A *protocol* defines how the exchange of information takes place over the Internet. Different types of information require different protocols. For example, the protocol used to send Web pages over the Internet (HTTP, or HyperText Transfer Protocol) differs from the protocol used to send e-mail messages over the Internet (SMTP, or Simple Mail Transfer Protocol). Because URLs can be used to represent different types of information, it is often necessary to specify the protocol.

These three components are required to fully specify an absolute URL. HTML tags that expect URL values allow you to use relative URLs, which are less specific. A relative URL might simply contain the resource portion of the URL, in which case the host name is assumed to be the same as for the Web page. For example, this is a legitimate relative URL for an image:

```
LgBear.gif
```

Because Web pages and other resources also exist in folders within a Web site, you may need to precede the name of the document with the name of its folder to specify a resource within a relative URL:

```
images/LgBear.gif
```

In this example, the file LgBear.gif is located in a folder named "images" on the Web server. If this relative URL is used in a Web page that is stored on the server with the host name *www.incthegame.com*, the URL is then equivalent to the following absolute URL:

```
http://www.incthegame.com/images/LgBear.gif
```

If you're worried that I'm straying too far from HTML with this URL information, let me point out that URLs are very important in HTML coding. They are used any time a resource is referenced externally. You've already been using URLs when specifying image files with the <img> tag. URLs are also used with hyperlinks in conjunction with the <a> tag, which you'll learn about next.

URLs and Web Resources

Throughout this chapter I've used the word *resource* a great deal, probably to the point that you're tired of it. The reason for my apparent obsession is that resources are incredibly important from the perspective of URLs and hyperlinks. Why? Well, a hyperlink is just a reference to a resource, which in turn is identified by a URL. To get the most out of hyperlinks, you must understand what kinds of resources are available as well as how to identify them with URLs. Following are the major types of URLs, along with a brief description of each:

- **Web page**—used to identify an HTML document available for downloading and viewing via HTTP
- **FTP**—used to identify a file available for download with FTP (File Transfer Protocol)
- **E-mail**—used to identify an e-mail address to which you can send an e-mail message
- **Newsgroup**—used to identify a newsgroup or message within a newsgroup
- **File**—used to identify a file on the local file system

Now that you know more about the main types of resources, the things you already knew will probably start to make more sense. Revisiting the URL you saw earlier, *http://www.incthegame.com/news.htm*, you see that the protocol for the Web page resource is specified as http. This is the protocol Web servers use to deliver pages to Web browsers, often called clients. The protocol changes when you use a different type of URL, such as an FTP or e-mail URL. The protocol name for FTP is ftp, the name for e-mail is mailto, the name for newsgroups is news, and the name for files is file. Following are sample URLs for each of these types:

```
ftp://michael:zed@ftp.incthegame.com/docs/resume.txt
mailto:info@incthegame.com
news:alt.bmx
file:///C:/Books/MSHTML/Source/Chap04/Tsali4.html
```

These examples demonstrate the different formats URLs can take; the format used depends on the type of the URL. In the case of the FTP URL, a user name (`michael`) and password (`zed`) are first provided, followed by the host name of the site containing the file (`ftp.incthegame.com`), followed by the path (`docs/`) and then the file itself (`resume.txt`).

The e-mail URL consists of the word `mailto` followed by the e-mail address of the recipient. It's up to the Web browser to invoke an e-mail program to handle the details of composing and sending the message. Internet Explorer will typically use either Outlook or Outlook Express to send e-mail through an e-mail URL.

The news URL consists of the word `news` followed by the name of a newsgroup. If you know the ID of a specific message within a newsgroup, you can specify it in lieu of the newsgroup name. In the example, the newsgroup `alt.bmx` is specified.

Note

For the uninitiated, *newsgroups* are special messaging systems on the Internet where you can hold open discussions with other people. Newsgroups were widespread prior to Web browsers and are still popular. Most Web browsers allow access to newsgroups. For example, to access newsgroups in Internet Explorer, you select Mail and News from the Tools menu, followed by Read News.

The final URL type is the file type, which consists of the word `file` followed by a path on the local hard drive. The path appears much as you might enter it in the Run window, which is accessible by clicking Run on the Start menu in Windows. The exception that sometimes catches us all is that the slashes are entered as forward slashes instead of as the familiar backslashes that are used in Windows paths. For example, a Windows path is specified using backslashes, like this: \Windows\Favorites. However, a URL path is specified using forward slashes, like this: /Windows/Favorites. Keep in mind that file URLs apply only to the local file system, which means you can't refer to remote files on the Internet. File URLs are what you use to open Web pages stored on your local hard drive, such as those you create as you work through this book.

Working with the `<a>` Tag

The magical HTML tag used to create hyperlinks is the `<a>` tag, which stands for "anchor." Anchoring is one of the uses of the `<a>` tag, which I'll tell you about in the next section. However, the most common use of this tag is creating hyperlinks to text and images.

You've already seen a few examples of this tag in action in previous chapters, and it's time to take a closer look at how it works.

Linking to Web Pages

A hyperlink created with the `<a>` tag consists of two items: the name of the hyperlinked HTML content and a target resource. The *hyperlinked HTML content* is text or an image and is enclosed within the `<a>` and `</a>` tags. The *target resource* for the hyperlink is specified in the `href` attribute of the `<a>` tag and consists of a URL that identifies the resource. Any of the URL types you learned earlier are okay to use with the `href` attribute, but the HTTP URL type is used to link to Web pages. Following is an example of such a hyperlink:

```
<p>
We offer many interesting products that you can
<a href="Order.html">order</a> from our online store.
</p>
```

In this example, the word *order* is the hyperlinked text that links to the Order.html Web page. This is a good example of a relative URL because no host name or path is specified for the target Web page. For the hyperlink to work properly, the Order.html file must be located in the same folder as the referring page. The same code could have used an absolute URL, which would look something like this:

```
<p>
We offer many interesting products that you can
<a href="http://www.thetribe.com/Order.html">order</a> from our
online store.
</p>
```

Notice how the full URL is specified in this example, including the protocol type, the host name, and the resource file name.

Linking to Other Resources

Creating hyperlinks based on the other URL types is similar to creating links to Web pages. Following is the same example code expanded to include an e-mail URL:

```
<p>
We offer many interesting products that you can
<a href="http://www.thetribe.com/Order.html">order</a> from our
online store. For additional information, please feel free to
send us <a href="mailto:info@thetribe.com">e-mail</a>.
</p>
```

This code demonstrates how to link to an e-mail URL using the `mailto` protocol type. As you can see, the `mailto` protocol type is followed by an e-mail address. When the user clicks the word *e-mail*, his Web browser will launch his e-mail program and start a new message with `info@thetribe.com` as the recipient.

Practical Linking with the \<a\> Tag

To see how the \<a\> tag works in the context of a real Web page, look over the following code. It shows a modified version of the mountain bike Web page you saw in the previous chapter and includes several hyperlinks to text and images:

```
<html>
<head>
   <title>Mountain Biking at Tsali</title>
</head>

<body background="DirtBack.gif">
<h2>My Tsali Mountain Bike Trip</h2>
<p>
Tsali is a system of mountain bike trails in western North
Carolina on the edge of the Smoky Mountains. I recently took a
trip there with a couple of friends. Following are pictures
from the trip:
</p>
<p>
<a href="Jump.jpg"><img src="SmJump.jpg" alt="Here I am
catching a little air." hspace="10" align="left"></a>
<a href="Cruise.jpg"><img src="SmCruise.jpg" alt="Here I am
cruising by Fontana Lake." hspace="10" align="left"></a>
In these photos, I'm catching a little air off of a jump
located on the Right Loop of the Tsali trail, as well as
cruising by <a
href="http://www.greatsmokies.com/community/fontana.htm">Fontana
Lake</a> on the Left Loop. The jump picture shows the last
in a series that provided a change of pace
from the fast descents and smooth climbs. The cruise picture
shows how the water in the lake was lowered due to dam
maintenance.
</p>
<p>
<br clear="left">
For more information on the Tsali trails, contact my friend <a
href="mailto:christheyeti@thetribe.com">Chris the Yeti</a>:
<a href="mailto:christheyeti@thetribe.com"><img
src="ChrisYeti.jpg" align="middle"></a>
</p>
</body>
</html>
```

In this code, you can see the external image hyperlinks that were already in the code from Chapter 3. The new hyperlinks include a link to a remote Web page containing information about Fontana Lake in North Carolina and a couple of e-mail links. One of the e-mail links is associated with the text "Chris the Yeti," and the other with the image file ChrisYeti.jpg. You can click either the text or the image to follow the e-mail hyperlink. Figure 4-3 shows this page as viewed in Internet Explorer.

Figure 4-3.
The mountain bike Web page shows several examples of using hyperlinks to link text and images with external images, Web pages, and e-mail addresses.

Anchor Hyperlinks

Although the `<a>` tag is commonly used to describe hyperlinks to other Web pages, it can also be used to identify anchors within a Web page. An *anchor* is a named point in a Web page that serves as a "bookmark" for the page. Put another way, an anchor is a reference to a specific location within a Web page. Anchors are invisible to the user and are used purely for linking purposes within a Web site. You create anchors using the `<a>` tag and the `name` attribute by specifying the name of the anchor in the `name` attribute, like this:

```
<a name="bbear">All About Black Bears</a>
```

In this code, the phrase *All About Black Bears* is identified as an anchor with the name `"bbear"`. Understand that this anchor is not a hyperlink; it serves as a target for a hyperlink. Once you've named an anchor, you can link to it with a hyperlink by using the `href` attribute of the `<a>` tag. The trick to referencing an anchor in a hyperlink is that you must precede the anchor name with the # symbol. Following is an example of using the `href` attribute to link to an anchor:

```
<p>
The mountains of Tennessee and North Carolina are home to
<a href="http://www.thetribe.com/animals.html#bbear">black
bears</a>.
</p>
```

Note

Anchor links can be relative, in which case you simply provide the # symbol and anchor name, or they can be absolute, in which case you specify a full URL with the # symbol and anchor name appended to the end.

In this code, the phrase *black bears* is linked to the anchor named bbear within the Web page:

```
http://www.thetribe.com/animals.html
```

Following this link, the Web browser will open the *animals.html* Web page and scroll to the anchor identified by the name bbear. Following is code for a more complete example that demonstrates how to use relative anchor hyperlinks:

```html
<html>
<head>
  <title>Mountain Bike Parts</title>
</head>

<body background="DirtBack.gif">
<h2>Inventory of Mountain Bike Parts</h2>
<p>
[ <a href="#brakes">Brakes</a> ]
[ <a href="#brakelevers">Brake Levers</a> ]
[ <a href="#brakepads">Brake Pads</a> ]
</p>
<h4><a name="brakes">Brakes</a></h4>
<ul>
<li>Avid Single Digit magnesium</li>
<li>Avid Arch Rival 50 Brakes</li>
<li>Avid Arch Supreme</li>
<li>Avid Disc Brake hydraulic</li>
<li>Avid Disc Brake Mechanical</li>
<li>Hayes Disc MC74 Hydraulic</li>
<li>Hayes Hydraulic disc</li>
<li>Hayes Cable disc</li>
<li>Magura Clara Hydraulic Disc Brakes</li>
<li>Magura Gustav Disc Brakes</li>
<li>Magura Louise XC Disc Brakes</li>
<li>Shimano XT Disc brakes</li>
<li>Shimano LX V-Brake</li>
<li>Shimano XT V-Brake</li>
<li>Shimano XTR V-Brake</li>
</ul>
<h4><a name="brakelevers">Brake Levers</a></h4>
<ul>
<li>Avid 2.0L Mag Levers</li>
<li>Avid SD-2.0L</li>
<li>Avid SD-1.9 L</li>
<li>Avid Ultimate L</li>
<li>Cane Creek Direct Curve V</li>
```

```
<li>Shimano 99 LX-V</li>
<li>Shimano 99 XT-V</li>
<li>Shimano 99 XTR-V</li>
</ul>
<h4><a name="brakepads">Brake Pads</a></h4>
<ul>
<li>Avid rim wrangler</li>
<li>Magura Pads</li>
<li>Ritchey Blk/Red</li>
<li>Ritchey V Pads</li>
<li>Shim. XTR-V</li>
<li>WTB Razor-V</li>
</ul>
</body>
</html>
```

This example contains code that might be suitable for an online bike shop. The code contains listings of mountain bike parts, broken down into categories. Below the title heading is a paragraph containing a simple navigation bar for jumping to parts of the inventory list. The navigation bar is created by using the <a> tag to establish links to relative anchors. The anchors themselves are created further into the document at each major heading. If this page sounds slightly complicated, just spend a moment studying the code and then look at Figure 4-4, which shows the page as viewed in Internet Explorer.

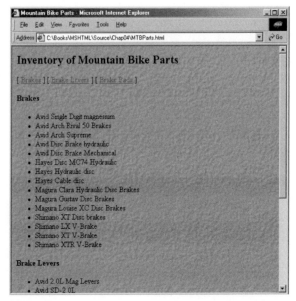

Figure 4-4.
Anchors provide a means of navigating to a specific location within a Web page.

Note

Anchors should refer directly to HTML content. In the bike shop example, the <a> tag should directly surround the text, as it does, instead of surrounding the text and the heading tags. The idea is that anchors identify a location within a document without regard for formatting. It's important to apply anchors directly to text or images; so far as anchors are concerned, formatting is secondary in importance.

Conclusion

Hyperlinks are the glue that bind together the massive collection of global Web pages that we call the World Wide Web. The concept of a hyperlink is quite simple, as you have learned, but it is a great example of how a simple concept applied on a huge scale can have profound results. The Web has clearly demonstrated that although information is important, providing access to information is where the proverbial rubber meets the road. You could take all the Web pages in existence and remove the links between them, and they would have virtually no value to anyone. It's the hyperlinks that make it possible to share our knowledge. Although this may sound like a speech at a nerd convention, it is the truth.

This chapter formally introduced you to hyperlinks. It explained the role they play in connecting Web pages with one another as well as with other Web resources such as images. An important part of the chapter explored URLs and the role they play in hyperlinks. We applied your newly gained knowledge and used the <a> tag to create hyperlinks. The chapter concluded by explaining how to use the <a> tag to create and reference anchors. All things considered, you should now have a solid grasp of hyperlinks and how they fit into the grand scheme of HTML.

Part 2

Beyond the Basics

Chapter 5

Visual Navigation
with Image Maps

Web fact for the day

If you lined up every Web address in existence, one after another, using the lettering size on a standard U.S. stop sign, the result would be 27,000 miles long—about 3,000 more miles than the circumference of Earth!

It's not easy to visualize the sheer quantity of Web addresses required to wrap around the world. It's even harder to imagine how you would keep the letters of the URLs floating together after you leave the continents to zoom across the vast oceans. Would you cruise along the equator or take the more challenging polar route with this massive collection of Web addresses? Regardless of how you decided to carry out this task, you would certainly need a compass and a good map. On that subject, this chapter is all about maps, albeit different kinds of maps than you would need to circle the globe with URLs.

This chapter introduces you to image maps—special images that are divided into sections, or regions. Each of the regions shown on an image map connects the page to another location on the Web site or on the Internet. You click different parts of an image map to follow different links. Image maps present a powerful option for navigating sites.

In this chapter, you'll learn about the significance of image maps and the types of Web pages they are commonly used in. You'll also find out about the different approaches to creating image maps, including one that is ideally suited to today's Web browsers. Finally, the majority of the chapter explores the creation of image maps through HTML coding—a surprisingly easy task considering how powerful image maps can be.

Image Map Basics

A couple of years ago, the hit Christmas toy was the *Tickle Me Elmo* doll, made by Fisher-Price. The selling point of the *Tickle Me Elmo* doll is that he giggles when you poke his belly. If you tickle Elmo anywhere else, he just sits there and does nothing. Thinking about Elmo's giggle zone might help you zero in on how an image map works.

Note

If you've never heard of the *Tickle Me Elmo* doll, I encourage you to check out your local toy store. Make sure no one is looking, and then give Elmo a good poke to the belly.

Another way to visualize an image map is as a color-by-numbers painting, with each region in the painting associated with a URL. Instead of painting a region a given color, you click it. Image maps can be used in a variety of different ways, the most common being for navigation bars and geometric maps. A good example of a geometric map with an image map is on the Nashville Predators NHL hockey team Web site. The seating chart for the arena, Gaylord Entertainment Center, is shown in Figure 5-1.

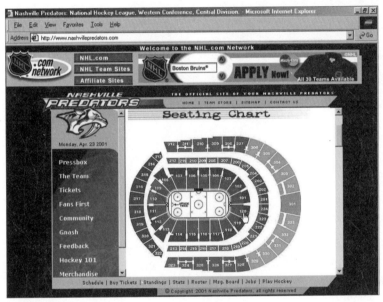

Figure 5-1.
The seating chart on the Web page for fans of the Nashville Predators is a good example of an interactive image map.

When you consider that single game tickets cost in the neighborhood of $20 to $80, this image map conveys valuable information. After you click one of the seating sections on the map, an image is displayed that shows the view of the ice from the section you clicked (see Figure 5-2 on the next page). This is a powerful and intuitive image map that helps provide information that is otherwise available only by visiting the arena.

To try out this image map for yourself, visit the Nashville Predators Web site at *http://www.nashvillepredators.com*.

As the figure reveals, image maps provide a unique option for navigating Web sites because they allow you to establish hyperlinks for individual parts of an image. By breaking an image down into several regions, it is possible to specify hyperlinks for each region and give an image a navigational context.

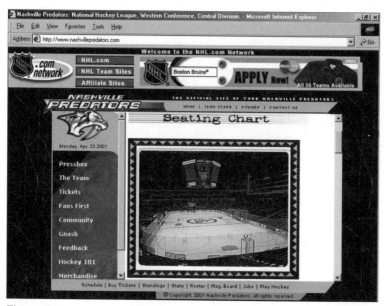

Figure 5-2.
After clicking a section in the seating chart, you see an image that shows the view of the ice from the selected section.

Two Approaches to Image Maps

Although you can create image maps several different ways using Web technology, two primary approaches have a dramatic impact on the way image maps work. Understand that when the user clicks an image map, the technology first determines the location of the mouse pointer on the computer screen, using the coordinates of the mouse click. Once the region is determined, the associated URL is used to open the Web page related to that region. The processing of the mouse-click coordinates is where the two image map approaches differ. One approach handles the processing on the client, which is the Web browser on your computer. The other takes place on the Web server. Let's take a look at why there are two different approaches to image maps.

Note

When I refer to "coordinates," I'm simply talking about an XY position on the screen. Coordinates identify the location of the mouse pointer relative to the browser window, or a point inside of an image. Coordinates are always measured in pixels, with the point 0,0 located in the upper-left corner of the browser window or image. This means that coordinate values increase to the right and down. So, if you started in the upper-left corner of an image (0, 0) and counted over 10 pixels and down 5 pixels, you would arrive at the point 10, 5.

Let the Server Do the Work

In the early days of the Web, browsers weren't crammed full of features. Much of the processing associated with interactive Web pages took place on Web servers. This server-based approach worked fine, but several weaknesses surfaced as the number of Web users grew rapidly. The number one problem with server processing is that it eats up valuable server resources. When you consider that a Web server may be called on to serve thousands of users at any given time, the idea of doing additional processing beyond serving pages becomes overwhelming. Figure 5-3 provides a visual summary of the processing of server-side image maps, which are image maps processed on a Web server.

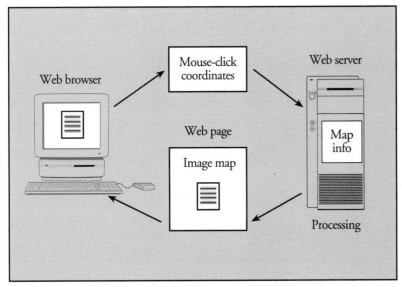

Figure 5-3.
With server-side image maps, a Web browser must deliver the mouse pointer coordinates to the server, where the processing takes place.

Maybe the Client Needs Some Responsibility

If a Web server is required to process a server-side image map, then we can reasonably expect that a Web browser is required to process a client-side image map. In fact, client-side image maps are processed entirely by a Web browser and basically result in a simple request for the target Web page from the server. In other words, a Web server has nothing to do with the processing of a client-side image map, which allows a browser to quickly process the information and improve the overall performance of the image map. Figure 5-4 on the next page provides a visual summary of client-side image map processing. Comparing this figure to Figure 5-3, you see that the map-image processing—the time-intensive activity—is moved from the server to the client.

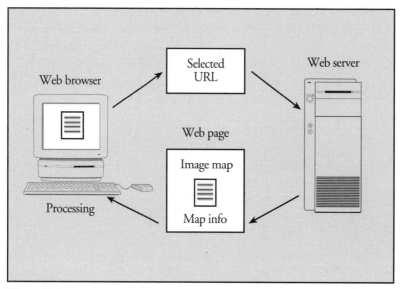

Figure 5-4.
With client-side image maps, all of the processing takes place on the client's Web browser, with only the URL of the associated page being delivered to the Web server.

Note

Because client-side image maps don't require any processing on the server, Web pages that use client-side image maps don't have to run in an online environment with a real Web server. This is a significant benefit of client-side image maps because it allows you to deploy Web pages in offline scenarios, such as on interactive CD-ROMs.

Another interesting distinction between client-side and server-side image maps is how the map information is specified. This information, as I mentioned earlier, consists of the geometric coordinates for the regions within the map, along with the URLs of the Web pages that are linked to each region. For server-side image maps, the map information is described in a special map file. The map file is placed on the Web server and referenced from an <a> tag that contains a reference to the image. Client-side map information is typically embedded directly in the Web page where the image map is located. Special HTML tags, which you learn about a little later in the chapter, describe the specifics of the map.

Note

Client-side map information can be placed in a different Web page for sharing purposes, but the code is still basically the same. For example, if you create an image map that is used in several Web pages, it is much better organizationally to store the map information in a file by itself so all of the pages can reference the information in one place. Otherwise you would have to duplicate the map information in every Web page.

I can tell you in no uncertain terms that client-side image maps are a significant improvement over server-side image maps. Therefore, the remainder of this chapter focuses on the creation of client-side image maps.

Using Image Map Development Tools

You'll be glad to know that creating client-side image maps isn't difficult. In fact, it is incredibly easy to create them with special graphical tools--no complicated programming or technical savvy needed. Several shareware image map editing tools are available, or you can use full-featured Web development tools, such as Microsoft FrontPage. Figure 5-5 shows a bicycle image ready to be converted to an image map by simply identifying hyperlink regions on the image.

Figure 5-5.
Microsoft FrontPage can be used to draw geometric regions for an image map.

In FrontPage, the tools shown along the bottom of the screen in Figure 5-5 allow you to draw geometric shapes to specify hyperlinked regions within the image. After drawing each shape, enter the hyperlink associated with the region in the Create Hyperlink dialog box that appears. Figure 5-6 shows the creation of a hyperlink for a Web page named wheels.html that is associated with circular regions drawn around the bicycle wheels.

Figure 5-6.
The Create Hyperlink dialog box allows you to enter a URL that specifies the Web page associated with an image map hyperlink.

You might be asking, if this book is about HTML, how can you endorse the use of a visual tool to create image maps? Because the end result of the visual graphical editing is HTML code that describes the image map. Additionally, the task of specifying the regions in an image map is a visual task, which is much easier to perform with a graphical tool. Following is the image map HTML code that is generated by FrontPage:

```
<p>
<map name="FPMap0">
<area href="wheels.html" shape="circle" coords="519, 278, 118">
<area href="wheels.html" shape="circle" coords="114, 291, 104">
<area href="brakes.html" shape="rect" coords="110, 164, 129,
217">
<area href="brakes.html" shape="polygon" coords="419, 185, 461,
227, 474, 209, 432, 167">
<area href="pedals.html" shape="rect" coords="312, 247, 333,
278">
<area href="pedals.html" shape="rect" coords="367, 325, 384,
344">
<area href="cranks.html" shape="polygon" coords="327, 271, 346,
323, 357, 315, 364, 334, 374, 324, 361, 299, 352, 293, 335,
259">
<area href="frame.html" shape="polygon" coords="152, 139, 305,
267, 316, 241, 332, 243, 356, 260, 370, 264, 387, 267, 381,
314, 521, 300, 513, 282, 397, 162, 418, 105, 401, 98, 398, 115,
179, 101, 161, 98">
```

```
<area href="stem.html" shape="polygon" coords="120, 69, 171,
94, 182, 90, 184, 71, 165, 67, 126, 49">
<area href="seat.html" shape="rect" coords="365, 7, 489, 32">
<area href="barends.html" shape="rect" coords="36, 48, 80, 76">
<area href="brakelevers.html" shape="rect" coords="59, 79, 104,
96">
<area href="grips.html" shape="rect" coords="78, 57, 115, 75">
<area href="grips.html" shape="polygon" coords="148, 54, 182,
54, 186, 64, 168, 67, 149, 57">
<area href="forks.html" shape="polygon" coords="136, 159, 104,
301, 124, 298, 128, 282, 145, 281, 172, 149, 153, 140, 143,
155, 140, 159">
<area href="seatpost.html" shape="polygon" coords="420, 36,
402, 98, 419, 100, 437, 36">
<area href="bottlecage.html" shape="polygon" coords="258, 205,
308, 248, 326, 223, 303, 198, 283, 216, 263, 198">
</map>
<img border="0" src="Bicycle.jpg" usemap="#FPMap0"
width="650" height="400">
</p>
```

Although this code might not entirely make sense to you at this point, a quick look reveals some clues about how image maps are described. Each area, or region, in the image map is specified as a shape followed by coordinates and values related to the position and size of the shape. Each area is associated with a single hyperlink to a location you go to when you click the area in the image.

On close inspection, you can see that several of the areas overlap each other. When you click in an overlapping region, the first area appearing in the code has precedence. You must take into consideration the order of the code when you create an image map with overlapping areas. I'll tackle this issue again in the next section when you construct image maps by hand in HTML code.

Coding Image Maps by Hand

You've seen HTML code for a client-side image map generated by FrontPage, but I haven't explained the specific HTML tags used to create image maps. This section describes the HTML tags and attributes that make image maps work.

Creating the Map

The primary tag used to create image maps is `<map>`, enclosing all the information associated with an image map. The `name` attribute of the `<map>` tag is used to identify the areas and hyperlinks for the map and to associate the map information with the map image itself. For example, following is code to create an image map named `bicyclemap`:

```
<map name="bicyclemap">
</map>
```

This code describes an empty map with no map information, not terribly useful. Map information within the `<map>` tag is coded using the `<area>` tag, which includes several attributes for describing regions within an image map. These are the main attributes of the `<area>` tag that are used to describe areas within an image map:

- `href`—URL of the resource, usually a Web page, linked to the area
- `nohref`—specifies that the area has no hyperlinked resource
- `shape`—geometric shape of the area
- `coords`—coordinates that describe the size and position of the shape of the area
- `alt`—text description of the area

The `href` attribute identifies the URL of the resource linked to the area, and it can contain either a relative or an absolute URL. The `nohref` attribute is used to specify that the area has no resource linked to it, which means that clicking the area does nothing. The `nohref` attribute is useful in situations when you don't want an area of an image map to serve as a hyperlink. Because there is no real value to assign to the `nohref` attribute, you code it in HTML using the following format:

```
nohref="nohref"
```

Once you've defined the hyperlink associated with an area, using the `href` or `nohref` attributes, you're ready to describe the shape of the area. The `shape` attribute is used to accomplish this task, and it can have one of the following values:

- `rect`—rectangle described by coordinates for the upper-left and lower-right corners
- `circ`—circle described by coordinates for its center, along with a radius
- `poly`—polygon described by a series of coordinates for connected points

Note

You might have noticed a discrepancy between these attribute values and those generated by FrontPage in the code shown earlier in the chapter. For example, FrontPage generates image map code using the shape value `circle` instead of `circ`. Both values work in most browsers, but it is generally accepted that the abbreviated forms of the shapes are safer to use. Most browsers also support the full names of the `rect` and `poly` shape values—`rectangle` and `polygon`. However, I encourage you to use the shortened versions.

These are the only shapes supported by the `shape` attribute, and they are the only shapes you can use in describing areas within an image map. While these shapes may seem limiting, you'll find that the `poly` shape type is extremely flexible and allows you to create complex shapes if necessary. The points used to describe each of the shapes are specified by the `coords` attribute, which contains a list of numbers separated by commas. The meaning of the numbers in the `coords` list varies according to the type of the shape. Next are the coordinate formats for each shape, illustrated in Figure 5-7:

```
shape="rect" coords="x1, y1, x2, y2"
shape="circ" coords="x, y, radius"
shape="poly" coords="x1, y1, x2, y2, x3, y3, ..."
```

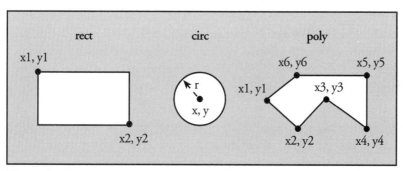

Figure 5-7.
The meaning of the numbers in the coords *list for each shape varies according to the specific shape.*

All of the numbers in the coords attribute used to describe the various shapes are specified in pixels relative to the upper-left corner of the image. The coordinates for the rect shape consist of two points—the upper-left corner of the rectangle and lower-right corner. The circ coordinates consist of the center of the circle and its radius. And finally, the poly coordinates consist of a list of points that are connected with lines to form a closed shape. Following are a few examples of how to describe shapes using the <area> tag in conjunction with the shape and coords attributes:

```
<area href="page1.html" shape="circ" coords="10, 10, 5">
<area href="page2.html" shape="rect" coords="5, 15, 40, 20">
<area href="page3.html" shape="polygon" coords="50, 5, 95, 45, 5, 45">
```

The first line of code creates a circular area at the point (10,10) with a radius of 5. The second line creates a rectangular area with its upper-left corner at the point (5,15) and its lower-right corner at (40,20). The last line of code creates a triangular polygon by connecting the points (50,5), (95,45), and (5,45) together.

One final useful attribute of the <area> tag is alt, which allows you to provide a text description of an area. When a user pauses the mouse pointer over an area with alt text, the text is displayed in a small window over the area. The alt attribute therefore provides a useful way of adding context to image maps. For example, to make them easily recognizable, you could use the alt attribute to associate the name of each state to the regions of an image map of the United States. This is an example of how you might use the alt attribute to describe a triangular area:

```
<area href="page4.html" shape="polygon" coords="50, 5, 95, 45, 5, 45"
alt="This is a triangular area.">
```

Associating the Map with an Image

You've learned how to describe the areas and URLs associated with an image map, but you haven't yet learned how to put this information together with an image to form a complete image map. Map information described in the <map> tag is associated with an image by using the usemap attribute of the <img> tag. The value of the usemap attribute contains a URL that identifies the map information for the image. Create the map information using the <map> tag, and associate it with an image using the usemap attribute of the <img> tag. Therefore, the creation of an image map is a two-step process:

1. Within the <map> tag, create the map areas with associated hyperlinks to URLs.

2. Associate the map information with an image by using the usemap attribute of the <img> tag.

Recall that every map has a name that is identified by the name attribute of the <map> tag. This name is what you use in the usemap attribute to associate a map with an image. If the <map> tag containing the map information is located within the same Web page as the image—typically the case—you specify the name of the map preceded by a # symbol, like this:

```
<img src="Jungle.gif" usemap="#junglemap">
```

In this code, the map named junglemap must be located in the same Web page as the <img> tag. You could also reference a map that is located in a separate document by including a URL to the map. The map name effectively works like an anchor, except that the image map is specified by the name attribute of the <map> tag, as opposed to using the <a> tag. The <a> tag doesn't enter the equation at all when using client-side image maps!

Constructing a Practical Image Map

To put together all of what you've learned about client-side image maps, it's worth studying a complete example. Following is code for a skateboard Web page that uses an image map to explain each part of a skateboard:

```
<html>
<head>
  <title>Anatomy of a Skateboard</title>
</head>

<body>
<h2>The Anatomy of a Skateboard</h2>
<p>
Click on the skateboard to learn more about each major part of
it.
</p>
```

```
<p>
<map name="skatemap">
<area href="wheels.html" shape="rect" coords="89, 155, 144,
195" alt="Wheel">
<area href="wheels.html" shape="rect" coords="455, 155, 510,
193" alt="Wheel">
<area href="Wheels.html" shape="rect" coords="461, 8, 517, 47"
alt="Wheel">
<area href="Wheels.html" shape="rect" coords="87, 5, 143, 44"
alt="Wheel">
<area href="Trucks.html" shape="rect" coords="437, 79, 501,
124" alt="Truck">
<area href="Trucks.html" shape="rect" coords="477, 47, 497,
155" alt="Truck">
<area href="Trucks.html" shape="rect" coords="102, 79, 170,
122" alt="Truck">
<area href="Trucks.html" shape="rect" coords="105, 47, 128,
156" alt="Truck">
<area href="Sticker.html" shape="rect" coords="503, 109, 552,
166" alt="Sticker">
<area href="Deck.html" shape="circ" coords="77, 100, 77"
alt="Deck">
<area href="Deck.html" shape="circ" coords="521, 101, 78"
alt="Deck">
<area href="Deck.html" shape="rect" coords="81, 21, 521, 181"
alt="Deck">
</map>
<img src="Skateboard.jpg" usemap="#skatemap" border="0">
</p>
</body>
</html>
```

To better understand how the areas of the image are organized, take a look at the skateboard Web page as viewed in Internet Explorer (Figure 5-8 on the next page). Especially note the small window appearing over the lower-right wheel; this is the text description provided by the `alt` attribute for that rectangular area.

You learned earlier in the chapter that areas are capable of overlapping in an image map, and that based on the order they were defined, areas take precedence over other overlapping areas. This is important in the skateboard image map because several of the areas overlap each other. For example, a large rectangle identifies the deck of the skateboard, which is the main body of the board. However, other components of the board appear above the deck rectangle, which means that their areas overlap the deck rectangle. To keep the deck rectangle from overriding the other areas, the smaller areas must be defined first, as evident in the HTML code for the page.

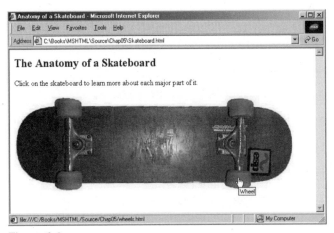

Figure 5-8.
The skateboard Web page is a good example of how an image map can be used to describe different parts of a photograph.

Another interesting facet of the skateboard Web page is how the deck area is described using both circles and rectangles. The ends of the skateboard are described using circles since the board has rounded ends. The middle part of the deck is then described using a large rectangle that overlaps half of each circle. This is significant because it shows how to model a complex shape using multiple simple shapes. There is nothing magical going on here, just a clever use of overlapping areas.

Each of the hyperlinks associated with the skateboard image map is linked to a Web page with a simple description of each part of the skateboard. Following is code for the Trucks page, which describes the role of skateboard trucks:

```
<html>
<head>
  <title>Anatomy of a Skateboard</title>
</head>

<body>
<h2>The Anatomy of a Skateboard : Trucks</h2>
<p>
Trucks are attached to the <a href="Deck.html">deck</a> of a
skateboard, and are used for steering.
<a href="Wheels.html">Wheels</a> are attached to the ends of
the trucks. Click <a href="Skateboard.html">here</a> to return
to the Anatomy of a Skateboard.
</p>
</body>
</html>
```

The Trucks Web page doesn't use image maps, but it does link back to other pages, including the main skateboard page. I wanted to show you this page because it helps demonstrate how image maps are used in the context of a complete Web site. I'll leave it up to you to think of something interesting to visually describe using image maps.

Conclusion

You have survived yet another chapter chock-full of strange and seemingly unrelated references designed solely for my own enjoyment. Between *Tickle Me Elmo*, bicycles, and skateboards, you're probably wondering if I have some fixation on fun. The truth is I do, but I always enjoy fun with a purpose. This is why the chapter weaved these topics into the discussion of image maps, which is arguably one of the most fun features of HTML. The capability of creating regions on a Web page that take you to different places when clicked is pretty neat, not to mention powerful.

This chapter introduced you to image maps and the role they play in adding interactivity to Web pages by way of images. Once you got the basics of image maps under your belt, you examined the difference between client-side and server-side image maps. This knowledge is necessary so that you appreciate the convenience of client-side image maps, along with being able to recognize a server-side image map when you see one. You saw how a visual Web development tool can make the creation of image maps quite easy. Not blindly embracing convenience, you marched on and learned about the HTML tags and attributes that make image maps tick. You wrapped up the chapter by coding a practical image map from scratch.

Chapter 6

Organizing Pages with Tables

Web fact for the day

In 1952, CBS made computer history. They used the first commercially available computer—UNIVAC I—to forecast the U.S. presidential election.

If the Fox news team had found that bulky UNIVAC and an empty Home Depot to house the monster, they would have no doubt used it in the 2000 presidential election. The 2000 election was a sad reminder that we aren't as high-tech as we think we are. The same country that invented a device to turn the lights on and off with the clap of a hand is still electing its leaders with paper punches. Let's solve this dangling chad business in the 2004 election: three claps for Ralph Nader, two claps for Harry Browne, or one big smack for wrestler-turned-politician Jesse Ventura.

Are you wondering what all this election talk has to do with tables? Seeing all that poll data on television and in the papers no doubt created a hunger for you to do your own polling. You may be waiting anxiously to display the results on a Web page in table form. Fortunately, this chapter shows you how tables work and how to create them in HTML code.

Tables are gridlike structures used to divide a Web page into rectangular regions. They were originally designed to organize tabular data of the kind you might find in a spreadsheet. As HTML evolved and more features were added, however, Web developers realized that tables could also solve page layout problems. This chapter explains how to use tables both as a page layout tool and as a means of organizing tabular data. By the end of this chapter you will have all the knowledge necessary to display in tabular form the results of a neighborhood poll about the next election.

Table Basics

The most obvious way to get acquainted with tables and their role in HTML is to think of them as spreadsheets. A spreadsheet consists of a grid of cells arranged in rows and columns of data of some sort. Tables are similar to spreadsheets in that they consist of cells that are arranged in rows and columns. A good example of a table used to organize tabular data is the election campaign finance totals in *www.OpenSecrets.org*. Figure 6-1 shows the Web page and what it reveals about the democratic process.

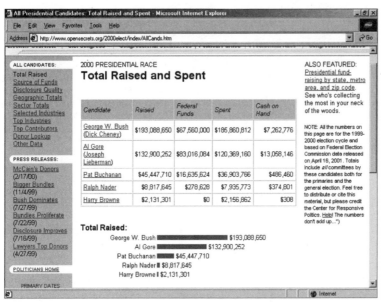

Figure 6-1.

The 2000 presidential election campaign finance totals, as presented by OpenSecrets.org, show how a table can be used to organize tabular data.

Although the OpenSecrets.org Web page shows the most logical use of Web page tables, they are used more often in a way that you may not know about: to control the layout of Web pages. Tables are extremely flexible and provide considerable control over the position of information. Unlike a spreadsheet, a table can be nested within another table, giving you more flexibility in organizing data. As an example, check out the Web page shown in Figure 6-2 on the next page, which is from my own board game Web site.

Looking at this Web page, you would probably never guess that a table defines its layout. In fact, two tables are used within the page to carefully position the text and images. The tables make it possible to specify the relative position of Web content. For example, by carefully designing the size and arrangement of cells within a table, you can create effects such as vertical navigation bars and text in two columns. To understand how tables are used in the Web page in Figure 6-2, check out the table diagram in Figure 6-3, also on the next page.

Figure 6-2.
The board game Web site uses tables to control the positioning of content on a page.

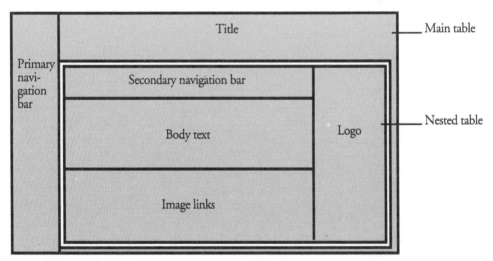

Figure 6-3.
By visualizing tables as diagrams, you can more easily understand how they control the layout of Web pages.

The table diagram in Figure 6-3 reveals that the structure of the *Inc. The Game of Business* Web page is a table nested within another table. The outer table defines the overall structure and layout of the page, and the more detailed inner table describes the arrangement of the body text in relationship to other content. Creating this type of table diagram before you begin coding a table in HTML gives you a useful guide. You will use this approach later in the chapter when you learn how to lay out pages with tables. But now let's move on to learning how to create tables with HTML table tags.

Getting to Know the Table Tags

Can you imagine life without tables? I'm referring to the real world now, not the virtual one. We'd be relegated to eating off the floor and holding business meetings in beanbag chairs. It's not a pretty thought. Just as we have furniture manufacturers to thank for making tables available in the physical world, we have HTML to thank for tables in Web pages. The basic HTML for tables comes in the form of a few tags:

- `<table>`—creates a table
- `<tr>`—identifies the beginning of a row within a table
- `<td>`—identifies a cell within a row

To create a table, start with the `<table>` tag. With the table initially created, you add rows to it by including as many `<tr>` tags as necessary. Then within each `<tr>` tag, you add `<td>` tags to identify each cell. Following is an example of how to use these tags to create a simple table:

```
<table>
<tr>
  <td>January</td>
  <td>February</td>
  <td>March</td>
</tr>
<tr>
  <td>April</td>
  <td>May</td>
  <td>June</td>
</tr>
<tr>
  <td>July</td>
  <td>August</td>
  <td>September</td>
</tr>
<tr>
  <td>October</td>
  <td>November</td>
  <td>December</td>
</tr>
</table>
```

This code creates a one-year calendar that contains months organized three across and four down. Figure 6-4 shows the resulting page.

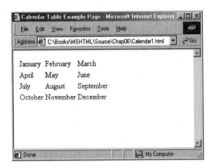

Figure 6-4.
The table tags make it easy to organize information into rows and columns.

Drawing Borders Around Tables

Although the calendar table in our example is functional, it could look better. One useful addition would be a *border* to visually divide the cells in the table. Conveniently, the `<table>` tag includes an attribute named `border`, which is designed specifically to accomplish this task. Set the `border` attribute to a number that determines the thickness of the table border, in pixels. To change the calendar Web page so that it has a border 2 pixels wide, you must change its `<table>` tag to:

```
<table border="2">
```

The resulting table is shown in Figure 6-5.

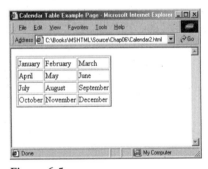

Figure 6-5.
The `border` *attribute of the* `<table>` *tag enables you to create a border around a table and between its cells.*

The default value of the `border` attribute is zero; no border appears if you don't use the attribute. In addition to improving the look of some tables, the `border` attribute can play an important role during the early design stages. Even if you don't want borders on your finished table, it is often helpful to temporarily insert them so you can see the layout of the table. Tables can get tricky, especially when you start nesting them, and borders provide an easy way to see exactly what is going on.

Heading Up Your Tables

In addition to the basic `<table>`, `<tr>`, and `<td>` tags, there is also a `<th>` tag that is used to create header cells. *Header cells* are cells with the contents centered and in a boldface font. They don't play a significant role in page layout, but you might find them useful when formatting tabular data with tables. Following is an example of a header cell in a new row of the calendar table:

```
<tr>
  <th>2001</th>
</tr>
```

This code formats the year of the calendar, 2001, as a header cell. So, "2001" will appear centered within the cell and in bold. However, the text won't be centered across the entire width of the table because it only occupies the first of three cells in the row. Figure 6-6 illustrates what I'm talking about.

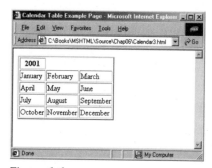

Figure 6-6.
The `<th>` tag allows you to automatically create a centered, boldface heading.

The problem with the table in Figure 6-6 is that the year of the calendar is displayed in the first cell of the first row, and the second and third cells in that row are empty. Why are there other cells, even blank ones, in the row, when there are no additional `<td>` tags in the code? The reason is that every row in a table is automatically sized to the maximum number of cells on any given row. In other words, find the row with the most cells, and that's how many cells will automatically be placed on every row. If on another row, for example, you specify fewer cells, the remaining cells will be empty. This approach may seem a little strange, but it would be difficult for HTML to handle tables any other way.

Spanning Cells

As with most problems in HTML, there is a simple solution to the automatic inclusion of unneeded cells in a table. The concept known as *cell spanning* involves letting one cell flow into another cell. In other words, it is possible for a cell to merge with adjacent cells and appear as if they are all one big cell. You can span cells vertically across rows using the rowspan attribute and horizontally across columns using the colspan attribute, leading to some interesting results. You apply the attributes to the number of rows or columns that a cell is to span. For example, to fix the header cell in the calendar table, you need to set the colspan attribute so that the cell spans three columns. Following is the new code for this cell:

```
<th colspan="3">2001</th>
```

Figure 6-7 reveals how this code causes the calendar year to span all of the cells in the first row of the table, which results in a perfectly centered table header.

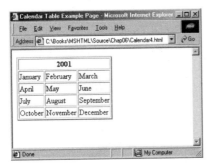

Figure 6-7.
The colspan attribute allows you to merge a cell with other cells, making the cells appear as one.

The rowspan attribute serves a purpose similar to colspan, except that it causes cells to merge vertically with cells in other rows. You can even combine the two attributes to merge cells in a rectangular fashion. You will learn later in the chapter that cell spanning plays a role in using tables to control the overall layout of Web pages.

Setting the Size of Tables

One topic worth tackling before you move on to the details of table formatting is the size of the table. The assumption at this point in the chapter is that Web browsers "intuitively know" how to size tables to perfectly fit their content. This assumption isn't far from the truth, although intuitive sizing isn't always a good thing. Generally speaking, a Web browser examines the content within a table and attempts to make the table as small as possible. The default size of a table is therefore just large enough to house its content. Although this frequently works out fine, you will want to exert control over the size of your tables in many situations.

The `<table>` tag offers an attribute that allows you to explicitly set the width of a table: `girth`. Just kidding. The real attribute is `width`, and it lets you specify the width of a table in pixels or as a percentage of the width of the displayed page. In pixels, the table is exactly as wide as the number of pixels in the `width` attribute. The only exception is when you set a width that isn't wide enough to hold the table's content. In this case, the table will ignore the width and adopt a breadth just wide enough to fit the content. You can think of the width of a table as either the number of pixels specified in the `width` attribute or the minimum number of pixels in width required to fit the content, whichever number is larger. To specify a table width in pixels, you provide a number in the `width` attribute:

```
<table border="2" width="400">
```

Note

Generally speaking, it's a good idea to keep the width of tables under 600 pixels. Most Web users have their screen resolution set to 800 x 600 pixels, which provides 800 pixels of screen width. When you factor in a Web browser scroll bar and some extra space around the edges of the page, it works out that even the largest tables should be no wider than 600 pixels.

This code sets the width of the table to 400 pixels, which means that the table will be 400 pixels wide unless it needs to be made larger to fit its content. The other approach to setting table width is to specify a percentage of the page size rather than a number of pixels in the `width` attribute, as the following code demonstrates:

```
<table border="2" width="60%">
```

Instead of setting the table width to a fixed value in pixels, this code causes the table to take on a width that is a percentage of the page width. The primary difference between this approach and the pixel approach is that the table width varies if the page size changes. For example, if the browser window is maximized at a screen resolution of 800 x 600, the page width will be approximately 800 pixels, so the table width will be 60 percent of that, or 480 pixels. However, if you resize the browser window so that it is only 500 pixels wide, the width of the table is cut to 300 pixels. Because of this variance in table size, the percentage approach to setting the table width is less predictable. On the other hand, it does have the positive effect of causing the table to appear in scale with the page. This is nice if you have a relatively large monitor with a screen resolution higher than 800 x 600.

Note

In case you're curious, there is also a seldom-used `height` attribute. In theory, this attribute allows you to set the height of tables. In practice, however, it yields inconsistent results, so I encourage you to avoid it.

You can set the width of individual cells by using the `<td>` tag. In reality, you are setting the width of the entire column, because cells in a column must all be the same width. For this reason, you can specify the `width` attribute in the first cell of a column.

The exception to this rule is when you have cells that span multiple columns, in which case it is necessary to stipulate the width of each cell.

Digging Deeper into Table Formatting

You can have fun with tables beyond creating them and defining a few cells. There is much more to table formatting than I've alluded to thus far. The next few sections explore some of the finer points of table formatting, and will no doubt leave you with enough skills to fill your Web pages with dazzling, functional tables.

Aligning Tables

Because tables typically must fit into the context of a complete Web page, it is necessary to consider their alignment, related to other content on the page. Fortunately, the alignment of tables is easily controlled with the align attribute of the <table> tag. This attribute can be set to one of the following values to control the alignment of a table:

- left—aligns the table at the left edge of the Web page
- right—aligns the table at the right edge of the Web page
- center—centers the table horizontally on the Web page

The align attribute also applies to individual cells within a table, which allows you to set the alignment of content within each cell. You can also set the alignment of an entire column by using the align attribute with the first cell in a column. Another interesting twist regarding alignment and cells is the valign attribute, which lets you set the vertical alignment of cells and rows. The valign attribute can be set to one of the following values:

- top—positions the cell content at the top of the cell
- middle—positions the cell content at the middle of the cell
- bottom—positions the cell content at the bottom of the cell

Note

In addition to these possible values for the valign attribute, Netscape Navigator also supports a baseline value that positions a cell at the baseline of the first line of text in the cell. The baseline of a line of text is the bottom of the text, excluding any letters that extend down below the others such as *g* and *y*.

Incidentally, the default value for the align attribute is left, and the default value of valign is middle.

To make sure you understand the practical usefulness of table alignment, let's take a quick look at an example. If you recall, I described some of my mountain biking exploits in Chapter 4 on a Web page named Tsali (Tsali is the name of the mountain bike trails). Although that page was formatted reasonably well given your knowledge of HTML at the time, you're now ready to improve the appearance and structure of that page with a table. Following is code that repositions the images and main paragraph on the page:

```
<table align="left">
<tr>
  <td>
  <a href="Jump.jpg"><img src="SmJump.jpg" alt="Here I am
  catching a little air." hspace="10" align="left"></a>
  </td>
  <td>
  <a href="Cruise.jpg"><img src="SmCruise.jpg" alt="Here I am
  cruising by Fontana Lake." hspace="10" align="left"></a>
  </td>
</tr>
<tr align="center">
  <td>
  Catching a little air
  </td>
  <td>
  Cruising Fontana Lake
  </td>
</tr>
</table>
```

You may not quite have the ability to visualize the final product based on HTML code just yet. Basically, this table adds captions for each of the two thumbnail images and aligns the table with the left edge of the screen. This causes the main paragraph of text in the page to flow around the right side of the table. Figure 6-8 shows the new and improved tabular format of the Tsali page.

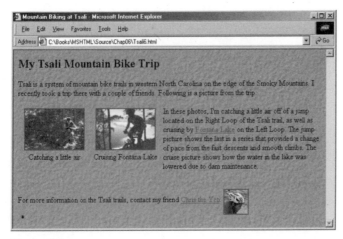

Figure 6-8.
The layout of the Tsali page is improved by using a table to add captions to the images and to flow the main paragraph of text around the right of the images.

For the record, I'm jumping ahead a little by showing how to use tables to describe the layout of Web pages. Later in the chapter you get a formal introduction to Web page layout with tables in the section titled, "Using Tables for Page Layout." For now, let's continue the discussion of table formatting by venturing into space.

Giving Tables Some Space

Have you ever been in line at a movie waiting for tickets and had someone crowding too close behind you? Maybe I just need more personal space than many people, but having strangers breathing down my neck is not my idea of a good time. On the other hand, if you're on a date, you may disagree. The point of this analogy is that tables often like a little breathing room, too. Sure, you could jam a table into a page right up against other content, but why not make it easy for everyone to see what you have to say?

The bad news is that the HTML specification does not provide any attributes for the `<table>` tag that allows us to directly accomplish this. But before you fall into a depression and start writing dark poetry in HTML, let me remind you that there is always another way. I repeat, because it will come in handy as you continue to develop HTML skills: "There is always another way." In this case, the other approach goes by the cutting-edge name of *pixel shims*.

If you're familiar with carpentry, you know that a shim is a small piece of wood used to fill a gap. A good example of using shims in carpentry is window installation in a new house. Because it is virtually impossible to size the window opening down to the millimeter to fit the exact dimension of the window, carpenters don't even bother trying. They shoot for an opening size that's within a quarter of an inch of the size of the window, which guarantees that the opening won't be too small. When they set the window in the opening, they drive wood shims in the gap and make a tight fit. This same logic applies to pixel shims used in a Web page.

Pixel shims are tiny blank images used to fill space in a Web page. Specifically, a pixel shim is a 1-pixel GIF image that can be resized to fill any rectangular area on the page. You create the shim with the color that looks good to you or even leave the shim transparent so the background of the page shows through. Also, pixel shims can be used to add space around a table. Look at the following revised Tsali page code, which uses pixel shims to spread out the table horizontally:

```
<table align="left">
<tr>
  <td rowspan="2" bgcolor="red">
  <img src="Shim.gif" width="15">
  </td>
  <td>
  <a href="Jump.jpg"><img src="SmJump.jpg" alt="Here I am catching a
little air." hspace="10" align="left"></a>
  </td>
```

```
<td>
<a href="Cruise.jpg"><img src="SmCruise.jpg" alt="Here I am cruising by
Fontana Lake." hspace="10" align="left"></a>
</td>
<td rowspan="2" bgcolor="red">
<img src="Shim.gif" width="15">
</td>
</tr>
<tr align="center">
<td>
Catching a little air
</td>
<td>
Cruising Fontana Lake
</td>
</tr>
</table>
```

Before you freak out over the size of this code, understand that I've added only two new cells in the first row, one at the beginning of the row and one at the end. The following code inserts the pixel shim as a cell in the table:

```
<td rowspan="2" bgcolor="red">
<img src="Shim.gif" width="15">
</td>
```

This code creates a pixel shim that spans two vertical cells, or the entire first column of the table. The same code is used to span the entire last column of the table as well. This may sound confusing, but Figure 6-9 should make it clear.

Figure 6-9.
Pixel shims are used to add space to the left and right sides of the table in the Web page about Tsali.

As the figure reveals, I did something interesting in this code. I deliberately set the background color for the shim cells to a contrasting color, red, so that you can see the effect of the pixel shim on the table. In this case, the code makes the end column 15 pixels wide. You can't see the pixel shim image in the figure because this one is a transparent GIF image, letting the red background show through. Use this trick to add extra space virtually anywhere on a page.

Individual cell spacing is also worth addressing. The `cellspacing` and `cellpadding` attributes of the `<table>` tag set the internal spacing of cells. The `cellspacing` attribute adds space between cells in a table but does not change the size of the cells themselves. The `cellpadding` attribute, on the other hand, adds space within the walls of a cell, around its content, on all four sides. Both attributes set the spacing in pixels.

Note

The default value for the `cellspacing` attribute is 2 pixels, and the default value for `cellpadding` is 1 pixel. You can set both attributes to zero to minimize the spacing of cells and pack them tightly together; no spacing or padding is applied to a cell in this case.

Dressing Up Tables with Colors and Images

Earlier, I mentioned using the `bgcolor` attribute to set the background color of cells in order to determine how they are being sized by the Web browser. This technique is valuable for testing purposes, as well as for setting the background color of cells as part of the design of a page. Using a solid color for a filled area of a page is much more efficient than using an image, because images must be downloaded before they can be displayed. Tables provide the perfect opportunity to use color as a design element by way of the `bgcolor` attribute. Following is an excerpt of code from the Tsali page, which has been modified so that the background color of the cell is set to maroon:

```
<td bgcolor="maroon">
Catching a little air
</td>
```

Note

In addition to setting the predefined colors in HTML, you can specify custom colors. You'll learn how in Appendix C, "Using Custom Colors."

Thanks to the convenience of HTML, you can extend the `bgcolor` attribute setting across entire rows with the `<tr>` tag. Taking it a step further, use the background color for an entire table by setting the `bgcolor` attribute in the `<table>` tag. It is possible to use the `bgcolor` attribute in several different tags to get different effects; the more detailed tag always overrides the more general tag. In other words, the background color specified in a `<td>` tag will override the background color set in the `<table>` tag. Following is an example of how to create a table that resembles a checkerboard, by carefully setting the background color of cells.

```
<table bgcolor="black" width="400" height="400">
<tr>
   <td bgcolor="red"></td> <td></td>
   <td bgcolor="red"></td> <td></td>
   <td bgcolor="red"></td> <td></td>
   <td bgcolor="red"></td> <td></td>
</tr>
<tr>
   <td></td> <td bgcolor="red"></td>
   <td></td> <td bgcolor="red"></td>
   <td></td> <td bgcolor="red"></td>
   <td></td> <td bgcolor="red"></td>
</tr>
<tr>
   <td bgcolor="red"></td> <td></td>
   <td bgcolor="red"></td> <td></td>
   <td bgcolor="red"></td> <td></td>
   <td bgcolor="red"></td> <td></td>
</tr>
<tr>
   <td></td> <td bgcolor="red"></td>
   <td></td> <td bgcolor="red"></td>
   <td></td> <td bgcolor="red"></td>
   <td></td> <td bgcolor="red"></td>
</tr>
<tr>
   <td bgcolor="red"></td> <td></td>
   <td bgcolor="red"></td> <td></td>
   <td bgcolor="red"></td> <td></td>
   <td bgcolor="red"></td> <td></td>
</tr>
<tr>
   <td></td> <td bgcolor="red"></td>
   <td></td> <td bgcolor="red"></td>
   <td></td> <td bgcolor="red"></td>
   <td></td> <td bgcolor="red"></td>
</tr>
<tr>
   <td bgcolor="red"></td> <td></td>
   <td bgcolor="red"></td> <td></td>
   <td bgcolor="red"></td> <td></td>
   <td bgcolor="red"></td> <td></td>
</tr>
<tr>
   <td></td> <td bgcolor="red"></td>
   <td></td> <td bgcolor="red"></td>
   <td></td> <td bgcolor="red"></td>
   <td></td> <td bgcolor="red"></td>
</tr>
</tr>
</table>
```

This code segment is long, but it's an excellent example of how you can use the `bgcolor` attribute creatively. Figure 6-10 shows the results of the checkerboard code.

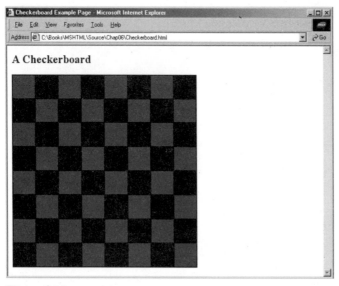

Figure 6-10.
The `bgcolor` attribute can be used to do interesting things, such as create a checkerboard.

In addition to background colors, you can set an image as the background of either a table or its individual cells. The `background` attribute that sets the background of an entire page is the same one you use to set the background of tables. To use this attribute, simply assign the name of the image. Following is an example of how to set the background of a cell to an image named Marble.gif:

```
<td background="Marble.gif">This is a cell!</td>
```

So, the background image for a table appears behind the table's content. In this example, the Marble.gif image shows up behind the text, "This is a cell!" This is fine, but remember not to use images that compete visually with the table content. Contrast makes text or other content stand out. It's more important for the user to be able to access the information on your Web pages than it is to have that user be impressed with aesthetics, especially ones that introduce too many distracting elements.

Note

One small caveat regarding a background image for an entire table: Internet Explorer and Netscape Navigator handle table backgrounds differently. Navigator doesn't support a true background image for a table, because it places the entire image in each cell. Internet Explorer, on the other hand, sets a single image for the entire table, which is more intuitive.

Revisiting Borders

Earlier in the chapter, you learned that the border attribute allows you to set the width of a table's border in pixels. Internet Explorer provides an additional attribute of the <table> tag that allows you to fine-tune the border's appearance and the parts of the table it's drawn around. This is the frame attribute, and it can be set to one of the following values:

- above—specifies border on the top of the table
- below—specifies border on the bottom of the table
- hsides—specifies border on the top and bottom of the table
- lhs—specifies border on the left side of the table
- rhs—specifies border on the right side of the table
- vsides—specifies border on the right and left sides of the table
- box—specifies border on all sides of the table
- border—same as box
- void—specifies no external borders on the table

Specifying the frame attribute values gives you some degree of control over how the border of a table is drawn. Following is an example from an NHL Hockey Standings Web page that uses the below value to fine-tune the border of a table:

```
<table border="2" frame="below">
<tr>
  <th align="left">Team</th>
  <th>Wins</th>
  <th>Losses</th>
  <th>Ties</th>
  <th>OT Losses</th>
</tr>
<tr>
  <td>Colorado Avalanche</td>
  <td>40</td>
  <td>12</td>
  <td>9</td>
  <td>3</td>
</tr>
<tr>
  <td>Detroit Red Wings</td>
  <td>39</td>
  <td>17</td>
  <td>7</td>
  <td>4</td>
</tr>
<tr>
  <td>Dallas Stars</td>
  <td>36</td>
  <td>22</td>
```

```
  <td>5</td>
  <td>2</td>
</tr>
<tr>
  <td>St. Louis Blues</td>
  <td>39</td>
  <td>16</td>
  <td>7</td>
  <td>4</td>
</tr>
</table>
```

Figure 6-11 shows the impact of the frame attribute on what the NHL Hockey Standings Web page looks like.

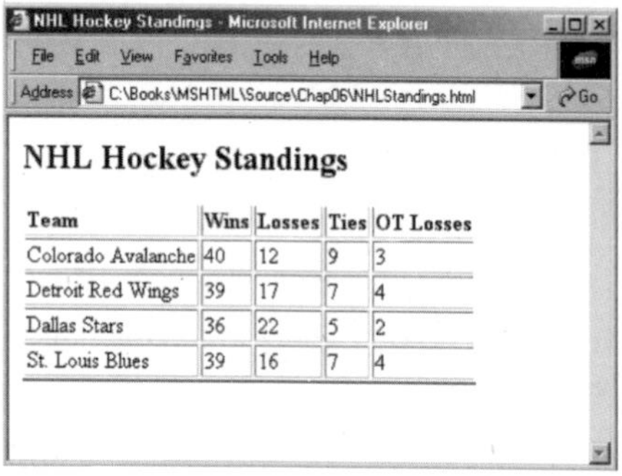

Figure 6-11.
The frame *attribute can be used to include specifics about the exact manner in which a border is drawn around a table.*

Using Tables for Page Layout

Tables are great for formatting tabular data such as that in the Web page with NHL hockey standings. You will also find them useful for laying out the general structure of your pages. Keep in mind that tables allow you to divide an area into rectangular segments. Where a single table might come up a little short, you can nest tables to get more interesting results. The next few sections of the chapter explore the use of tables for page layout.

Working Out the Design

Before you design a Web page, sketch the page on paper—not hundreds of words, just the general format of the page and where major elements of the page will reside. For example, if you plan on having a navigation bar with buttons down the left side of the page, show it in the sketch. You may also have a title image in mind that is positioned along the top of the page. From there, you may decide to format the body of the page as two-column text like a newspaper article. It's all up to you, but by sketching it on paper you can form a better understanding of what you'll need to include in your HTML code.

Another huge benefit of the paper-sketch approach to Web page design is that it allows you to visualize the structure of any tables needed to carry out the design. As you've learned, tables can get somewhat tricky at the code level and are often hard to picture. Figure 6-12 shows a sketch of a sample Web page structure and how the layout can be achieved with a few nested tables.

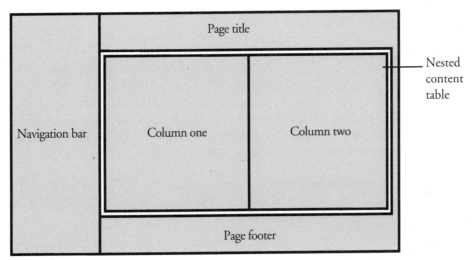

Figure 6-12.
A simple sketch made before you do any HTML coding reveals how a few tables can be nested to form the layout of a Web page.

Putting the Table Together

With your sketch in hand, you'll find the actual coding of the table pretty straightforward. The most important thing is to set a border for all of the tables so that you can see what is happening in the browser as you test the layout. Beyond that, the coding is primarily a process of studying the sketch and creating rows and columns within tables to accommodate the design. Keep in mind that you will probably need to span rows and columns in some situations to get the desired effect. You may even need to nest a table or two within another table. Look at this HTML code, corresponding to the sketch you saw in the previous section:

```
<table width="600" border="1">
<tr>
  <td width="60" rowspan="3">Navigation Bar</td>
  <td>Page Title</td>
```

```
</tr>
<tr>
  <td width="540">
  <table width="540" border="1">
  <tr>
    <td>Column One</td>
    <td>Column Two</td>
  </tr>
  </table>
  </td>
</tr>
<tr>
  <td width="540">Page Footer</td>
</tr>
</table>
```

First notice that I've set the width of certain parts of the table to specific values. This helps to eliminate any browser inconsistencies when it comes to sizing a table with respect to the current browser window size. Next notice how the navigation bar is created by spanning the first cell down through all three rows in the table. Another table is then used to break up the content area of the page into two columns. Figure 6-13 shows the results of viewing this newly coded table in Internet Explorer.

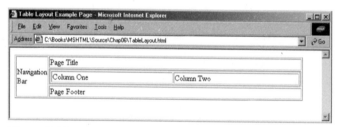

Figure 6-13.
Taking a page layout sketch from concept to reality can be as simple as creating a few tables.

Adding the Content

The real fun of seeing a page layout come together is when you add the actual content of the page. The table design you saw in the previous section is an excellent starting point for adding content and building a Web page of your own. Rather than provide you with all the specifics and take the fun out of the experience, I encourage you to take the template I've provided and build your own page from it. Just keep in mind that a navigation bar typically consists of equal-sized images that serve as hyperlinks to other parts of a Web site. Also, you will probably want to use the footer of the page to place a copyright notice identifying the Web page as your own intellectual property. The rest of the creative process is up to you, so have at it!

Conclusion

I'd be willing to bet that you've learned as much about tables as you can absorb at one time. That happens to work out well because I've written as much about tables as I can at one time! This chapter covered a considerable amount of territory in introducing you to tables and exploring the details of how they are used to organize the overall structure of Web pages and tabular data. I'm confident that you're now comfortable enough with tables to begin putting them to use in your own Web pages.

This chapter began its assault on tables by laying the ground rules and explaining why tables are an important part of your HTML coding arsenal. From there, you learned about the main HTML tags employed in creating tables: `<table>`, `<tr>`, and `<td>`. You then dug a little deeper into the formatting specifics of tables. You learned how to do some interesting things such as aligning tables, controlling the space within and around cells, and setting a background color or image for a table. The chapter concluded by examining the role of tables in simplifying Web page layout.

Chapter 7

Gathering Information with Forms

Web fact for the day

Twenty-five percent of Americans with e-mail accounts say they *very often* send e-mail messages for personal communication instead of making a phone call.

I can personally attest to that fact. Thanks to e-mail, I've maintained personal relationships with people with whom I probably wouldn't have, if we had relied solely on the telephone to stay in touch. I'm not saying we shouldn't talk to each other and enjoy traditional social interaction. It's just that e-mail makes it convenient to ask questions and share information without interrupting people or putting them in a position that forces an immediate response. In case I haven't hammered home the point, I'm a major fan of e-mail.

E-mail often serves as the basis for processing information in forms, hence its significance in this chapter. Forms are the HTML equivalent of the traditional fill-in-the-blank paper forms that we all know and love. For example, consider the pile of paperwork associated with filing your taxes. All those pages and pages of documents are, in fact, forms.

HTML provides a rough equivalent of paper forms that allows you to enter information and send it to a Web server for processing. In many cases, a form is designed so that the information is sent to an e-mail address. The recipient examines the information and decides what to do with it. This chapter explores the inner workings of forms and how they are created, along with how you can put them to good use in your Web pages.

Understanding Forms

The whole premise behind a Web page is that you have information that you'd like to share with the world. You code it in HTML and people view it by using a Web browser. The central idea is that you share information with others. You probably didn't realize that the Web also works the other way: people can share information with you through your Web pages. This is possible thanks to *forms*, which are collections of fields on your

Web pages where visitors enter information, which is subsequently collected and delivered to you. You can process the information you received and perform wondrous things— such as storing it in a database.

If you've ever ordered anything off the Web, you've probably encountered forms. They are regularly used in online shopping carts when you enter your shipping address and payment information. Another common use of forms is in searching Web sites. Figure 7-1 shows the Smart Search page on eBay, which uses a form for powerful searches on the online auction site.

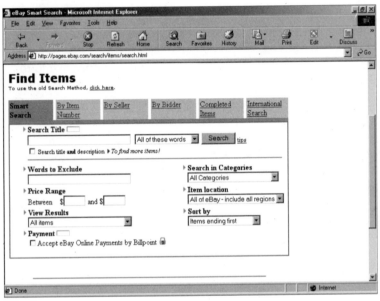

Figure 7-1.
The eBay Smart Search page uses a form to allow you to specify several criteria for controlling searches of online auctions.

Notice that on the eBay Smart Search page, you enter text in several text boxes. You also choose from a few drop-down menus, which are identified by the small arrows to the right of each box. Perhaps most important is the Search button, which triggers a search when clicked. The form gathers the information entered in the boxes and uses that data to search for matching auction items. This is an excellent use of a form, showing how they can be used in practical situations.

The *boxes* on the eBay form are referred to as *controls*, which come in various types. You will learn about the different form controls later in the chapter, but I want to take a quick moment to show you how to use a few of them in the context of a real form. To create a form, use the `<form>` tag, which requires several attributes to function properly. One is the `action` attribute, which determines what happens to the information entered on the form. There are a couple of other important `<form>` attributes, but let's jump ahead and look at the code for the form:

```html
<form enctype="text/plain" action="mailto:me@tailspintoys.com"
method="post">
Name:
<input type="text" name="username"><br>
City, State:
<input type="text" name="userlocation"><br>
Comments:
<textarea name="comments" rows="3" columns="40" wrap="">Type
your comments here!</textarea><br>
<input type="submit" value="Finished">
<input type="reset" value="Start Over">
</form>
```

This code represents a simple form for a *guest book* that you might want to add to your Web site. A Web guest book works much like a printed guest book in that people enter their name, address, and possibly a few comments about your Web site. Figure 7-2 shows what this form looks like in action.

As you can see in the figure, I opted for function over fashion by not adding any HTML code to improve the layout. The result: the form isn't pretty, but it works. Substitute your e-mail address in the `action` attribute of the `<form>` tag, fill out the form, click Finished, and the form data will be delivered to you by e-mail.

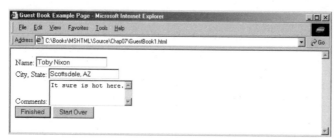

Figure 7-2.
This guest book form is an example of a simple form that could use a little layout help.

Most Web browsers warn you before sending information for processing by a form. This is primarily a security precaution in case you've entered sensitive information such as credit card numbers or your age. Also, the e-mail message containing the form data displays your e-mail address as the return address. Depending on who you are submitting it to, you might not want to reveal your e-mail address. The only alternative is to cancel the form submission. Figure 7-3 shows the security message that pops up when you submit a form in Internet Explorer.

The guest book form sends the form information to you by e-mail, the simplest way to process the data. Figure 7-4 shows how the form information is formatted and stored in an e-mail message.

Figure 7-3.
When you submit a form, most browsers prompt you before sending along the information, as a security precaution.

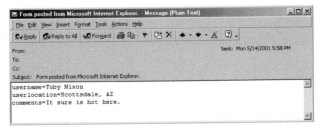

Figure 7-4.
When a form is designed for processing as e-mail, the form information is carefully packaged into an e-mail message.

The e-mail in the figure highlights an important aspect of forms: form information always consists of pairs of names and values. For example, in the guest book example there are three named properties that have been assigned a value. More specifically, the username property has been assigned the value Toby Nixon. Not surprisingly, this is the text entered by the user in the form control named username.

Look at the form's HTML code, and you'll see that there's a control with its name attribute set to username. This technique of associating values with named controls is how form information is packaged and delivered in e-mail. It is also how information from a form is delivered to special programs that perform additional processing, as you will learn in the next section.

Don't worry if the HTML code for the guest book form doesn't make sense yet. It's not supposed to! I wanted to give you a glimpse of the code for a form so that you would have a basic understanding of what goes into one.

Processing Forms with Scripts

In the guest book example form, the form action was set to send the form data to an e-mail address. Although this is perfectly fine for retrieving information from the user, there are many situations where it's beneficial to process the information using a special program called a *script*. For example, the eBay Smart Search form that you saw earlier uses a script to carry out the search, based upon the search criteria entered in the form.

These scripts are typically referred to as CGI scripts, because they are designed to adhere to a Web communication standard known as the Common Gateway Interface (CGI). CGI scripts are usually written in a programming language called Perl.

Even though you aren't going into the details of creating your own CGI scripts, it's worth a look at how you might use existing CGI scripts to process your forms. It turns out that there are lots of free CGI scripts on the Web that you can use in your Web pages. First, look at how a script is used in the context of a form.

Using Scripts

As I mentioned, the `<form>` tag has an attribute named `action`. The `action` attribute was used in the guest book example to identify the e-mail address that is to receive the form information. The `action` attribute is actually more flexible than this and can be used to specify a script for processing a form. Check out the following line of code, which shows how you might process a form using a CGI script named `StoreIt.cgi`:

```
<form action="http://www.tailspintoys.com/cgi-bin/StoreIt.cgi">
```

In this code, the `action` attribute is set to the URL of the CGI script. When you click the Finished button for the form, the form information is delivered to the `StoreIt.cgi` script to be processed. The specifics of this processing are up to the script, which is why you need some knowledge of a programming language such as Perl or C++ to create your own scripts. But it's also possible to use scripts that someone else has written. For example, check out the following code:

```
<form method="post"
action="/cgi-bin/demos/visitorbook/visitorbook.cgi">
```

This is the starting `<form>` tag for a CGI script that results in a more powerful guest book, which stores the guest information in a database rather than delivering it by e-mail. Of course, the `visitorbook.cgi` script is responsible for handling the details of storing the information in the database. This software is named VisitorBook LE, and is made available by FreeScripts.com (*http://www.freescripts.com/*). Figure 7-5 shows what the demo form for this script looks like as you enter information into the guest book.

In the code for the `<form>` tag establishing the `visitorbook.cgi` script as the processor for the guest book form, the script is stored several directories beneath a directory named `cgi-bin`. `Cgi-bin` is a common directory on most Web servers, used to store CGI scripts. In many cases, using a CGI script is as simple as placing the .cgi file in the `cgi-bin` directory and referencing the file in the `action` attribute of the `<form>` tag. Now that you have a basic understanding of how scripts are used, let's see where you can find them.

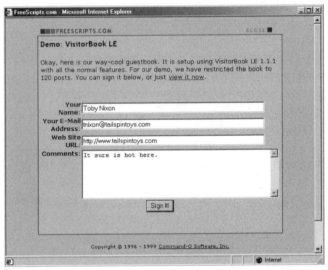

Figure 7-5.
The VisitorBook LE CGI script stores form information in a database, and includes a demonstration form for testing the script.

Finding Scripts

If you're the type of person who gets up at the crack of dawn Saturdays to hunt for yard sale bargains, you'll do well when it comes to finding free CGI scripts. Good CGI scripts are even easier to find than something useful at a yard sale. Following are several Web sites that I highly recommend visiting to find all kinds of interesting CGI scripts:

- The CGI Resource Index: *http://cgi.resourceindex.com/*
- ScriptSearch.com: *http://www.scriptsearch.com/*
- Matt's Script Archive: *http://www.worldwidemart.com/scripts/*
- FreeScripts.com: *http://www.freescripts.com/*
- CGI City: *http://www.icthus.net/CGI-City/*

Most of the CGI scripts available on these Web sites are free for you to use. Just make sure that you credit the author appropriately if the documentation for the script mentions it. Many times script authors simply ask you to notify them of your site so that they can provide a link to it; they see it as a feather in their cap that someone is using their script. It's essentially a win-win situation.

Borrowing Scripts

Unless you are running your own Web server, you may find that your Web hosting service doesn't allow the use of custom CGI scripts. There are a number of reasons why they might impose this restriction, the most important being the security risk of having a custom application running rampant on their servers. Some Web hosting services offer their own CGI scripts, which is ideal because the scripts are probably free and guaranteed to work with the Web server. If your Web hosting service doesn't allow custom scripts and doesn't offer any scripts that serve your needs, consider using a form hosting service.

A *form hosting service* is a special service that handles forms for Web sites and provides the CGI scripts that process the forms. You typically reference a form and a CGI script that is stored at the form hosting service. Following are several form hosting services that you might consider for your form processing needs:

- Response-O-Matic: *http://www.response-o-matic.com/*
- Responders.com: *http://www.responders.com/*
- FormSite.com: *http://www.formsite.com/*
- HostedScripts.com: *http://pages.hostedscripts.com/*
- Revamp.net: *http://www.revamp.net/*

Most of these services are free. They may be worth checking into if you plan on using forms throughout your Web pages and you can't host your own scripts. On the other hand, if you don't mind receiving form information by e-mail with no frills, you can forego scripts completely. It's up to your individual needs.

Getting to Know Form Controls

As you now know, forms consist of entry fields such as text boxes and check boxes, as well as buttons. These form elements are called controls, and they are the building blocks of forms. A form without any controls is not a form; it's like a sentence without words. There are several different controls that you can use in the creation of forms. Each is designed to collect a certain type of information from the user. Following are the controls available for you to use in creating forms:

- Text box
- Password box
- Text area
- Check box
- Radio button
- Menu
- Button

The next few sections examine these controls in more detail, including how to use them in forms. After learning more about them, you will create a complete form that shows how they work in a practical application.

The Text Box and Password Box Controls

The text box and password box controls allow the user to enter one line of text. The only difference between the two controls is that the password box control hides the typed text by showing bullet-characters instead. This allows you to enter confidential information such as passwords without someone being able to look over your shoulder and see what you've typed. However, no other security is employed by the password box control. This means that the Web page is not secure and could be vulnerable to hackers.

Note

Information on a Web page that is not secure is transmitted in an unencrypted form that Web hackers could view. Secure Web pages are encrypted, which means that even if someone hacks into the information, he or she won't be able to read it. A secure Web page is like the newer cordless telephones that encrypt the conversation digitally before sending it between the handset and the base. This prevents nosy people with scanner radios from eavesdropping on their neighbors' conversations.

You use the `<input>` tag to create both text boxes and password boxes. Each control is differentiated by the `type` attribute of the input tag, which you set to either `text` or `password`. In addition to the `type` attribute, most form controls also have `name` and `value` attributes for identifying the name of the control and its initial value, if any. This name/value pair is delivered to the Web server upon submitting a form and, if a CGI script was named in the `action` attribute, this name/value pair is processed by that script. Following is an example of creating a text box control using the `<input>` tag:

```
<input type="text" name="username" value="">
```

This code might be used to create a text box that allows someone to enter a user name for access to a Web site. It might also make sense to add a password box:

```
<input type="password" name="userpass" value="">
```

Notice that the type of the control is set to *password* in this example, and the name of the control is assigned a unique value. Also, the `value` attribute in both controls is set to empty (indicated by the pair of double quotes), which results in the controls having no initial values. This is actually the default setting of the `value` attribute, but I set it explicitly to show you how it's done.

Two other attributes are of interest with respect to text boxes and password boxes: `size` and `maxlength`. They establish the size of the box in characters and the maximum number of characters that can be entered in the box. I'm not sure why you would ever set these attributes to different values; you will want the user to see the full text they are entering. Following are the text box and password box examples with the size and maxlength attributes set:

```
User Name:
<input type="text" name="username" value="" size="12"
maxlength="12"><br>
Password:
<input type="password" name="userpass" value="" size="8"
maxlength="8">
```

In this code, the text box is 12 characters in size and the password box is only 8 characters in size. Figure 7-6 shows how these two controls look when added to an empty form.

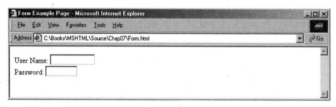

Figure 7-6.
The text box and password box controls allow you to retrieve text input from the user in a form.

If you want to allow the user to enter more than a single line of text, a text box is not your best option. However, there is a form control that handles this chore, which you will learn about next.

The Text Area Control

For those occasions when you want to allow the user to enter several lines of text, the text area control is the control of choice. It can accommodate several lines of text and automatically adds scroll bars if the user enters more text than can visibly fit in the control. To create a text area control, use the <textarea> tag along with a few attributes.

The familiar name attribute is used to name the control, and the rows and cols attributes set the size of the control. The value of the rows attribute should be set to the number of lines of text that can fit in the control, while the cols attribute specifies the maximum width of text in the control, in characters. An additional attribute, wrap, causes the text to automatically wrap to the next line when the user types beyond the width of the control. It isn't necessary to assign an actual value to the wrap attribute.

The text area control is unique among form controls because it doesn't use the value attribute. And, unlike the other form controls, the text area control requires a closing </textarea> tag to complete the control in HTML code. The reason for this is that you can initialize the text in the control by placing text between the starting and closing <textarea> tags. Following is an example of how to create a text area control that is initialized with a short sentence:

```
<textarea name="comments" rows="4" cols="40" wrap="">
Please enter your comments here.
</textarea>
```

This code could be used to create a comment box on a form that gives the user room to enter several lines of text. Specifically, the text area control is set up so that it can accommodate 4 lines of text 40 characters wide, clearly visible in Figure 7-7.

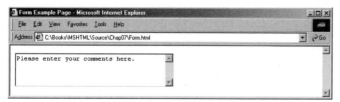

Figure 7-7.
The text area control allows you to retrieve multiple lines of text from the user.

Note

Text area controls hold up to 32,700 characters. Of course, if you have people typing that much information into a form, you may need to talk with them instead of communicating by form.

The Check Box Control

If you need to prompt the user for a response that has an answer of *Yes* or *No*, or *True* or *False*, you might consider using a check box control. It displays a simple box that the user can click to check or click to remove the check. The `<input>` tag is used to create check box controls, along with the familiar `type`, `name`, and `value` attributes. For check box controls, set the `type` attribute to `checkbox`. There is also a `checked` attribute that you can use to indicate that a check box control should be initially checked. You don't need to set a specific value for the `checked` attribute.

Keep in mind that the only information displayed for a check box control is the check box itself, even if you set the `value` attribute. The significance of the `value` attribute is that it's delivered to the Web server when a form is submitted if the control has been checked. If you don't set the `value` attribute, a value representing *on* is sent to the Web server if the control is checked. Although this works fine if you are using a check box control by itself, it presents a problem if you are using the control as part of a group. You will learn about check box grouping shortly. For now, look at this code, which creates a single check box control:

```
<input type="checkbox" name="emaillist" checked="">
Check the box to join our e-mail list.
```

In this code, a check box control prompts users to join an e-mail list. Notice that the actual text prompt is entered just after the `<input>` tag. Figure 7-8 shows what this control looks like in action.

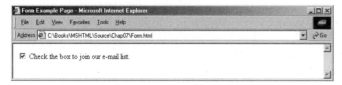

Figure 7-8.
The check box control allows you to prompt the user for simple Yes/No or True/False information.

As previously mentioned, it's possible to group several check boxes as a set. This is useful if you have multiple pieces of related information that you want the user to be able to turn on and off on a form. When you use check box controls in a group, specify the same value for the `name` attribute for all the controls. Set unique values for the `value` attribute of each control. When the user makes his or her selections and submits the form, each of the checked values is passed along to the server. Following is an example of how you might use several check box controls together in a group:

```
<input type="checkbox" name="addons" value="sunroof">Sun roof
<input type="checkbox" name="addons" value="alloywhls">Alloy
wheels
<input type="checkbox" name="addons" value="heatseats">Heated seats
<input type="checkbox" name="addons" value="abs">ABS
<input type="checkbox" name="addons" value="spoiler">Rear spoiler
```

This code creates a set of check box controls that might be handy on a car shopping Web page, where the potential buyer enters add-ons for a new car. Figure 7-9 shows what these controls look like in a form.

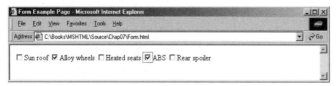

Figure 7-9.
Multiple check box controls can be used together as a set to prompt the user for multiple pieces of information.

The Radio Button Control

Although you can select multiple pieces of information from a group of options presented in check box controls, you may want to limit the selection to one item in certain situations. This is where the radio button control comes into play. It is designed for use in groups, but you can select, or turn on, only one control at any given time. The radio button control is named after old car stereos that had a row of buttons you could set to different radio stations. The trick was that when you pushed one button it would automatically unpush the previously pushed button, so that only one button was pushed at a time. If you've never seen this type of car stereo, be thankful because they weren't very user-friendly.

You create a group of radio button controls in the same manner as you create groups of check box controls, as you learned in the previous section. In case you've had a memory lapse, you create a radio button control using the <input> tag. However, you must set the type attribute to *radio*. To create a group of radio buttons, set the name attribute for each control to the same value, providing unique values for each value attribute. You can set the checked attribute for one of the controls if you'd like it to be set initially. The idea behind a group of radio buttons is to have just one of them set, so it's a good idea to set one of them initially using the checked attribute.

Like check box controls, radio button controls appear on the page as individual graphical icons, with no text. To make each control meaningful to the viewer of the page, you need to include text next to it. Following is an example of the code required to create a group of radio buttons:

```
<input type="radio" name="size" value="s">Small
<input type="radio" name="size" value="m" checked="">Medium
<input type="radio" name="size" value="l">Large
<input type="radio" name="size" value="xl">Extra large
```

This code creates a set of controls that might be useful in allowing the user to select a pizza size for orders on a pizza delivery Web page. Figure 7-10 shows what these radio button controls look like in a form.

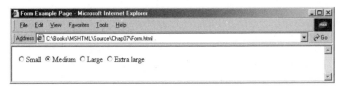

Figure 7-10.
The radio button control allows you to create groups of mutually exclusive items—a fancy way of saying that only one item in a group can be selected at a time.

The Menu Control

The menu control accomplishes roughly the same task as the radio button control; it allows the user to select from a group of options. But, the items associated with a menu control appear in a dropdown list that the user reveals by clicking the arrow. Also, a single menu control houses all the items that a user can select. You don't have to do anything special to associate them as a group, as you do with the check box and radio button controls.

Note

HTML menu controls are identical to the graphical user interface controls known as combo boxes and dropdown lists, found in operating systems such as Windows.

To generate a menu control, use the `<select>` tag to create the menu itself. It's important to use the `name` attribute with this tag to give the menu a name that will be associated with the menu selections when the form is processed. You can also specify the height of the unopened menu, in lines of text, by using the `size` attribute. By default, menus are one line of text, meaning that only one item is visible in the menu when it is not opened.

The other attribute you might use with the menu control is the `multiple` attribute, which specifies that multiple items in the menu can be selected, as opposed to allowing only one item to be selected at a time. Following is an example of how you might start a simple menu with the `<select>` tag:

```
<select name="color">
```

That wasn't too difficult, now was it? The next step in setting up a menu is to create the individual menu items, using the `<option>` tag and its `value` attribute. The `value` attribute of the `<option>` tag assigns a unique name to each menu item. Study this example of a complete menu:

```
Select a color:
<select name="color">
<option value="red">Fire engine red
<option value="yellow">Canary yellow
<option value="blue">Ocean blue
<option value="green">Forest green
<option value="black">Black onyx
<option value="gray">Gun metal gray
<option value="white">Pearl white
</select>
```

The first thing to notice about this code is that the phrase `Select a color:` is added before the `<select>` tag to indicate the purpose of the menu. The `<option>` tags are used within the starting and ending `<select>` tags to identify each of the items in the menu.

Note

Keep in mind that the `size` attribute of the `<select>` tag can be used to make an unopened menu larger. The default size of one, for example, means that the menu shows only one line of text. Of course, all menus open to reveal a dropdown list upon being clicked.

Figure 7-11 shows a menu control after it's been clicked. If you want more flexibility in your menus, use the `<optgroup>` tag to create submenus within a menu. To create a submenu, you surround a group of menu items with starting and ending `<optgroup>` tags.

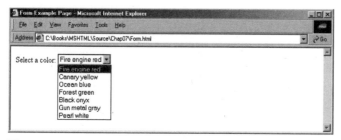

Figure 7-11.
When you click a menu control, it opens to reveal a dropdown list of items that can be selected.

The Button Controls

The form controls you've learned about are important in establishing a means of retrieving information from the user. Yet none of them provides control over the entire form. Here's where the button controls come into play. You can use two types of form buttons: Submit and Reset. It's important for every form to have a Submit button, which sends the form data to the Web server for processing. The Reset button, on the other hand, is used to reset a form to its default setting. It's the equivalent of obtaining a new piece of paper when you're filling out a paper form. Although it's not as critical as the Submit button, you'll want to include a Reset button on your forms as a convenience to the user.

To create a Submit button you use the `<input>` tag and set the `type` attribute to `submit`. Set the text that will appear on the button by setting the `value` attribute. Following is an example of creating a Submit button:

```
<input type="submit" value="Place Order">
```

This example might apply to an order entry form where the user clicks the Submit button to enter an order in an online store. To add a Reset button to the same form you again use the `<input>` tag, but this time you set the `type` attribute to *reset*. Here's an example of how you might code the Reset button:

```
<input type="reset" value="Start Over">
```

You can see that the Reset button is created the same way as the Submit button. Figure 7-12 shows how both buttons appear within a form.

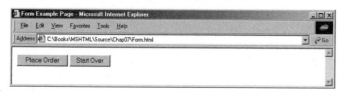

Figure 7-12.
The Submit and Reset buttons allow you to submit a form for processing and reset the form controls to their default values, respectively.

To make your button controls look spiffier, use the `style` attribute with the `<button>` tag. The `style` attribute uses style sheet settings to alter the buttons' appearance. You will learn about style sheets in Chapter 11, "Style Sheet Basics," so for now I'll show you just the basics. The `<button>` tag is necessary for creating buttons with a custom appearance. When you use the `<button>` tag to create Submit and Reset buttons, you must set the `type`, `name`, and `value` attributes all to either `submit` or `reset`. The button text is placed between starting and ending `<button>` tags. If you're confused, the following code should clear things up:

```
<button type="submit" name="submit" value="submit"
style="font:18pt Helvetica; background:green">Place Order
</button>
<button type="reset" name="reset" value="reset"
style="font:18pt Helvetica; background:red">Start Over
</button>
```

This code uses the `<button>` tag and `style` attribute to customize the font and background color of the Submit and Reset buttons.

Lastly, you can customize the appearance of buttons with images. Just as you place the text of a button between the starting and ending `<button>` tags, you can place an image between these tags. The following code demonstrates how you might add an image to a Submit button:

```
<button type="submit" name="submit" value="submit"
style="font:18pt Helvetica; background:green">
<img src="Order.gif">Place Order
</button>
```

This code is similar to that of the previously customized Submit button. In fact, the only difference is the addition of the `<img>` tag between the starting and ending `<button>` tags. Adding an image to a button control is that simple!

Creating Forms

We've finally gotten to the point of actually creating a complete form that can do something useful. The form you will create in this section is a feedback form that allows your Web site visitors to leave detailed information by way of the form. In addition to reinforcing what you've learned throughout the chapter, it should serve as a practical example of how to create complete forms with different types of form controls.

Establishing the Form's Action

As you may recall, forms are created by using the `<form>` tag and a few attributes to describe the form. The `action` attribute is important because it determines how a form is processed. The `action` attribute is often set to a CGI script that resides on your Web server. If you don't have access to a CGI script and want to receive form information by e-mail, set the action attribute to your e-mail address by preceding the address with the word *mailto* followed by a colon. You will see how this is accomplished in a moment.

You also need to be concerned with the method attribute of the <form> tag. The method attribute determines how information entered in the form is delivered for processing. If you specify *post* for this value, the data will be delivered to the CGI script or e-mail address specified in the action attribute.

The other setting you can use for the method attribute is *get*, which sends the form information to the Web server as part of the URL for the Web page with the form. This get technique is commonly used by search engines. It's why you often see a huge line of jumbled text in the address bar of your browser when you perform a search. For the purpose of this chapter, we're going to stick with the *post* approach to processing form information.

If you opt to have data delivered to an e-mail address, I recommend using one other attribute of the <form> tag: enctype. This attribute allows you to specify how the data is formatted for processing. In the case of e-mail, it's good to format the information as plain text. Set the enctype attribute to *text/plain*. The result of this setting is that the information will appear directly in the body of the e-mail message in plain text.

Following is the complete <form> tag for the feedback form:

```
<form enctype="text/plain" action="mailto:me@tailspintoys.com"
method="post">
```

Of course, this form isn't of much use without controls. Read on.

Note

Don't forget to plug in your own e-mail address in the action attribute.

Laying Out the Controls

The heart of any form is the controls used to obtain information from the user. The feedback form is no different. The first step is to find out what kind of feedback the user is likely to be interested in providing. You want to know if this is a happy or irate user. That's a good opportunity to use a set of radio buttons, as the following code demonstrates:

```
What is the nature of your comment?<br>
<input type="radio" name="nature" value="praise"
checked="">Praise
<input type="radio" name="nature" value="suggestion">Suggestion
<input type="radio" name="nature" value="problem">Problem
<input type="radio" name="nature" value="complaint">Complaint
```

This code creates a set of radio buttons to find out the nature of the user's comment. Notice that I've cleverly made the Praise button the default option, which might give the user a hint that we prefer and expect positive feedback. It's also important to find out

what specifically the user wants to leave feedback about. This is a great place to use a
menu, as the following code reveals:

```
What specifically would you like to comment on?<br>
<select name="specific">
<option value="website">Web site
<option value="company">Company
<option value="products">Products
<option value="services">Services
<option value="other">Other
</select>
```

There's nothing tricky about this code; it's just a basic menu with several items to
select from. Now that you have some information about the feedback, you can give the
user an opportunity to leave detailed comments with a text area. The following code
shows how the text area is created:

```
Please enter your comments below:<br>
<textarea name="comments" rows="6" cols="60"
wrap=""></textarea>
```

As you can see, the text area gives the user room to enter 6 lines of text that are 60
characters wide. Of course, if you run across a particularly verbal person, the text area will
automatically use scroll bars to allow for more text.

You're not likely to encourage anonymous feedback, so the next step is obtaining
contact information, including the user's name, e-mail address, phone number, and fax
number. Text box controls work great for this, but it's somewhat difficult to line up the
controls properly with labels to the left of them. For this reason, a table comes in handy
as a layout tool for aligning the text box controls, as the following code shows:

```
How can we get in touch with you?<br>
<table>
<tr>
  <td>Name:</td>
  <td><input type="text" name="name" size="40"></td>
</tr>
<tr>
  <td>E-mail:</td>
  <td><input type="text" name="email" size="40"></td>
</tr>
<tr>
  <td>Phone #:</td>
  <td><input type="text" name="phone" size="20"></td>
</tr>
<tr>
  <td>Fax #:</td>
  <td><input type="text" name="fax" size="20"></td>
</tr>
</table>
```

The purpose of the table in this code is to align the controls with each other, greatly improving the table's appearance. This will be clearer when you see the end result of the form.

The last piece of necessary information is the site visitor's preference about being contacted quickly in response to his or her feedback. This requires a Yes or No answer, so a check box control is the obvious choice. The following code shows how a check box control is used to obtain this information:

```
<input type="checkbox" name="asap">Please contact me as soon as
possible regarding this feedback.
```

No control is complete without a Submit button. And while you're adding a Submit button, you might as well throw in a Reset button so that the user can clear the form. Following are these two buttons for the feedback form:

```
<input type="submit" value="Submit Feedback">
<input type="reset" value="Start Over">
```

That concludes the controls for the feedback form. You had already learned the ins and outs of each one, so this section was pretty straightforward.

The Complete Form

Before you move on to test the Feedback form, it's worthwhile to see the HTML code for the complete form. It shows all the different form controls in context. Here is the complete code for the feedback form:

```
<form enctype="text/plain" action="mailto:me@tailspintoys.com"
method="post">
<p>
What is the nature of your comment?<br>
<input type="radio" name="nature" value="praise"
checked="">Praise
<input type="radio" name="nature" value="suggestion">Suggestion
<input type="radio" name="nature" value="problem">Problem
<input type="radio" name="nature" value="complaint">Complaint
</p>
<p>
What specifically would you like to comment on?<br>
<select name="specific">
<option value="website">Web site
<option value="company">Company
<option value="products">Products
<option value="services">Services
<option value="other">Other
</select>
</p>
```

```
<p>
Please enter your comments below:<br>
<textarea name="comments" rows="6" cols="60"
wrap=""></textarea>
</p>
<p>
How can we get in touch with you?<br>
<table>
<tr>
   <td>Name:</td>
   <td><input type="text" name="name" size="40"></td>
</tr>
<tr>
   <td>E-mail:</td>
   <td><input type="text" name="email" size="40"></td>
</tr>
<tr>
   <td>Phone #:</td>
   <td><input type="text" name="phone" size="20"></td>
</tr>
<tr>
   <td>Fax #:</td>
   <td><input type="text" name="fax" size="20"></td>
</tr>
</table>
</p>
<p>
<input type="checkbox" name="asap">Please contact me as soon as
possible regarding this feedback.
</p>
<p>
<input type="submit" value="Submit Feedback">
<input type="reset" value="Start Over">
</p>
</form>
```

Granted, most of this code is repeated from the control layout section, but it helps to see all the code together. Note that the paragraph tags (<p>) are used to provide space between each section of the form. I know you're itching to see the completed form in a Web browser, so let's take it for a test drive.

Testing the Form

As you know, the feedback form is designed to obtain information from a visitor to your Web site and pass it along to you by e-mail. Figure 7-13 shows the feedback form as it first appears when you open the page in a Web browser.

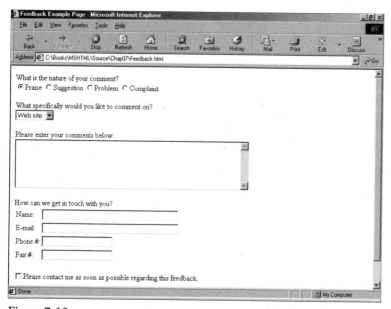

Figure 7-13.
Visitors to your Web site leave feedback that is sent to you by e-mail.

I took the liberty of filling out the form and submitting it by clicking the Submit Feedback button. The information I entered is shown in Figure 7-14.

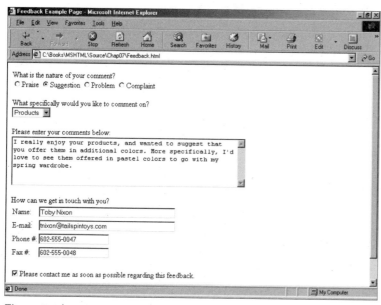

Figure 7-14.
Using the feedback form is as simple as entering information and clicking the Submit Feedback button.

After the feedback is submitted, it's packaged into an e-mail message and delivered to the e-mail address specified in the `action` attribute of the `<form>` tag. Figure 7-15 shows the resulting e-mail message, revealing how the form information is combined with form control names to yield name/value pairs.

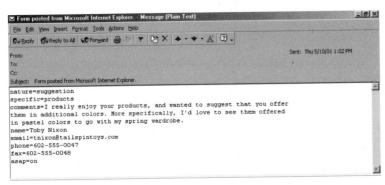

Figure 7-15.
The information in the feedback form is packaged into an e-mail message and delivered to you.

To use this form on your Web site, simply change the e-mail address in the `action` attribute of the `<form>` tag to your own. You're now set to receive feedback from visitors to your site.

Advanced Form Tips and Tricks

Now that you have a solid understanding of forms and how they are used to get information from people who visit your Web site, I'd like to highlight a few interesting form tips and tricks. They aren't organized in any particular order, so please take them at face value.

Creating Read-Only Controls

The accepted use of form controls is for retrieving information from people visiting your Web pages, but it's also possible to create read-only controls that are used to display information. Although the concept of a read-only form control may seem counter-intuitive, there are a few circumstances where it could come in handy. For example, you might want to dynamically display calculations made by a script. You learn how to use controls in this manner later in the book in Chapter 14, "Dynamic HTML." Regardless of why you might want to create a read-only control, I want to point out that it's possible.

To create a read-only control, set the `readonly` attribute inside the control's tag. This attribute doesn't require any special value, so you can just set it to empty text (""). Following is an example of how you might create a read-only text Box control:

```
<input type="text" name="stats" value="" readonly="">
```

Hiding Controls

Just as creating a read-only control might seem strange, how about creating controls that are hidden from view? I'm not kidding. It's entirely possible and sometimes useful to hide a control so that the user can't see it. It has to do with scripting, which you haven't learned much about yet. Suffice it to say that there's a time and place for hidden controls, even if it isn't readily apparent.

To hide a control, set the `type` attribute to `hidden`. It's a unique type of control, not just a property associated with the controls you've learned thus far. In other words, you can use the `readonly` attribute to make any control read-only, but you must create a control of type `hidden` to create a hidden control. Following is an example of how to create a hidden control:

```
<input type="hidden" name="ssn" value="123-456-7890">
```

Organizing Controls into Field Sets

In the feedback form you saw earlier, the form controls were organized into paragraphs, providing spacing and making the form easier to understand. There's a more formal approach that provides an interesting effect. I'm referring to field sets, groups of controls that are set off by themselves. They don't play any functional role in forms; they simply help to organize the controls visually.

To group controls in a field set, surround them with start and end `<fieldset>` tags. This draws a box around the controls. Another tag that's ideal in conjunction with the `<fieldset>` tag is the `<legend>` tag. The `<legend>` tag creates a title for the field set. The `<legend>` tag is placed right after the start `<fieldset>` tag and must enclose the name of the field set. You can also specify the `align` attribute within the `<legend>` tag to align the legend to the `left` or `right` of the field set box. If this sounds confusing, maybe the following code will clear things up:

```
<form enctype="text/plain" action="mailto:me@tailspintoys.com"
method="post">
<fieldset>
<legend align="left">User Information</legend>
Name:
<input type="text" name="username"><br>
City, State:
<input type="text" name="userlocation"><br>
</fieldset>

<fieldset>
<legend align="left">Comments</legend>
<textarea name="comments" rows="3" columns="40" wrap="">Type
your comments here!</textarea><br>
</fieldset>
```

```
<input type="submit" value="Finished">
<input type="reset" value="Start Over">
</form>
```

In case you don't recognize this code, I'll tell you that it's the Guest Book form code from the beginning of this chapter. I've modified it to use field sets. Figure 7-16 shows how the field sets are used to organize the form controls.

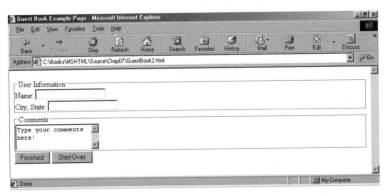

Figure 7-16.
Field sets are used to organize form controls into groups that are surrounded by borders.

Setting the Tab Order of Controls

Although many of us are content to click and drag for hours on end, it's a little known fact that not all computer users are enamored of the mouse. For this reason, consider the ramifications of forms for people who are in love with their keyboards. The way to navigate through a form using the keyboard is to repeatedly hit the Tab key, taking you through the form one control at a time. So controls in a form are assigned a *tab order*. By default, the tab order of the controls is the same order as their order of appearance in the HTML code for the form.

To change the tab order of form controls, use the `tabindex` attribute with the control's tag. This attribute can be set to any number between 0 and 32,767; however, it's important that each control have its own unique tab index value. The low-numbered controls are activated first on a form, with the navigation proceeding in order to higher numbered controls. Following is an example of how you could set the tab order for Submit and Reset buttons:

```
<input type="submit" value="Place Order" tabindex="50">
<input type="reset" value="Start Over" tabindex="51">
```

In this code, the Place Order button will be activated first because it has a lower tab index than the Start Over button. You can use a similar approach to set the tab order of all the controls in a form.

Providing Keyboard Shortcuts

Another aspect of keyboard trickery that you can use on your forms is keyboard shortcuts. They allow the user of a form to jump directly to a given control by invoking a key combination such as the Alt key plus some other key (Windows users). In theory, Macintosh users would use the Command key plus another key to carry out keyboard shortcuts, but currently keyboard shortcuts aren't supported on the Mac. Even so, it won't hurt to create the shortcuts for Windows users, and Mac folks likely will benefit from them at some point in the future.

To create a keyboard shortcut for a control, use the accesskey attribute of the control's tag. Set the accesskey attribute to a letter or number that identifies the key that the user must press in addition to the control key (Alt, Command, or other). Following is an example of how to set keyboard shortcuts for a couple of text box and password box controls that you saw earlier in the chapter:

```
User Name (Alt-U):
<input type="text" name="username" value="" size="12"
maxlength="12" accesskey="u"><br>
Password (Alt-P):
<input type="password" name="userpass" value="" size="8"
maxlength="8" accesskey="p">
```

Notice in the code that in addition to using the accesskey attribute to set the keyboard shortcuts, I also mentioned that shortcuts are available in the labels preceding the controls.

Note

Be careful to choose keyboard shortcuts that don't interfere with the Web browser's built-in shortcuts. For example, the File menu in most browsers is accessed by a control key (Alt, Command, or others) and the letter f. For this reason, avoid setting a keyboard shortcut with the letter f. As with the letter f in *File*, avoid using the underlined character in the other option names on the browser's menu bar.

Conclusion

You probably have a newfound respect for all those Web sites that ask you for information. This chapter explored the inner depths of forms, used to turn the tables on conventional Web page design by obtaining information from the user, as opposed to presenting it to them.

The chapter began with some theory on forms and the significance they have for Web pages. You moved on to the somewhat complex topic of form processing, which ultimately boils down to scripts. Because the development of form-processing scripts is a topic beyond the scope of this book, I pointed you in a few directions where you could find scripts. After script basics, you were introduced to the various controls that serve as the building blocks of forms. From there, you built a complete form that can be used to obtain feedback from visitors to your Web site. The chapter concluded with a handful of tips and tricks for improving your forms.

Chapter 8

Integrating Multimedia with Your Web Pages

Web fact for the day

The first video game was Pong, created in 1972 by Nolan Bushnell, who subsequently founded Atari.

If you've never heard of Pong or Atari, we really have our work cut out for us in this chapter. Nintendo, Sega, and now Microsoft are the household names in video games. But in the late 70s and early 80s, there was only Atari. The Atari 2600 home video game system was the ultimate in entertainment for those lucky enough to own one in the early days of video games. I'm fortunate to have grown up in the age of Atari and Pong during the evolution of video games.

I'm once again in the tricky position of justifying a strange beginning to a chapter about HTML—but I've got it covered. In many ways, video games are the end-all multimedia application. If you think about it, most modern video games include amazing graphics and sound coupled with live action video and other interesting special effects. If you've had trouble sorting out what the word multimedia means, blow a few bucks at an arcade; I guarantee that you'll get it.

In HTML, multimedia refers to the mixing of audio, video, and Web pages. Standard HTML allows you to work with text, images, and even animated images. But I've held off mentioning sound and traditional video until now. This chapter explores the possibilities of adding sound and video to your Web pages by using HTML. So pull that microphone and video camera out of the upstairs closet and brush up on your directing skills. Action!

Understanding Plug-ins and Helper Applications

If you've ever seen a Glade air freshener in a bathroom, you know what I'm talking about when I refer to a *plug-in*. Web browsers have their own version of plug-in—but with no scent and no useful purpose in a bathroom. Browser plug-in programs display Web content that the browser can't. Much multimedia content falls outside the realm of standard browser support, so it's safe to say that plug-ins are frequently used. You may not even realize that your browser is using a plug-in because it typically appears in the browser window. In other words, you won't see another program launch when a plug-in is activated.

Note

If you've spent any time on the Web, you've probably run across an Adobe Acrobat file, which requires the plug-in named Adobe Acrobat Reader. If you don't have the appropriate plug-in, your browser usually tells you where you can obtain it on the Web.

A Web browser examines the file extension of the multimedia file to figure out how to handle its content. This file extension is sufficient for the browser to determine what kind of file it is and whether or not it's necessary to use a plug-in. As an example, when a browser encounters a file with a .jpg or .gif file extension, it recognizes the files as standard browser images and has no problem displaying them. But if a browser encounters a file with a .pict or .tif file extension—non-standard in browser terms—the browser will search for the plug-in that you can use to view the image. For the record, PICT and TIFF are image formats not commonly used in Web pages. This primarily has to do with the fact that these image formats don't compress image sizes as effeciently as JPEG or GIF, so they are more appropriate for desktop publishing where image size isn't such a critical issue.

If a plug-in for a certain file type isn't available, the browser will look for a helper application. A helper application differs from a plug-in; it's a separate program launched independently of the browser. Just as you might use Windows Media Player to play a video or MP3 music file, a helper application is launched outside of the browser to display an image or video or play a piece of audio.

Note

MP3 is a music format that allows you to store and play digital music on your computer. MP3 music is now supported on several portable digital music players, and was popularized in the media through the legal battle between the music recording industry and the popular Napster music file-sharing service.

Because it's less distracting to see a media file displayed directly within a Web browser, the browser attempts to find a plug-in and then looks for a helper application if the search fails. If neither exists for a given media file, the browser typically prompts you to save the file to your local hard disk.

A browser generally recognizes files from an established type known as Multipurpose Internet Mail Extensions or MIME. This collection of file types was used originally to encode different types of files so that they could be sent easily as e-mail messages. Today, MIME types are also used as the basis for identifying files for browsing purposes. Table 8-1 contains the different MIME types that you will likely encounter as you work with multimedia files.

Table 8-1. **Common MIME Types**

File Extension(s)	MIME Type	Media Type
`.gif`	`image/gif`	Image
`.jpg, .jpeg, .jpe`	`image/jpeg`	Image
`.tif, .tiff`	`image/tiff`	Image
`.pic, .pict`	`image/pict`	Image
`.xbm`	`image/x-xbitmap`	Image
`.wav`	`audio/x-wave`	Audio
`.au, .snd`	`audio/basic`	Audio
`.aiff, .aif`	`audio/aiff`	Audio
`.mpg, .mpeg, .mpe`	`video/mpeg`	Video
`.qt, .mov`	`video/quicktime`	Video
`.avi`	`video/x-msvideo`	Video

MIME types are used to identify different types of multimedia files that often appear on the Web. The MIME type names listed in Table 8-1 are somewhat cryptic; it's not important for you to remember them. Just understand that each type of multimedia format has an associated type that a browser uses to determine what to do with the file. You can see in the last column that each of the MIME types boils down to one of three fundamental types of media: an image, a piece of audio, or a video. A few may be directly supported in your browser, but others may require a plug-in to view or listen to them. Others may require a helper application if no plug-in is installed. It depends on the browser you are using and what plug-ins you have.

Note

Not all file types have MIME types associated with them. If a Web browser encounters a file type that doesn't have a MIME type, it uses the operating system's file associations to search for a helper application.

Working with Sound

Computers are digital machines. All their information is stored as a series of 0's and 1's. This means that sound on a computer is also digital. However, sound in the real world isn't digital, and it must be converted to be stored and played on a computer. The process of converting a real-world sound to a digital computer sound is known as *sampling*. Sampling made its mark on the music industry in the 80s when rap artists sampled rhythm and blues melodies and drum beats and used them in their own songs. After lengthy litigation, sampling is now permitted, provided that you have permission from the original artist.

Sampling is important because sounds must be sampled in order to be playable within a Web page. The manner in which a sound is sampled determines both its quality and its size. There is a significant trade-off in determining the ideal sampling approach to achieve maximum sound quality without requiring a huge sound file. It's tough to get CD quality sound out of smaller sound files. Plus, large sound files result in long download times. This is not a good thing!

The length of a sound proportionately affects its size. And some sounds are too long to trim down to a reasonable size. Some sounds are, theoretically, infinite in length. On Internet radio, a station broadcasts digitally over the Internet in real time. There is no way to limit the size of the sound file, as the broadcast is continuous. In fact, it's hard for the user to tell if there is a sound file.

This brings us to the distinction between two types of sound on the Web: static sounds and streaming sounds. *Static sounds* are sounds that must be downloaded completely before you can start listening to them. They are good for storing short sound clips.

Streaming sounds can be played while they are being downloaded. Their primary benefit is that they can be quite long, and they can be played without waiting until the entire sound has been downloaded. The key is that you should use static sounds for shorter sound clips, and rely on streaming sounds for sounds with longer download times. Live audio broadcasts on the Web are treated as streaming sounds. Although streaming sounds are ideal in many ways, there is a drawback: they often require a special audio server, and they are more difficult to prepare.

Note

RealNetworks makes RealProducer, a special program that simplifies the task of creating and using streaming sounds. You will learn more about RealProducer and streaming RealMedia sounds later in the chapter.

Don't forget that you can't use copyrighted sounds without the copyright owner's written permission. For example, you must obtain permission to use sounds sampled from copyrighted movies or audio recordings. It is no different from using copyrighted software without permission or a licensing agreement. So, be careful when sampling sounds from copyrighted sources; it's illegal to place your entire MP3 collection on your Web site.

Note

Some sound collections that you might assume are in the public domain are actually copyrighted. Most collections come in the form of an audio CD containing a variety of sound effects. Read the fine print, and make sure you can legally use the sounds, or get written permission from the publisher.

Creating Your Own Sounds

Because the majority of the sounds out there are copyrighted, you may want to create your own sounds for your Web pages. You can record with a microphone or use sample sounds from a stereo cassette deck or VCR. The microphone is the easiest route; many multimedia computers come equipped with one. If you have some sounds in mind from a prerecorded cassette, CD, DVD, or home movie, you will need to connect an external sound source to your computer. To sample a sound, you use a special program called a sound editor. If your computer came with a microphone and a sound card, it probably has a sound editor already installed. In fact, all Windows computers come with a simple sound editor called Sound Recorder.

Note

If you have a Creative Labs sound card, your computer probably has Wave Studio already installed. It is a full-featured sound editor with interesting effects to spice up sounds.

Cleaning up a sampled sound for use on the Web is basically the same, regardless of where you sample sounds. Sample the sound and play it back to make sure that it sounds okay. It's likely that the sound will be either too loud or too soft. You can judge the volume of the sound by looking at the sound's waveform in a sound editor.

The *waveform* of a sound is its graphical appearance plotted over time. If the sound waveform goes beyond the top or bottom of the waveform display, you know it's too loud. If you can barely hear it, it's too soft. You can either adjust the input level for the sound device and resample the sound, or use amplification effects provided by the sound utility. Amplification effects allow you to make a sound louder or softer.

The best way to fix the volume problem is to adjust the input level of the sound device and resample the sound. For example, in Windows you can easily adjust the microphone or line input level using the Volume Control application (see Figure 8-1 on the next page). Note that the content of the Volume Control window is determined by the audio hardware and software on your computer and may look a bit different from the figure.

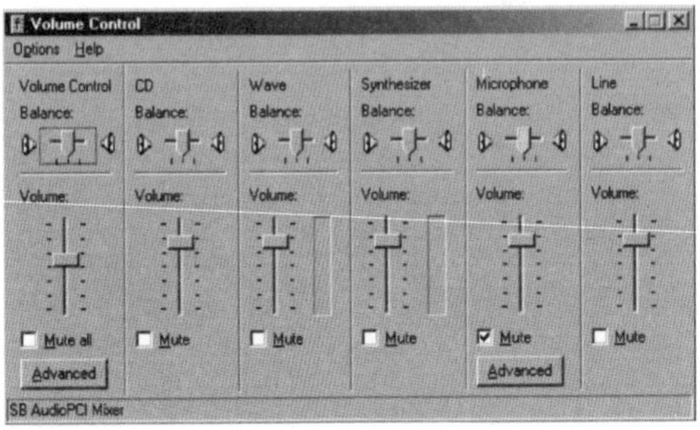

Figure 8-1.
The Windows Volume Control application allows you to alter the level of the microphone and line input.

When you have the volume of the sound at a level you like, clip the sound to remove unwanted portions. Clipping a sound means zooming in on the waveform in a sound editor and cutting out unwanted silence or other sounds. This is important because it removes unneeded parts of a sound, such as silence at the beginning and end. The shortened sound plays more quickly.

Once you have a sound clipped it should be ready to roll, but first check out the effects that are available with your sound utility. Simple effects range from reverb to echo; advanced effects include fading and phase shifts. It's up to your imagination and discerning ear.

Finding Sounds

If you don't have the vocal skills of Michael Winslow—the self-proclaimed master of 10,000 sound effects in the *Police Academy* movies of the 80s and 90s—don't despair. You may need to seek an outside sound source. The best source for prerecorded sounds is the sound archives on the Web, but many different sound archives are available, with a vast array of sounds. Keep in mind that you need to be careful about the copyrights of these sounds also. In general, sounds in an archive are safe to use, but double-check.

The best place to find sounds is probably the Microsoft Design Gallery Live, also great for clip art and other Web site images. It has numerous sounds, and is unique in that you can search the sounds by keyword. Figure 8-2 shows the Design Gallery Live Web site, located at *http://dgl.microsoft.com/*.

Another good place to find sounds is the World Wide Web Virtual Library, which maintains an audio page with links to sound archives. It is located at *http://www.comlab.ox.ac.uk/archive/audio.html*. Yet another good sound source is the Yahoo! audio archive, located at *http://dir.yahoo.com/Computers_and_Internet/Multimedia/Audio/Archives/*. And finally, as if those Web sites aren't enough, Excite has sound archives, which you can listen to at *http://www.excite.com/computers_and_internet/multimedia/music_and_sound/sound_archives/*. Examples of what you'll find on these archive sites are animal sounds, military sounds, spoken phrases, and sound effects of all kinds, from bubbling liquids to chirping insects.

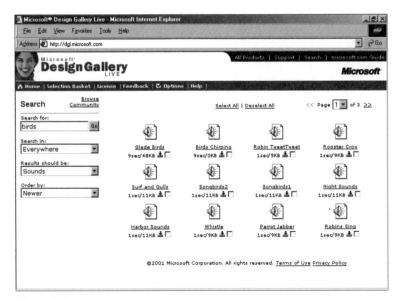

Figure 8-2.
Microsoft's Design Gallery Live serves as an archive of sounds that you can search using keywords.

Archived sounds may be stored in different formats. Currently the most common is the WAV format, Microsoft's standard Windows sound format. Sounds stored in the WAV format are also known as *wave* files, or simply *waves*. All WAV sounds are static sounds. RealAudio and RealMedia are two other sound formats widely used on the Web. RealAudio is used for static sounds, and RealMedia for streaming sounds. If you plan to place short sound clips in your Web pages, your best bet will be to find sounds in WAV or RealAudio formats.

Note

Another sound format you may run across in your search is the Musical Instrument Digital Interface (MIDI) format, used to store music in very small files. MIDI files usually have the .mid file extension. They can be used in most browsers to provide simple music without taking up much space.

Adding Sounds to Your Pages

Finally, we get into the fun stuff! Let's use HTML code to add sound to a Web page. Note that there are three approaches to using sound, which differ with respect to how a sound is played when the browser encounters it in a Web page. Following are the ways you can use a sound in a Web page:

- Link to the sound, in which case it will be played in an external helper application
- Embed the sound, in which case it will be played by the browser or a plug-in
- Set the sound as the background sound, in which case it will be played by the browser or a plug-in as soon as the page is opened

129

Many users find it annoying when a Web page starts playing sounds immediately upon being opened in a browser. You should strongly consider giving the user the option of playing a sound. This is primarily an issue when it comes to background sounds, which we will get to in a moment.

Linking to Sounds

Linking to a sound from a Web page is the cleanest, simplest way to use sounds on the Web. Playing the sound is optional for the user, and the browser relies on a helper application to play that sound. To link to a sound from a page, use the familiar <a> anchor tag. You may recall that the href attribute of this tag is used to identify the target of the link, in this case the URL of the sound file. Following is an example of how you link to a sound using the <a> tag:

```
<p>
Click <a href="Funny.wav">here</a> to listen to a funny
sound clip!
</p>
```

This code reveals how easy it is to link to sounds in your Web pages. You may find it more interesting to link sounds to an image such as an ear or a speaker. Following is example code from a Web page that uses small images as links to sounds of animals that live in a pond:

```
<html>
<head>
  <title>Pond Friends</title>
</head>

<body>
<h2>Pond Friends</h2>
<table cellspacing="20">
<tr>
  <td>
  <img src="Pond.jpg">
  </td>

  <td>
  <p>
  This is a picture of my backyard pond. Several different
  types of animals live in the pond, and they all make
  distinctive sounds. Following are a few of the animals that
  inhabit the pond:
  </p>
```

```
<bl>
<li>Frogs <a href="Frog.wav"><img src="Speaker.gif"
border="0"></a></li>
<li>Mosquitos <a href="Mosquito.wav"><img src="Speaker.gif"
border="0"></a></li>
<li>Ducks <a href="Duck.wav"><img src="Speaker.gif"
border="0"></a></li>
</bl>
</td>
</tr>
</table>
</body>
</html>
```

Figure 8-3 shows how this Web page uses a small image of a speaker to serve as the link to sound clips.

Figure 8-3.
The Pond Friends Web page uses a small speaker image to serve as a link to animal sounds.

Okay, I lied a little on the Pond Friends Web page—my pond doesn't have ducks. However, it does have hefty koi, which are colorful Japanese fish that are more appealing than ducks. Sorry, Donald. Back to the sound aspects of the Pond Friends Web page. Click one of the speaker images and a helper application is launched to play the sound, as shown in Figure 8-4 on the next page.

If you don't like the idea of using a helper application to play sounds, you may want to consider embedding sounds in your pages. That just happens to be next on our agenda!

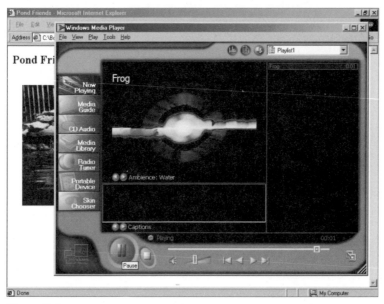

Figure 8-4.
Click one of the speaker links in the Pond Friends Web page, and a helper application is launched to play the appropriate sound.

Embedding Sounds

A browser can play a sound embedded in a Web page without the aid of a helper application. In some ways, this is more appealing for the user, because it doesn't involve another window popping up in the way. On the other hand, browsers are more limited in the types of sound files that can be played as embedded sounds. Stick with the WAV format and you'll probably be just fine. To embed a sound in a Web page, use the `<embed>` tag. The URL of the sound file is specified in the `<embed>` tag by using the `src` attribute. Following is an example of how to embed a sound using the `<embed>` tag and the `src` attribute:

```
<embed src="Frog.wav">
```

Although this code works fine, it results in the sound being played automatically when the page is first opened in the browser. It also results in the display of a large multimedia console with play, pause, and stop buttons, along with a volume control. These are neat features, but you usually want an embedded sound to take up minimal space.

These problems are solved with additional attributes of the `<embed>` tag: `width`, `height`, and `autostart`. The `width` and `height` attributes allow you to set the size of the multimedia console; a minimum size of 25 by 25 pixels leaves enough room for a play button, ideal for most embedded sounds. The `autostart` attribute allows you to set whether or not the sound is played automatically when the page is opened. Following is an example of how the previous embedded sound example might be modified using these attributes:

```
<embed src="Frog.wav" width="25" height="25" autostart="false">
```

Note

The `<embed>` tag also supports the `align` attribute, serving the same purpose as with the `<image>` tag. It aligns the multimedia console for the sound with respect to any surrounding content.

Following is the Pond Friends Web page that you saw earlier, now modified to use embedded sounds instead of linked sounds:

```
<html>
<head>
  <title>Pond Friends</title>
</head>

<body>
<h2>Pond Friends</h2>
<table cellspacing="20">
<tr>
  <td>
  <img src="Pond.jpg">
  </td>

  <td>
  <p>
  This is a picture of my backyard pond. Several different
  types of animals live in the pond, and they all make
  distinctive sounds. Following are a few of the animals that
  inhabit the pond:
  </p>
  <bl>
  <li>Frogs <embed src="Frog.wav" width="25" height="25"
  autostart="false"></li>
  <li>Mosquitos <embed src="Mosquito.wav" width="25"
  height="25" autostart="false"></li>
  <li>Ducks <embed src="Duck.wav" width="25" height="25"
  autostart="false"></li>
  </bl>
  </td>
</tr>
</table>
</body>
</html>
```

As you can see, this code no longer includes the anchor tags, but uses `<embed>` tags to embed the sounds on the page. Figure 8-5 on the next page shows how the resulting page now displays small play buttons for each sound, as opposed to the speaker image link.

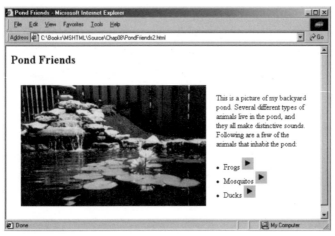

Figure 8-5.
The embedded sounds on the Pond Friends Web page are identified by small play buttons that play a sound when clicked.

When you click any of the play buttons, the appropriate animal sound is played directly in the browser. This is more convenient for the user than linked sounds, provided the browser supports the embedded sound format.

Note

Though you will need Version 7 (or later) of Windows Media Player for any of these examples, I've noticed that some of the earlier releases of Version 7 do not support this use of the width and height attributes to access the Media Player's control bar. In Windows Media Player, open the Help menu and select About Windows Media Player. Ensure the Version number is 7.00.00.1956, or greater. If it is not, then log onto the Internet, open the Help menu, and select Check For Player Upgrades; your version of Media Player will be updated and these examples should play accurately for you.

One last <embed> attribute to know is the loop, which allows you to loop a sound multiple times. Specify a number of repetitions in the loop attribute. Or set it to true, and the sound will continue to loop until the user clicks the stop button on the multimedia console. This assumes you've made the stop button accessible by using a larger value for the width attribute. Otherwise, the user won't be able to stop the sound without leaving the page. If your intent with the loop attribute is to establish a background sound, such as music that plays continuously, consider setting it as the background sound for the page.

Using Background Sounds

I dislike recommending solutions that are only applicable to a specific browser, but I must point out that Internet Explorer supports a tag for background sounds: <bgsound>. A background sound is one that is played when the user first opens a Web page, similar to an embedded sound with its `autostart` attribute set to `true`. However, background sounds don't have a visual presence on the page, so you don't have to worry about sizing the multimedia console. Like embedded sounds, the `<bgsound>` tag has a loop attribute that can be set so that a sound plays a certain number of times. Or set the `loop` attribute to `infinite`, in which case the sound will play until the user leaves the page. Following is an example of how you might set a background sound for a page:

```
<bgsound src="Music.wav" loop="infinite">
```

It's important to use a relatively subtle sound. Otherwise, you run the risk of driving people away from your site. Some people, myself included, are genuinely annoyed by most background sounds. Also consider that many people work in office environments where unexpected sounds can be a problem. They may enjoy listening to music while surfing the Web but dislike hearing someone else's background sounds at the same time.

Working with Video

Back in the early 80s a horror movie caused quite a stir in my family. *Savage* involved a killer stalking kids in the backwoods of Tennessee. You probably haven't heard of this movie, because it was created by a couple of 12-year-old kids with an 8mm movie camera and no budget. I was one of those kids, and somewhere I still have the original 8mm reels of film used to capture my first foray into film-making. Today's technology makes it easy to make homemade movies, and I haven't ruled out rounding up the neighborhood kids to film *Savage II*.

Virtually anyone can buy a digital video camera for under $1,000 and create videos and movies. Inexpensive video editing software makes it relatively painless to edit video, add professional wipes and fades between scenes, and overlay music and sound effects. Video has entered the digital age and opened up the possibility for the next Steven Spielberg to emerge from any home studio. Knowing how many aspiring Spielbergs are out there, I'm not surprised that video has made its way onto the Web.

Like sounds, videos can be either static or streaming. The majority are streaming, because video files are much larger than sound files. Waiting for a video file to download can be a real drag; lucky you are if you have an extremely fast Internet connection. I have a cable modem, fast by most standards, and some videos still take too long to download.

Creating Your Own Videos

As I said, it's easier than ever to create your own videos if you have access to either a traditional video camera or one of the newer digital models. You'll need a special video card in your computer, with a connector for hooking the camera to the computer and transferring the video. Newer Macintosh computers typically come standard with video inputs for pulling video from a camera, along with video editing software. If you have a PC without such a graphics card, you can install one or use an external video input device. One is the Dazzle Digital Video Creator, which plugs into your computer's universal serial bus (USB) port and captures videos from a video camera, allowing you to edit them on your PC.

Note

Most computers these days include USB ports, which allow you to connect different kinds of devices to your computer. For example, many digital cameras communicate with computers using a USB port.

Regardless of the hardware and software used to create videos, the end result is basically the same. You end up with a video file that can be played back using a video player. Popular formats for static video files include MPEG, AVI (promoted by Microsoft), and QuickTime (promoted by Apple). MPEG videos have a file extension of .mpe, .mpg, or .mpeg; AVI videos use .avi; and QuickTime movies use a file extension of .mov or .qt. All three formats are supported, although each requires a plug-in determined by which browser you're using.

Finding Videos

If you don't aspire to be the next Martin Scorsese, you might consider existing videos for your Web pages. Streaming video is used on the Web more than static video, so there aren't as many video archives. Videos take up a lot of space and it's tough to maintain a generic video archive. There are a few sources; you just have to hunt for them. Keep in mind that most video archives are specific to a certain topic, such as movies or sports.

Some of the best sources are movie-related Web sites. For example, Jurassic Punk is a Web site at *http://www.jurassicpunk.com/*, which includes videos of the latest movie trailers. This is a great way to find out about new movies. Another movie-related site with loads of videos is Jim Carrey Online—mostly his movie clips. Carrey fans will be in Carrey heaven at *http://www.jimcarreyonline.com/videoclips/*.

If you're looking for something more educational, check out Volcano World, which has several video clips of erupting volcanoes. The video section of Volcano World is located at *http://volcano.und.nodak.edu/vwdocs/movies/movie.html*. Also take a look at the National Oceanic and Atmospheric Administration (NOAA) Web site located at *http://www.pmel.noaa.gov/vents/geology/video.html*. The New Millennium Observatory off the coast of Oregon filmed these intriguing videos of underwater volcanoes.

Adding Videos to Your Pages

You'll be glad to learn that adding videos to your Web pages is virtually identical to adding sounds. The next two sections explore the details of adding videos to Web pages, revealing the similarities of coding sound and video in HTML.

Linking to Videos

The tag that allows you to link to videos from your Web pages is the <a> anchor tag, which you used earlier in the chapter to link sounds. Not surprisingly, the href attribute of this tag is used to identify the URL of the video file. Next is an example of how to link to a video using the <a> tag:

```
<p>
Fortunately, junior's first home run was immortalized on
<a href="HomeRun.avi">video</a>.
</p>
```

In this code, the word video serves as the text that links to the video file HomeRun.avi. When you click the word video to activate the link, the HomeRun.avi video is displayed by a helper application such as Windows Media Player.

Similar to the technique for sounds, used earlier in the chapter, it is also possible to link to a video with an image. Following is an example of code from a Web page that uses a small image of a piece of film as the link to a hockey video:

```
<html>
<head>
  <title>Hockey Skills</title>
</head>

<body>
<h2>Hockey Skills</h2>
<p>
Hockey is a game of considerable skill. One of the toughest
skills to develop is that of a quick, powerful, yet accurate
shot. Some shots go so far beyond the realm of normal skill
that they are just about unbelievable. This video clip
demonstrates what I'm talking about. <a href="HockeyShot.avi">
<img src="Film.gif" border="0"></a>
</p>
</body>
</html>
```

Figure 8-6 shows how this Web page looks when viewed in Internet Explorer.

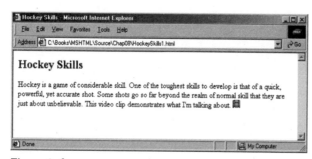

Figure 8-6.
The Hockey Skills Web page uses a small film image to serve as a link to an incredible hockey video.

When you click on the little film image on this page, a helper application plays the video, as shown in Figure 8-7.

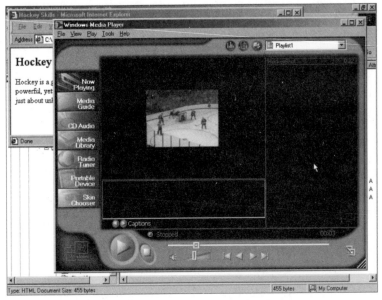

Figure 8-7.
When you click the film link in the Hockey Skills Web page, a helper application is launched to play the video.

As with playing sounds, you may prefer to embed videos directly within a page so that they aren't played by a helper application. If so, you'll be interested in the next section. Keep in mind that video formats vary considerably, which means that browsers are more likely to delegate the specifics of supporting different video formats to helper applications. On the other hand, some plug-ins do play embedded video.

Embedding Videos

To embed a video in a Web page, you use the `<embed>` tag, which is the same tag you used earlier in the chapter to embed sounds. The URL of the video file is specified in the `<embed>` tag by the `src` attribute. Following is an example of how to embed a video using the `<embed>` tag and the `src` attribute:

```
<embed src="HomeRun.avi">
```

Embedded videos have the same issues as embedded sounds in how they are presented to the user. The same attributes of the `<embed>` tag alter the presentation and control of the videos: `width`, `height`, `autostart`, and `loop`. The `autostart` attribute allows you to set whether the video is played automatically when the page is opened, and the `loop` attribute determines how many times the video is played. Unlike the `width` and `height` attributes for embedded sounds, these attributes are critically important for embedded videos because they determine the viewing area of the video.

Following is the Web page titled Hockey Skills from the previous section, now modified to use an embedded video:

```
<html>
<head>
  <title>Hockey Skills</title>
</head>

<body>
<h2>Hockey Skills</h2>
<p>
Hockey is a game of considerable skill. One of the toughest
skills to develop is that of a quick, powerful, yet accurate
shot. Some shots go so far beyond the realm of normal skill
that they are just about unbelievable. This video clip
demonstrates what I'm talking about.<br>
<embed src="HockeyShot.avi" width="200" height="200"
autostart="false"></a>
</p>
</body>
</html>
```

This code no longer includes the anchor, but instead uses the <embed> tag to embed the video on the page. Figure 8-8 shows how the video is displayed on the page when viewed in a Web browser.

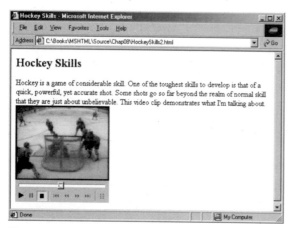

Figure 8-8.
The embedded video is shown directly on the Web page called Hockey Skills.

Along with playing the video on the Web page, you can also control the video using the multimedia console buttons along the bottom of the video image.

Tinkering with Streaming Media

Thus far in the chapter you've been dealing with static sounds and video clips that must be downloaded before you can hear or view them. In practice, it's often more efficient to use streaming sound and video because many sound and video clips are long enough to make downloading a slow and painful process. Fortunately, it is relatively straightforward to create streaming versions of static sounds and video clips.

Choose a streaming format before you consider how to carry out the conversion. Microsoft is solidly behind the Windows Media Format, which supports both streaming sound and video. Another popular one is the RealMedia format by RealNetworks. Like the Windows Media Format, RealMedia can be used for either streaming sound or video.

Preparing Multimedia Files for Streaming

Because most sound and video originates as a static file, the most common way to create streaming multimedia content is to convert a static sound or video file into a streaming format such as Windows Media Format or RealMedia. Microsoft offers a tool called Windows Media Encoder that automates this process. RealNetworks has a similar tool, RealProducer. I'll demonstrate using Windows Media Encoder to create streaming multimedia files in the Windows Media Format.

Windows Media Encoder is available for free from Microsoft's Windows Media Web site at *http://www.microsoft.com/windows/windowsmedia/*. After downloading and installing the tool, you can convert a static sound or video file to the streaming Windows Media Format. Run Windows Media Encoder and read the directions on the opening window, as shown in Figure 8-9.

Figure 8-9.
Windows Media Encoder begins by asking you how you'd like to use the tool.

To convert a static multimedia file, select the first option in the Windows Media Encoder opening window. Then, you'll be using the New Session Wizard, which makes things much easier. Click OK, and the New Session Wizard will appear as shown in Figure 8-10.

The New Session Wizard asks you a series of questions to automatically set up the conversion of a static multimedia file to a streaming Windows Media equivalent. Select the last option in the New Session Wizard, then click Next. This results in the display of the File Selection page of the New Session Wizard, as shown in Figure 8-11.

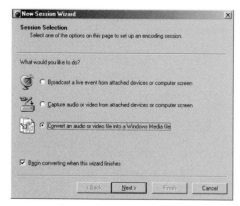

Figure 8-10.
The New Session Wizard within Windows Media Encoder guides you through the creation of streaming multimedia content.

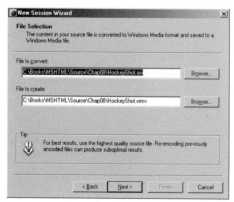

Figure 8-11.
The File Selection page of the New Session Wizard prompts you to specify the name of the multimedia file that you want to convert to Windows Media Format.

To select a file for conversion, click the Browse button and find the file on your hard drive. Once you've found the file, click Next to continue. The next step is the Output File Distribution, as shown in Figure 8-12.

Figure 8-12.
The Output File Distribution page of the New Session Wizard prompts you to select the type of Web server you'll be using to serve the new file.

Although this part of the wizard sounds complicated, it really isn't. All it's asking you is whether you plan to use a Windows Media server to deliver your streaming files. Unless you know for certain that you'll be using a Windows Media server, you'll probably want to select the second option, which indicates that a standard Web server will serve the file. After selecting this option, click Next to proceed to the Profile Selection page of the wizard, as shown in Figure 8-13.

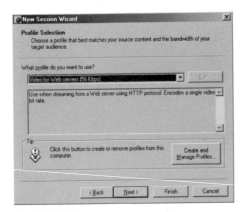

Figure 8-13.
The Profile Selection page of the New Session Wizard prompts you to select the profile of the new file, essentially the connection speed at which you expect the file to be viewed.

The Profile Selection page prompts you to select the connection speed of the target visitor of your Web site. This is important because the quality of the resulting file must be carefully adjusted according to the speed at which the file will be downloaded. Select Video for Web servers (56 Kbps) if you want to target the widest range of users (those who have standard dial-up modems). This results in lower quality sound or video, but it's the only way to make the streaming file available to users with the current-generation traditional dial-up modems. If you want to support only users with faster connections such as cable and DSL modems, you can select a faster option. After you've selected the profile and clicked Next, the Display Information page of the wizard is displayed, as shown in Figure 8-14.

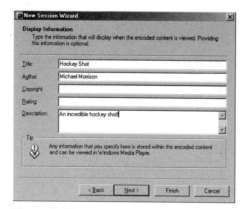

Figure 8-14.
The Display Information page of the New Session Wizard prompts you to enter information about the multimedia file, such as the title, author, and description.

Note

Cable and DSL (Digital Subscriber Line) modems allow you to connect to the Internet at much higher speeds than traditional dial-up modems.

The Display Information page allows you to enter information about the multimedia file for viewing by the user. Enter a title for the file, along with the author, a copyright notice, a rating, and a brief text description. Once you've finished, click Next to continue to the last step of the New Session Wizard, as shown in Figure 8-15 on the next page.

The Settings Review page of the wizard allows you to go over the settings you've made for the conversion before moving forward. To perform the conversion, click Finish. After Windows Media Encoder churns on the file for a few moments, you'll see the Encoding Results window, which summarizes the results of the conversion, as shown in Figure 8-16, also on the next page.

You now have a streaming media file with a .wmv file extension, ready to be added to a Web page and streamed to users.

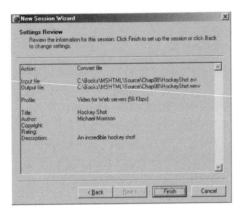

Figure 8-15.
The Settings Review page of the New Session Wizard allows you to review the settings for the file conversion before you convert it.

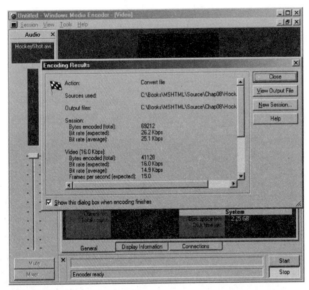

Figure 8-16.
The Encoding Results window shows the outcome of the file conversion.

Linking to Streaming Multimedia Files

The previous section revealed why it's necessary to perform a conversion on a static multimedia file to use it as a streaming file. The good news is that you can link to a streaming multimedia file with little effort. The only difference between linking a streaming file and a static file is that streaming files require an additional helper file. This *metafile* helps describe the streaming file. The metafile for a streaming file can be complicated, but this simple example shows what a minimal metafile looks like:

```
<asx version="3.0">
    <entry>
        <ref href="HockeyShot.wmv">
    </entry>
</asx>
```

Windows Media metafiles are stored in a special XML format, and have a file extension of .asx. Don't worry about the meaning of the metafile tags now; just keep in mind that the streaming media file is identified in the `href` attribute of the `<ref>` tag. These tags will make more sense when you learn about XML in Chapter 17, "Understanding XML."

When adding a streaming multimedia file to a Web page, you link to the metafile instead of the streaming file. Following is some familiar code that demonstrates how to link to a streaming video clip:

```
<p>
Hockey is a game of considerable skill. One of the toughest
skills to develop is that of a quick, powerful, yet accurate
shot. Some shots go so far beyond the realm of normal skill
that they are just about unbelievable. This video clip
demonstrates what I'm talking about. <a href="HockeyShot.asx">
<img src="Film.gif" border="0"></a>
</p>
```

Notice in the code that the .asx metafile is specified in the `href` attribute, as opposed to the .wmv streaming media file that you created in Windows Media Encoder. This wraps up the basic requirements of adding streaming multimedia files to your Web pages. You now understand enough to link to streaming sound and video clips from your Web pages.

Note

It's also possible to embed streaming multimedia files in your Web pages, but it's considerably more involved than linking to streaming files.

Other Types of Multimedia

In addition to the multimedia file types mentioned in this chapter, there are other types that you might run across on the Web. Following are some of these types of multimedia:

- Java applets and animations
- Flash movies and animations
- Virtual 3-D worlds

Although all of these are interesting in their own right, it's too ambitious to cover all of them in this chapter. There are tons of Java books out there for learning how to use Java applets and animations. You can also check out the official Web site for Java at *http://java.sun.com/*. Flash is another widely used technology for simple animations as well as full-blown cartoons and games. To learn more about Flash and how to use it in your Web pages, visit the Macromedia Web site at *http://www.macromedia.com/*.

And finally, there are several technologies for creating and adding virtual 3-D worlds to your Web pages. One such technology comes in the form of a browser plug-in called Rover and a special XML-based language—3DML—used to describe 3-D worlds. Rover and 3DML are products of Flatland Online and are very cool technologies. Go to the Flatland Web site at *http://www.flatland.com/*.

Conclusion

I'll bet you never realized that multimedia was such a rich area of Web development. Multimedia has been gaining in popularity on the Web quite rapidly in the past few years. The only thing stopping multimedia from literally becoming the Web is the limited connection speeds imposed by current modems and networks. Multimedia content takes up lots of space, taking a long time to download at the slower connection speeds associated with traditional modems. Higher-speed connections, such as those offered by cable and DSL modems, are opening the door for more multimedia-rich Web sites. This chapter gave you the fundamental knowledge to begin creating such sites.

The chapter began by explaining the role of plug-ins and helper applications in the multimedia landscape of the Web. From there, you moved on to learning about sound, including how to create sounds of your own, how to find sounds on the Web, and how to add sounds to your Web pages. The focus of the chapter then shifted to video, where you learned how to work with video in your Web pages. You also learned how to use a Microsoft tool to convert static multimedia files into streaming files that the user can view or listen to, without having to download the file first. The chapter concluded by briefly covering a few other multimedia types and where you can learn more about them.

Chapter 9

Graphical Tools and HTML

Web fact for the day

Nintendo's Game Boy, based on a technology more than a decade old, has more computing power than the combination of all the computers used to put the first man on the moon.

Does this mean that NASA and Nintendo plan to put a man on Mars with a network of Game Boy Advance devices? Probably not. I think it's safe to say that Nintendo is too busy fighting for video game domination on this planet to focus on Mars. But what this interesting tidbit about Game Boy technology tells you is that technological progress is always on the move.

You already knew this, but it's worth pointing out that graphical Web development tools have advanced rapidly in the past few years. Just as video game technologies now eclipse the best NASA technologies of decades past, today's graphical Web tools blow away the best publishing and multimedia software of only a few years ago.

What does any of this have to do with HTML? Well, HTML is the fundamental language used to develop Web pages, so graphical Web tools must edit and manipulate HTML code. Although the focus of this book is clearly on coding Web pages with HTML by hand, it's important to learn how graphical Web tools fit into the Web development equation. Even if you choose to become an HTML whiz, you will no doubt find some of these tools useful in certain situations.

Note

There are other Web tools such as pure graphics programs that don't directly deal with HTML, but instead allow you to create and fine-tune images for use in Web pages.

Why Use a Graphical Tool?

In case you haven't noticed, people don't think the way computers do. Computers think of everything in terms of steps and instructions. When you get down to it, everything in a computer boils down to a number. People tend to think in terms of physical things and how they relate to one another, resorting to numbers only when it's absolutely necessary. One of the principal challenges in any computing system is bridging this gap between *computer thought* and human thought. One situation where this gap is readily apparent is in HTML code.

The very word *code* reveals that HTML is not something natural to human expression. To get a desired visual effect on a Web page, you have to use HTML to write code that the computer can comprehend and act upon through the Web browser. Even though HTML uses tags that are understood by most people, a certain degree of thought goes into formatting a page using HTML, as opposed to sketching the same page on a piece of paper.

The ultimate Web development tool would allow you to sketch a page and skip the HTML coding. Supercomputers and artificial intelligence may some day make this a reality. But for now we have graphical Web development tools that help transfer a Web page design from your head to HTML, a format that the computer can understand.

Graphical Web development tools work like a word processor or desktop publishing software. In fact, early Web development tools followed the lead of desktop publishing tools used for printed publications. Just as the word processor of desktop publishing tools allows you to visually lay out a printed page containing images, text, and other visual elements, a graphical Web tool allows you to lay out a Web page with similar elements. These kinds of tools are sometimes referred to as WYSIWYG, or What You See Is What You Get. Essentially, what you see on the screen is close to what you will see on the final page. Building a Web page this way is significantly more intuitive than hacking away at HTML code.

Then why learn HTML when you can construct Web pages graphically by using a Web development tool? The answer is that no tool can replace the efficiency and accuracy of hand coding HTML. In other words, you will need to know HTML at some point even if you plan to use a graphical Web development tool religiously. If you plan to be an HTML purist and snub graphical tools for the most part, you will still encounter situations where a graphical tool can save you time. You have the best of both worlds when you know how to leverage a graphical Web development tool with your HTML coding and understand when each can improve the Web development process.

Getting Acquainted with Graphical Tools

My family has a somewhat tragic and often entertaining history with tools. I'm talking about traditional construction tools such as hammers, saws, ladders, etc. My uncle lost a few fingers in a strange table saw accident, while I witnessed my dad fall from an attic to the ground floor of his house with a ladder in tow. I've personally crashed while pushing a fully loaded wheelbarrow, so I don't have much room to talk. This is just a theory, but it may be that if my family spent a little more time getting acquainted with tools, we would all be safer for it. This brings us to graphical Web development tools, with which I want to acquaint you before you run out and hurt yourself.

When I talk about graphical Web development tools, I'm referring to HTML-based tools such as Microsoft FrontPage and Macromedia DreamWeaver. But they are not the only graphical tools available for Web development. Imaging tools are other development tools that you'll find useful in creating Web pages with images. They allow you to create and edit images and image maps. When you couple them with a graphical Web page design tool, you have a complete Web development toolset that goes a long way in helping you to create compelling Web pages. A handy set of tools will allow you to spend more of your time focusing on the design of pages. The next few sections explore some of the popular tools used to build Web pages.

Image Editing Tools

I have a friend named Keith whose eyes appear red in every photograph taken of him. I've pondered the possibility of a demonic influence at work, but the truth is that red-eye in photographs is caused by the reflection of the camera's flash off the retina of the eye. I'm not sure why some people are more prone to photographic red-eye than others, so I'll continue to look into the notion of a demonic influence on my friend. I mention the red-eye problem because software can now easily correct it in digital photographs. The software that makes this magical feat possible is the image-editing tool.

With the transition from traditional cameras to digital ones, image-editing tools have become very popular. You no doubt have an image-editing tool already if you own a digital camera. They become important for Web development because they allow you to resize, crop, and otherwise manipulate images for your Web pages. Most image-editing tools also support multiple image file formats such as GIF, JPEG, and PNG (Portable Network Graphics). Some comprehensive image-editing tools offer powerful image manipulation features such as the automatic removal of red-eye, along with many other special effects.

Following are several popular image-editing tools to consider using for your Web pages:

- Microsoft PhotoDraw
- Jasc Paint Shop Pro
- Adobe Photoshop

Microsoft PhotoDraw is a powerful image-editing tool sold as a separate piece of software or bundled with Microsoft Office 2000 Premium. PhotoDraw is geared toward the creation of images for publication either on the Web or in print, so it's quite versatile. One of the program's neat features is the capability of creating Web-specific images such as banners and navigation buttons. Figure 9-1 shows the PhotoDraw graphics templates that are used to create Web-specific images.

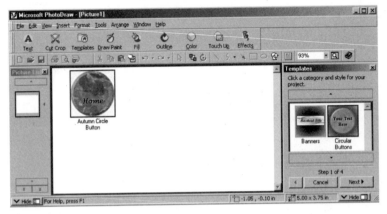

Figure 9-1.
Microsoft PhotoDraw is a powerful image-editing tool that you can use to create Web-specific images such as banners and buttons by following a series of steps.

By following the simple series of steps presented in PhotoDraw, you can create Web images with little effort. Figure 9-2 shows how PhotoDraw allows you to customize the appearance of a button by changing the background image.

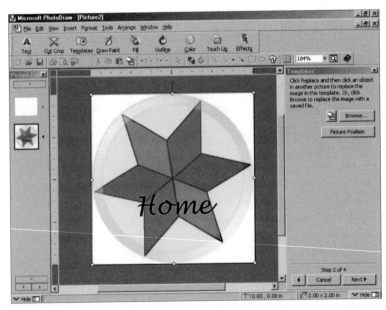

Figure 9-2.
PhotoDraw allows you to modify the appearance of a button quickly and easily.

Of course, most buttons have text that corresponds to their purpose, so it is important to be able to change the text of a button. With PhotoDraw, you can do this, as well as alter the text's font, size, and position. Figure 9-3 shows how the text of a button can be modified to have more impact.

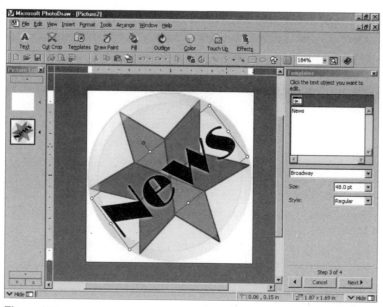

Figure 9-3.
PhotoDraw also lets you change the text on a button to create custom navigation menus for your Web pages.

The Web image features of PhotoDraw are only part of the many interesting aspects of the tool. One of its strong points is the ability to layer multiple images on top of each other to form a single composite image. This feature is not new to high-end graphics tools, but you will find it useful as you tinker with creating graphics for Web pages. To find out more about PhotoDraw, visit the PhotoDraw site on the Web at *http://www.microsoft.com/office/photodraw/*.

I don't mean to sound like an infomercial for Microsoft PhotoDraw. It is but one of many powerful image-editing tools on the market that you might consider for the creation and editing of Web images. Another popular Windows tool is Paint Shop Pro, by Jasc Software. It originated as a shareware graphics software package that evolved into a full-blown retail application. This shareware history is what made it popular among those of us who couldn't afford expensive graphics software.

In keeping with its shareware roots, an evaluation version of Paint Shop Pro is available from the Jasc Software Web site at *http://www.jasc.com/*. The program includes a variety of image-editing features that are on par with those found in PhotoDraw. The Paint Shop Pro software package also includes a tool called Animation Shop that allows you to create animated images. Animated images can be tricky to create without the help of a good tool, and Animation Shop is just the one to simplify the process.

This discussion would not be complete without mentioning Adobe Photoshop, the preeminent image-editing tool. It's been around a long time, and it is hands-down the most powerful image editor available today. But this power and flexibility come with two significant costs: a steep learning curve and a big dent in the wallet. I'm not saying you can't work through a few tutorials and get up to speed with Photoshop in a reasonable amount of time, but it's definitely a more complex tool than PhotoDraw or Paint Shop Pro. On the other hand, there isn't much you can't do in Photoshop, which is why it's so widely used by professional artists, photographers, and Web designers.

If you can afford the high price tag and learning curve, then by all means, use Photoshop for your Web graphics needs. Otherwise, you might want to consider one of the two options I've mentioned here, or browse around for one of the many other image-editing tools. To learn more about Photoshop, visit the Adobe site on the Web at *http://www.adobe.com/*.

Image Map Tools

In Chapter 5, "Visual Navigation with Image Maps," you learned how valuable a graphical tool can be in creating image maps. It is extremely tedious to create image maps by hand in HTML. You'll find that an image map tool will help a great deal, regardless of whether you are creating pages with a graphical Web page tool or by hand in straight HTML code. I already showed you how to use the built-in image map features in FrontPage in Chapter 5. Now I'd like to unveil another handy tool designed solely for creating and editing image maps: CuteMAP.

CuteMAP is a tool by GlobalSCAPE that allows you to create image maps graphically, freeing you from calculating and coding the areas of an image map by hand. Figure 9-4 shows the familiar skateboard image example from Chapter 5 as viewed in CuteMAP.

When you create a project in CuteMAP, the program prompts you to select an image to use as the basis for the image map. The image is then displayed in the CuteMAP window, along with the HTML code. That CuteMAP displays the HTML code is significant because it allows you to cut and paste image maps into your own Web pages. It's also educational because you can see the HTML code being generated as you work through the creation of an image map.

If you elect not to use a full-featured Web design tool such as FrontPage, which includes a built-in image map tool, I highly recommend CuteMAP for your image map creation needs. To find out more about CuteMAP, visit the Globalscape Web site at *http://www.globalscape.com/*.

Note

Unfortunately, the CuteMAP image map tool is available only for the Windows platform. However, there are a few image map tools available for the Macintosh platform. One of these tools is MapMaker, which you can download online at *http://www.kickinit.net/mapmaker/*. Macromedia DreamWeaver for the Power Mac also includes a built-in image map tool. You might also visit your favorite Macintosh shareware Web site and search for additional image map tools if these don't suffice.

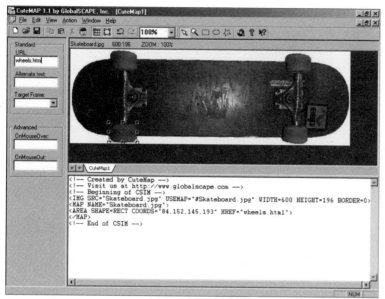

Figure 9-4.
The CuteMAP image map tool allows you to create image maps graphically.

Web Page Design Tools

If you start creating complex Web pages with only a text editor, you will find Web design exceedingly tedious and messy. You might want to consider using a graphical Web page design tool to avoid some of the drudgery of HTML coding, and to allow you to focus on the visual aspects of your pages. Many people have the attitude that graphical tools allow you to be blissfully ignorant of HTML. But it's not a good idea to limit yourself to only graphical tools if you plan to create Web pages with any flair.

Graphical Web design tools such as Microsoft FrontPage give you the freedom to build Web pages visually, resorting to HTML only when necessary. You learned in the previous section that coding image maps can be tiresome. Another facet of Web design that isn't particularly entertaining in straight HTML code is creating tables. You learned in Chapter 6, "Organizing Pages with Tables," that coding tables in HTML by hand isn't necessarily difficult, but using a graphical design tool can make the process much smoother and more intuitive. Figure 9-5 on the next page shows how it is possible to visually create a table in FrontPage.

You will learn later in the chapter that FrontPage also makes it possible to view the HTML code for a Web page. This is helpful if you are using only the table and image mapping features of FrontPage. You can use FrontPage to create just the tables and image maps, and then copy and paste the code generated by FrontPage into your hand-coded HTML files. This is a reasonable trade-off between graphical and nongraphical Web page design. It avoids the hassle of manually coding highly visual Web elements in HTML and retains complete control over your Web pages.

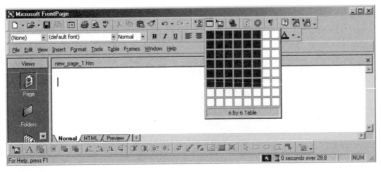

Figure 9-5.
FrontPage allows you to create tables by dragging the mouse and visually indicating the number of rows and cells.

If I've convinced you to consider using a graphical Web design tool, you'll be glad to know that there are numerous options. Following are several popular ones:

- Microsoft FrontPage
- Adobe GoLive
- Macromedia DreamWeaver

I found it easier to distinguish the price and target user of each product than to fairly compare their respective features. In truth, any of these tools will likely serve your purpose well into the future because they are all quite powerful.

FrontPage and GoLive are worth a look, because they are professional quality Web design tools but are simple enough that beginning Web designers can get started quickly. Be aware that GoLive offers more features than FrontPage, but costs twice as much. FrontPage also comes bundled with several Microsoft Office suites. If you are an Office user, you might already have FrontPage as part of Office. There are benefits to using FrontPage with Office, because of its integration with other Office applications. For more information about FrontPage, visit the FrontPage Web site at *http://www.microsoft.com/ frontpage/*. To learn more about GoLive, visit the Adobe Web site at *http://www.adobe.com/*.

Just as Adobe Photoshop offers a high-end, high-priced solution for image editing, Macromedia DreamWeaver offers a high-end answer in a graphical Web design tool. DreamWeaver quickly became the Web design tool of choice for many professional Web designers a few years ago, and it is still going strong. If you are an aspiring professional Web designer, you might want to consider spending the money for DreamWeaver. Short of that ambition, you might be better served with FrontPage, GoLive, or some other Web design tool.

Keep in mind that GoLive and DreamWeaver are available for both Mac and Windows, but FrontPage is available only for Windows. There are many other Web design tools; I've only highlighted the most popular ones.

HTML Editors

The last type of Web tool I want to mention is an HTML editor—the one tool that you can't live without. So far I've assumed that you're using a no-frills text editor such as Windows Notepad to code your Web pages. Although Notepad or some other text editor is certainly suitable for coding Web pages, there are other options that offer significant benefits.

HTML editors are special text editors designed specifically for editing HTML code. They offer benefits such as context-sensitive highlighting, a fancy way of saying that the HTML code is colored differently to help distinguish tags from other types of content. I've listed two popular HTML editors that you might consider if you go beyond a simple text editor such as Notepad:

- GlobalSCAPE CuteHTML

- Allaire HomeSite

In addition to serving as more powerful options to traditional text editors, these HTML editors also are great educational tools. They help you write HTML code, which helps you get acquainted with tag usage. As an example, look at Figure 9-6, which shows how CuteHTML allows you to place an image on a Web page using an intuitive dialog box.

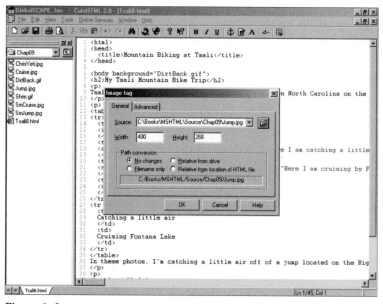

Figure 9-6.
The CuteHTML editor allows you to "write" HTML code by entering information about an HTML element in a dialog box.

HomeSite and CuteHTML aren't technically graphical Web design tools. They don't support WYSIWYG Web page editing, but they do provide graphical features that improve the development of HTML code. For example, CuteHTML includes a visual table creation feature that is similar to the one you saw in FrontPage. Figure 9-7 shows how tables are created using this feature in CuteHTML.

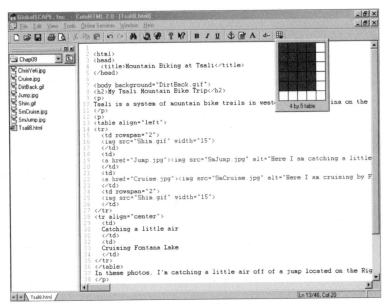

Figure 9-7.
Creating tables in CuteHTML is as simple as dragging the mouse to indicate the number of rows and columns.

HomeSite and CuteHTML aren't the only HTML editors out there. Rather than give you a long list of HTML editors, I'm simply giving you an idea of what is possible with these kinds of tools. By all means, look around for other options. If you consider HomeSite, visit the Allaire Web site at *http://www.allaire.com/*. Learn more about CuteHTML by visiting the GlobalSCAPE Web site at *http://www.globalscape.com/*.

Note

Like the CuteMAP image map tool you learned about earlier in the chapter, CuteHTML is available only for the Windows platform.

Working with HTML in FrontPage

Because Microsoft FrontPage is perhaps the most prevalent graphical Web design tool among beginner and intermediate Windows users, I want to explore how to carry out a few tasks that you'll find useful even if you aim to be an HTML purist. By HTML purist,

I mean that you decide to stick with hand-coding your Web pages in a text editor or HTML editor so that you have maximum control over what goes on them. Following are a few common HTML coding chores that I find useful to carry out within FrontPage:

- Previewing Web pages
- Creating tables
- Creating image maps
- Publishing Web pages

The next few sections describe how to use FrontPage to make each of these Web design tasks easier to manage. If you don't have FrontPage and you intend to use a different graphical Web design tool, you can rest easy knowing that you can probably perform similar steps in your tool of choice for a similar result. If you're hardcore about HTML coding and avoiding all graphical tools, more power to you. But I recommend that you continue reading just to find out what you might be missing.

Using Different Views

In an attempt to accommodate both beginner and advanced Web page designers by providing both a high-level and low-level approach to editing Web pages, FrontPage offers several different views of a page. You can edit the page using a WYSIWYG editor that displays the page more or less as it will appear in a browser, or you can edit the HTML code directly. The WYSIWYG view in FrontPage is considered the *normal* view, because most users will avoid HTML coding at all costs. But not you! You can also use Preview, the view that allows you to see the page exactly as it will appear in a Web browser. To summarize, following are the three views supported in FrontPage:

- Normal
- HTML
- Preview

These views are displayed as tabbed panes within the main area of the FrontPage workspace. Figure 9-8 on the next page shows the Tsali mountain bike Web page as viewed in the Normal view of FrontPage.

As you can see in the figure, the Tsali Web page is displayed roughly as it will appear in a Web browser. The obvious difference is the outline around the table, which is necessary for you to see the table for editing purposes. To change the view and edit the Web page as straight HTML code, click the HTML tab below the page. Figure 9-9, also on the next page, shows the HTML view of FrontPage, which allows you to directly edit the HTML code for the Web page.

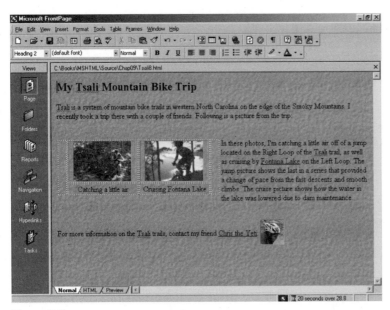

Figure 9-8.

The Normal view in FrontPage provides a WYSIWYG editor that displays a Web page in a form that resembles its final browser appearance.

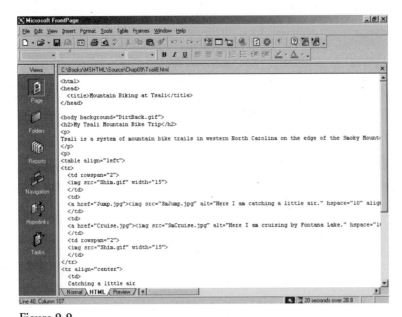

Figure 9-9.

The HTML view in FrontPage provides an HTML editor that allows you to directly edit the HTML code for a Web page.

The other view in FrontPage is the Preview view, which allows you to see a page as it will appear in a browser. Its advantage is that you view the page directly in FrontPage, so you don't have to actually run a Web browser separately. To switch to the Preview view, click the Preview tab below the Web page. Figure 9-10 shows the Preview view in FrontPage, and how it displays a page as it will appear in a Web browser.

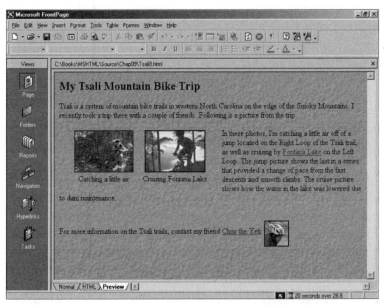

Figure 9-10.
The Preview view in FrontPage allows you to view a Web page as it will appear in a Web browser.

The neat thing about the views in FrontPage is that you can quickly switch between them by clicking the tabs below the view window. This makes it possible to try out different things in HTML view and quickly see the results in Preview. And if you want to use the WYSIWYG editor to help create a table or an image map, you can hop over to it and then jump back to the HTML view to see the resulting HTML code. I encourage you to experiment with the views in FrontPage and get a feel for how they let you build and test Web pages.

Note

Most graphical Web design tools, including FrontPage, generate HTML code that seems un-necessary. The reality is that these tools typically require special tags to carry out some of their more advanced features, which you may or may not be interested in using. If you avoid using these features, you can typically avoid the automatic insertion of the sloppy looking code. Regardless of how careful you are, some of this code may end up in your pages. You can decide to ignore it or delete it by hand in the HTML view.

Creating Tables

As you learned earlier in the chapter, creating a table in FrontPage is straightforward, thanks to the visual table creation feature that allows you to click and drag the mouse to determine the number of rows and columns in a table. You already saw what this looked like earlier in the chapter, so I'll spare you another figure. What I haven't mentioned is that it's also possible to enter content in a table in FrontPage, using the WYSIWYG editor. For example, if you want to create a table to catalog your monthly budget for a family Web site, you would first create a table by clicking the Table button, then dragging to define the dimensions of the table. After creating the table, make sure you are in the Normal view. You will see the outline of the table with rows and columns delineated. Click in each cell of the table and start typing away to add the budget content. Keep in mind that you can highlight cells and format the text using the FrontPage menus and toolbars. Once you're finished entering the budget numbers, you should have a page that is similar to the one in Figure 9-11.

The interesting aspect of the table creation process is when you pop over to the HTML view and take a look at the HTML code generated for the table, as shown in Figure 9-12. Of course, the most exciting part of creating any Web page is seeing the finished result, which is possible by simply switching to the Preview view, as shown in Figure 9-13.

Earlier I mentioned that the multiple views of FrontPage can be used in conjunction to provide a powerful Web development environment. This table creation example serves as a great demonstration of this point.

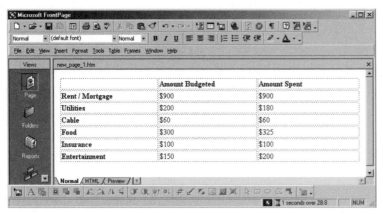

Figure 9-11.
Because the Normal view of FrontPage is a WYSIWYG display, entering text into table cells is simply a matter of selecting the cell and typing.

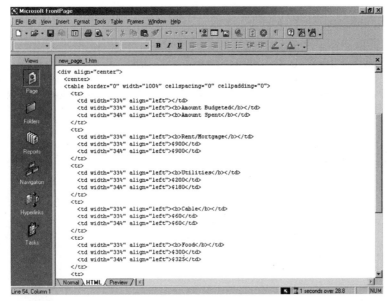

Figure 9-12.
The HTML view provides a means of studying or modifying HTML code generated by FrontPage for the newly created table.

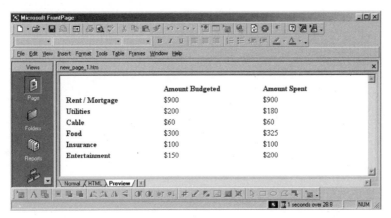

Figure 9-13.
The Preview view displays the newly created table in all its glory.

Creating Image Maps

Like tables, image maps can be a pain to code by hand in HTML. For this reason I strongly recommend using a graphical Web design tool such as FrontPage to create and edit image maps. You learned how to work with image maps in FrontPage in Chapter 5, "Visual Navigation with Image Maps." Note that the same use of the multiple FrontPage views comes in handy with image maps as well as with tables.

Publishing Your Pages

One last facet of FrontPage, and most graphical Web design tools for that matter, is the publication of pages to the Web. In Chapter 1, "HTML Essentials," you created your first Web page and published it to the Web using the Microsoft Web Publishing Wizard. Tools such as FrontPage eliminate the need for the Web Publishing Wizard by including a built-in feature for publishing Web pages. The advantage is that you complete the design, test, and publication phases of Web site development from within the same application. In other words, with a tool such as FrontPage, you can quickly publish pages after editing them without using any other tool or utility. You will learn much more about publishing pages using FrontPage and other software utilities in the next chapter, "Publishing Pages on the Web."

Conclusion

After reading this chapter you're probably pondering the purchase of a tool belt and workbench to accommodate all the tools you've learned about. Fortunately, HTML tools are all software and won't take up any space in your garage. If you still want to buy a tool belt as a cool fashion accessory, be my guest!

The purpose of this chapter was to give you an introduction to HTML tools in order to open your eyes to the variety of options available to you as a Web page designer. All Web designers have preferences for certain tools they find useful, because of how those tools mesh with their HTML coding efforts. Now that you know what's on the market and what the typical features are, you can begin assembling an HTML toolkit that appeals to your own Web development style.

This chapter began by extolling the virtues of graphical Web design tools and why you might consider using them. From there, I presented several different fundamental types of tools, and introduced you to popular tools of each type that are heavily used at all levels of Web development. The chapter concluded by focusing specifically on Microsoft FrontPage as a graphical design tool, and pointed out several facets of FrontPage that would make it a valuable part of your Web development tool kit.

Chapter 10

Publishing Pages on the Web

Web fact for the day

Individuals around the world take about 2,700 original photographs every second, far more than the number generated by publishers or other commercial groups. This adds up to more than 80 billion new images a year on more than 3 billion rolls of film.

Before you rush to the phone to call your broker and buy Eastman Kodak stock, let me caution you that we are in the midst of a rapid shift from traditional printed photography to digital. Many people, myself included, have made the move to digital cameras and are now cataloging photos on their hard drives instead of in photo albums. Although printed photos aren't going away entirely, there is something incredibly empowering about "developing" your own digital images.

Just as digital photography effectively allows you to become the photo lab tech, the Web allows you to become the printing press operator. There has been much hoopla surrounding e-commerce and how we'll all be Internet billionaires in a few years, but the reality is that the growth of self-publishing is one of the most significant contributions of the Web. Never before has it been possible for people with modest means to present their ideas for the entire world to see. Granted, I'm using the word "ideas" rather loosely, because there are plenty of personal Web pages floating around that are devoid of any meaningful thought. Even so, I'm all for empowering individuals regardless of how they choose to use that power. In this chapter, you exercise your power to self-publish by learning how to publish your own Web pages on the World Wide Web. Make me proud!

Web Publishing Basics

In introducing HTML, Chapter 1 addressed Web publishing by quickly showing you how to publish your own Web page. Although you covered the steps required to use a specific Web publishing tool, I glossed over the details of the Web publishing process. Now it's time to dig deeper into Web publishing and find out what is really happening when you make your presence known on the Web. Let's start off by reviewing two important terms from Chapter 1:

- Web client—a Web browser that displays Web pages after receiving them from a Web server

- Web server—a special computer on the Internet that delivers Web pages to Web clients

The relationship between a Web client and a Web server is pretty simple: the client (Web browser) asks the Web server for a certain Web page, and the server obliges by delivering the page to the client. This relationship is important to Web publishing because you must understand how and where to place your Web pages to make them accessible by Web users. More specifically, you must copy your pages to a Web server, allowing your pages to be viewed by anyone with a Web browser.

You probably don't have a Web server sitting around the house. So, your first task is to choose whether you will install Web server software on a computer with a permanent Internet connection or use a Web hosting service. Most likely you'll be using a Web hosting service unless you are developing a business Web site. You might also have the capability to publish Web pages through your Internet service provider (Microsoft Network, America Online, Earthlink, or others).

Note

Technically speaking, one type of permanent Internet connection is the cable modem. This might lead you to believe that you can install a Web server on a computer with a cable modem connection and run a Web site. In fact, this scenario is technically possible, but most cable Internet providers don't allow it. That's because it can result in problems if too many people browse your pages at once. If you're still considering bending the rules, keep in mind that if everyone ran a Web site using a cable modem connection, the connection speed would probably slow to a crawl.

Although Web pages must be stored on the hard drive of a Web server computer, the actual development of the pages takes place on your local computer. If you are hosting your own Web server, then your local computer may perform both the development and the distribution functions. When you're ready to publish the pages on the Web, you copy them to a Web server. You learned in Chapter 1 how this is accomplished on the Windows platform with Microsoft's Web Publishing Wizard. If you aren't using a Windows computer or don't have access to the Web Publishing Wizard, you can use an FTP (File Transfer Protocol) program to send the Web page files to a server using FTP. Some popular Windows FTP programs are WS_FTP and CuteFTP. For the Macintosh, Fetch is a popular FTP program. You can also use a graphical Web development tool such as Microsoft FrontPage or Macromedia DreamWeaver, which include built-in publishing features.

A potential source of confusion regarding publishing Web pages is that Web servers often aren't computers that you will see and interact with. Don't get me wrong: a Web server looks like a normal computer. But you usually have no idea where the Web server for your Web site is located, especially if you use a Web hosting service. Do you know the exact location of the phone company's central office that services your phone line? Probably not. The same situation applies with Web servers because it really isn't important where the Web server is physically located. In lieu of knowing its physical location, you interact with a Web server by using its Internet address. An Internet address is basically an online version of a mailing address.

Note

If you're working on a business Web site, there may actually be a Web server in your building. In this case you may be able to walk up and interact with it, perhaps against the wishes of the network administrator. However, most individuals and many smaller companies can't justify the expense of the permanent Internet connection that is required for Web servers. Most Web hosting companies are good at minimizing the inevitable technical problems to ensure that your site stays up and running.

When you publish pages using the Web Publishing Wizard, an FTP program, or a graphical Web development tool, you must specify the address of the Web server for your Web site. Your Web hosting service will have provided the address to you. If you have your own domain name, you will enter it as the address of the Web server. For example, when I modify my board game Web site, I specify the Web server as *http://www.incthegame.com* (Figure 10-1). The Web publishing software (FrontPage in this case) will then ask for a user name and password, which I must enter so that I can publish the updated pages.

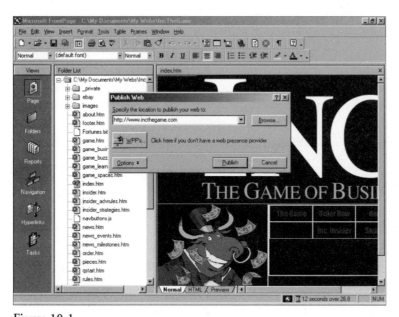

Figure 10-1.
The Publish Web window of Microsoft FrontPage prompts you to enter the address of the Web server for the Web site being published.

If you have a Web site as part of your AOL (America Online) Internet account, you will specify *http://members.aol.com* as the address of the Web server. You then enter your AOL user name/ID and password, and the pages are published. The AOL Web server automatically stores the pages in the appropriate location within the AOL Hometown community. I will go into more detail regarding AOL as a Web hosting service in the next section of this chapter.

The goal of this section isn't to give you a detailed play-by-play analysis of how the Web publishing process works for a specific Web server or Web publishing program. There are so many different possible configurations that it is virtually impossible to discuss them all. Instead, I want to give you the fundamentals of Web publishing and how it works so that you can successfully publish your Web pages with any tool on any Web server. Let's move on and take a look at the options available for hosting your Web pages.

Finding a Good Home for Your Web Pages

The first car I ever bought with my own money is a Honda Civic. I spent a considerable amount of time researching the car and determining exactly which options and features I wanted. I'm speaking of the car in the present tense because I still own it. My wife and I have taken such good care of it that we can't bear the thought of giving it to someone and that person not giving it the same care, so it continues to sit in our garage as a quite expensive sentimental object. Maybe someday we'll get up the courage to let it go, and we'll screen potential candidates to make sure that they meet our high standards of car care. You should be as picky about finding a good home for your Web pages as I am about finding a good home for my trusted Civic. There are some hard questions that enter into the picture when you face the important decision of where to place your Web pages. Following are the major options, listed in order of decreasing cost, that are available to you, the Web page owner:

- Host your own Web server ($$$$$)
- Pay for a Web hosting service ($$$$)
- Use the Web hosting service built into your Internet account ($$$)
- Use a free Web hosting service ($$)
- Store the pages only on your local hard drive ($)

Of course, decreasing cost corresponds with decreasing power and flexibility. The old adage, "You get what you pay for," definitely holds true for Web hosting. Notice that at this point I haven't made any recommendations regarding how you should host your Web pages, regardless of how much money you have buried in the back yard. But I will. Rest assured that two of the options on this list can be safely ruled out by the vast majority of individual Web page designers.

Hosting Your Own Web Site

If you're struggling on the dating circuit and looking for a way to impress a potential mate, I can think of no better way than hosting your own Web server. Whereas luxury cars were the status symbols of the 80s and 90s, the new millennium has ushered in information management as a status symbol all its own. As you show your date around your house, think about the captivating effect that the whirring hard drive of a Web server will have as you casually say, "And, this is the server room." Trust me, if you've got a Mercedes, ditch it and get a Web server!

Truthfully, I have serious doubts that anyone but an aspiring e-business tycoon will have the need for his or her own Web server. Hosting your own Web server involves buying a special computer with special server hardware, and then paying a hefty monthly fee for a dedicated Internet connection. None of this is cheap, so unless you fell for the joke about a Web server helping your love life, I don't recommend it as a realistic option.

On the upside, if you do have money to burn, a Web server of your own provides the most flexibility, because you can use it however you wish. Practically speaking, this means you can install any kind of special server software that a traditional Web hosting service might not allow. Web hosting services tend to be very hesitant to try new things because network stability is a huge issue for them.

Paying for a Web Hosting Service

If you've ruled out the possibility of running your own Web server, then the next option you might consider is paying for a Web hosting service. This type of Web hosting service is different from your normal Internet account in that it is solely for hosting Web pages. Literally thousands of companies offer Web hosting services, and their prices and service levels vary considerably. These are a few of the most popular larger Web hosting services:

- Earthlink (*http://www.earthlink.net/*)
- Yahoo! (*http://website.yahoo.com/*)
- Network Solutions (*http://www.networksolutions.com*)

Network Solutions is also the company responsible for the registration of Internet *domain names*.

Note

A domain name is a unique name that identifies your Web site to the world. Although it is possible to host your Web site as part of someone else's domain name, it's pretty cool to have a name all your own. For example, I own the domain names `michaelmorrison.com` and `michaelmorrison.net`. Domain names are somewhat like real estate, in that only so many of them are available. If you have a name in mind for a Web site, I encourage you to spend a little money and register the domain name for it now, assuming it's still available.

Having your own domain name is one of the factors that will likely affect the type of Web hosting you choose. For example, most Internet services that include built-in Web hosting don't allow you to use your own domain name. Instead, you store your Web site within a folder on the domain of the Internet provider. Figure 10-2 shows an example on AOL of the personal Web site name `trailhiker` appended to the AOL domain name `hometown.aol.com`. There's nothing wrong with your Web site having another domain name, other than that it isn't quite as succinct. And, of course, it doesn't carry the prestige of having your own `.com`.

Figure 10-2.
A Web site hosted under an AOL Internet account has the `hometown.aol.com` *domain name, as opposed to having its own name.*

Note

The primary parameter that affects Web hosting services is the amount of space available for Web pages. In other words, you should note the amount of storage space they provide when comparison-shopping Web hosting services. Keep in mind that text takes up little space, so the space issue mainly comes into play if you're using a large number of photos or multimedia files such as videos.

If you do decide to pay for a Web hosting service, you can expect to pay somewhere in the range of $15 to $75 per month. If you don't plan on doing any e-commerce on your site, you can easily come in on the low end of this price range. The monthly cost moves to the high end of the range when you have shopping cart features and process credit cards. Also, don't forget that there is a fee associated with registering a domain name, which you will learn about later in the chapter.

Hosting with Your Internet Account

For the vast majority of individuals who simply want a presence on the Web, the best option is to use free Web features that accompany most Internet accounts. For example, my @Home cable modem Internet account includes 10 megabytes (MB) of free Web space that I can use to store a Web site. However, like most Internet services, @Home doesn't allow you to use a domain name of your own. This means that your Web site appears as a folder beneath the members.home.net domain. For example, if I use the user name bagheera and create a Web site in my @Home account, the Web site would be accessible as *http://members.home.net/bagheera*. This isn't as slick as having your own domain name, but it may serve your purpose just fine. And you can't beat the price!

One thing to keep in mind about using Web features built into your Internet account is that your Internet service provider may require you to use a standard template for your pages. This is certainly a reasonable approach for some people, because it makes creating Web pages simple. On the other hand, because you're reading this book, I would guess that you're looking for a more hands-on approach that gives you the flexibility to modify and improve on simple designs. For this reason, you will probably want to look for an option that allows you to create your own pages and then transfer them directly to the Internet service's Web server. Most Internet service providers support this option for people who, like you, are on their way to becoming HTML gurus.

Using a Free Web Hosting Service

It's possible that you don't have an Internet account at home and therefore don't have the luxury of using built-in Web features. Or maybe you have a big family, and the kids have already hijacked the free Web space that came with your Internet account. Either way, if you're looking for a low-cost option for creating a Web site, there's actually a no-cost option that you might want to investigate. I'm referring to free Web services, such as Yahoo! GeoCities (*http://geocities.yahoo.com*) and BigStep (*http://www.bigstep.com*). These types of services offer completely free Web hosting; the only "payment" is the appearance of small ads when someone visits your Web page. You decide whether this a problem.

Similar to the built-in Web features that accompany most Internet services, the features offered by free Web hosting services lean toward the use of standard templates to construct your Web pages. BigStep, for example, doesn't allow you to create your own Web pages from scratch using HTML. However, Yahoo! GeoCities does, which is why I encourage you to check it out if you're looking for a no-cost Web hosting solution. There are many other similar services out there, but I'll leave it up to you to hunt them down. You might try a Web search for the phrase "free Web hosting" and see what you can find.

Foregoing Web Hosting Entirely

If you're the kind of person who wants the utmost in privacy and is secretive to the point of compulsion, then you might consider foregoing Web hosting entirely. In this scenario, you'd create your Web pages and keep them on your local hard drive. Of course, the drawback is that you will be the only person to see your Web pages—unless you call your friends and family over to check out the pages directly on your own computer. Realistically, this isn't much of an option, because then your pages aren't really part of the World Wide Web. Nonetheless, I want you to know that I'm leaving no stone unturned in terms of giving you options for your Web pages.

Obtaining a Domain Name

Several times throughout the chapter I've alluded to the fact that you can register your own domain name and host your Web site in style. A certain air of mystery surrounds domain names and where they come from, so please allow me to take you behind the scenes and reveal the tricks of the domain name trade.

In reality, obtaining a domain name is a straightforward process. The only trick is making sure that the name is available before attempting to register it; you'd be surprised how many domain names are already taken. To find out if your domain name is available, visit the Network Solutions Web site at *http://www.networksolutions.com*. The Network Solutions home page includes a text edit field that allows you to enter the name of your domain and see if it's available (Figure 10-3). Make sure to enter the domain name without the extension (.com, .net, and others), and then select the extension from the list next to the name.

Unfortunately, you'll probably find that your name is already taken. There isn't much you can do about this except try a different extension such as .net or .org, instead of .com. Keep in mind that domain names are essentially rented from Network Solutions, which means that they can expire and become available again. This happened with my domain name, michaelmorrison.com. When I first tried to register it a couple of years ago, it was taken. I kept checking the status every few months—a seemingly futile effort— and I couldn't believe it the day the name came up as available. Apparently the previous owner didn't renew, so the name went back on the block.

Note

As of this writing, the available domain extensions are .com, .net, .org, .cc, and .tv. However, new extensions, .biz and .info, should be available in the near future.

Once you've found a domain name, you can register it on the Network Solutions Web site by entering information about yourself. Registration fees are calculated on a yearly basis, which means that you pay to reserve the domain name for years at a time.

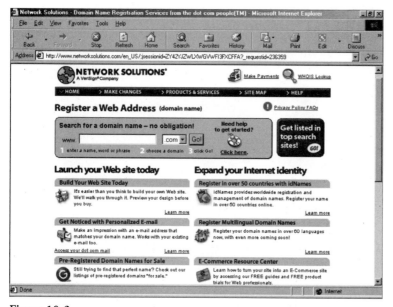

Figure 10-3.
You can enter a domain name and check its availability on the home page of the Network Solutions Web site.

The minimum amount of time you can reserve a name is one year, which breaks down into the following costs for the five current domain name types:

- .com—$35
- .net—$30
- .org—$25
- .cc—$50
- .tv—$50

Please understand that these prices are controlled by organizations that are free to change them at any time. I'm sharing them with you so that you have a ballpark idea of what it costs to get your own domain name. The registration fees for domain names come down considerably if you're willing to register a name for a longer period of time. The longest time frame you can register a domain name is 10 years, which currently saves you 40 percent of the normal yearly price if you calculate the yearly cost times 10.

Once you've registered your domain name, you'll need to inform your Web hosting service so that it can take the appropriate steps to associate your Web pages with the domain name. Most Web hosting services will register the name for you as part of the hosting set-up process if you want to handle everything in one step.

Personally, I recommend going through Network Solutions because you can register the name even if you aren't ready to build the Web site yet. For example, you could register your domain name and wait to build your Web pages until you finish reading this book.

The significance of registering now is that your domain name is safe and secure, and you don't have to worry about someone else absconding with it. Network Solutions also offers Web hosting services you may want to check into.

Note

I'd like to remind you that I don't have any affiliation with Web hosting services or any other Internet-related services, for that matter. I'm merely giving you suggestions and ideas based upon my own experiences. I encourage you to do your own research in finding what type of service solution best meets your needs.

Selecting Web Publishing Software

Once you've decided how to host your Web site and maybe even registered a domain name, you'll need to consider the software you plan to use to publish the finished Web pages on the World Wide Web. There are two major types:

- FTP clients
- Graphical Web development tools

These terms should look familiar to you, as we discussed them earlier in the chapter. As you'll recall, FTP clients are special programs that support the transfer of files across the Internet using the File Transfer Protocol (FTP). FTP clients allow you to transfer files of any type, but they are commonly used to transfer Web pages to Web servers.

Graphical Web development tools are complete software environments that support every phase of Web development from HTML editing to Web page publishing. Whether or not you use the HTML editing features of a graphical Web development tool, you might find such a tool useful for publishing pages you've created by hand in HTML. FrontPage is a good example of a Web development tool that makes it easy to publish Web pages.

In addition to FTP clients and graphical Web development tools, you can also use a special Web publishing tool such as the Microsoft Web Publishing Wizard to publish your Web pages. The Web Publishing Wizard is essentially an FTP client designed solely for transferring Web pages to a Web server. For more information on how to use the Web Publishing Wizard, please refer to the step-by-step Web publishing procedure in Chapter 1.

Conclusion

If you've never pondered the impact of the Web on the sharing of independent thought, I hope this chapter has stirred you to take advantage of the opportunity to spread whatever thoughts you have to share. On the other hand, maybe you don't have any grand ideological plans for your Web pages, and you just want to create a Web page with pictures of your terra cotta ashtray collection. Regardless of your motives for publishing on the Web, the reality is that it's not difficult to take Web pages that you've created on your local computer and transfer them to a Web server for the whole world to see.

This chapter presented the different options available for publishing your Web pages on the Web. If you were excited about learning more HTML tags and attributes, this chapter may have been a letdown. Maybe I can cheer you up with the news that the next chapter delves back into the minutiae of HTML, introducing you to style sheets. Until then, I encourage you to spend some time choosing a Web host and taking a stab at publishing some of your own Web pages.

Part 3

Adding Style to Your Pages

Chapter 11

Style Sheet Basics

On the other hand, if you stare at a computer screen for long hours every day without sufficient breaks, it probably will help you along the path to near-sightedness. Although it won't improve your vision, you can spice up your Web pages with style sheets and at least make the experience more pleasurable. Style sheets are used to control the appearance of Web content, and are the recommended means of formatting Web pages for viewing. The governing body for the Web, the World Wide Web Consortium (W3C), is pushing style sheets to control fonts, colors, and other aspects of Web page formatting.

This chapter introduces you to style sheets, and defines their role in improving the appearance of Web pages. Along with learning the basics of style sheets, you will also learn several techniques for introducing style sheets into your Web pages. This chapter doesn't cover the whole gamut of style sheets but it is a good jumpstart. The next chapter covers the details of various styles.

What Are Style Sheets?

As you've seen throughout this book, you can create Web pages with the colors of your choice. Altering the color of a piece of Web content is a formatting task that applies only to how the content looks when viewed in a Web browser. Consequently, you should make a clear distinction between the information in a Web page and the formatting code used to describe its appearance. The benefit of dividing formatting code from content in a Web page is that it makes the Web pages easier to alter and maintain. For example, consider the following code, which sets the color of several non-adjacent paragraphs of text to green:

```
<h3>Rules</h3>
<p><font color="green">
Q : Can I sell employees to other players, transfer them
between businesses, or turn them back in to the Employee Pool
for money?
</font></p>
<p>
A : No, you cannot sell employees to other players or
transfer them between different businesses. Employees can be
turned back in to the Employee Pool (laid off) but you don't
receive any money.
</p>

<p><font color="green">
Q : What happens if I land on the Corporate Headhunter space
and I can't use all of the employees I receive?
</font></p>
<p>
A : The employees must be returned to the Employee Pool.
</p>

<p><font color="green">
Q : Can I use a corporation as part of a matching pair to
form another corporation?
</font></p>
<p>
A : No. Corporations can only be formed when you have two
matching small businesses and the one you are incorporating
is fully employed.
</p>
```

This code is part of a Frequently Asked Questions (FAQ) Web page for a financial board game. If you look closely, you'll notice that each question is formatted to appear in a green font. This is accomplished using the `<font>` tag and the `color` attribute, and it helps to distinguish the questions from the answers when the page is viewed. Figure 11-1 on the next page shows the *Inc. The Game of Business* FAQ page as viewed in Internet Explorer.

It's difficult to see the different colors in the figure, but you can see how the questions and answers are arranged on the page. A subtle problem arises when the page expands to contain additional questions and answers. The `<font>` tag must be applied to each of the questions over and over. It's easily handled in HTML code, but what if you decide to change the color of the questions to blue, or maybe use a different font for the questions? In either of these situations, you would have to go through the HTML code and make changes to each individual question. This is necessary because the formatting code, `<font>`, is tightly linked to the content of the page—the question text.

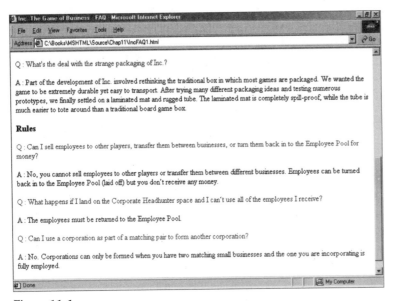

Figure 11-1.
The Inc. The Game of Business FAQ page uses the `<font>` tag to set the color of different paragraphs of text.

Style sheets have a solution that links formatting code with Web page content. You define specific styles that can then be used to format Web page content. They can apply to an entire Web page, to specific portions of a page, to specific tags, and even to specific instances of a tag. In short, style sheets offer a great deal of flexibility. They accomplish this by maintaining an arm's length of distance between them and the content of a Web page. To understand how this works, consider the following code that simplifies the FAQ page with a simple style sheet:

```
<style>
  p.question { color:green }
</style>
```

This code contains a simple style sheet that establishes a specific class of `<p>` tag named *question*. Any time a `<p>` tag is used and its `class` attribute is set to `question`, the text in the paragraph will be displayed in green. Following is an example of how this style sheet is used in the FAQ Web page code:

```
<h3>Rules</h3>
<p class="question">
Q : Can I sell employees to other players, transfer them
between businesses, or turn them back in to the Employee Pool
for money?
</p>
<p>
A : No, you cannot sell employees to other players or
transfer them between different businesses. Employees can be
turned back in to the Employee Pool (laid off) but you don't
```

```
receive any money.
</p>

<p class="question">
Q : What happens if I land on the Corporate Headhunter space
and I can't use all of the employees I receive?
</p>
<p>
A : The employees must be returned to the Employee Pool.
</p>

<p class="question">
Q : Can I use a corporation as part of a matching pair to
form another corporation?
</p>
<p>
A : No. Corporations can only be formed when you have two
matching small businesses and the one you are incorporating
is fully employed.
</p>
```

Notice that in this code, the `<font>` tag is mysteriously absent. Instead, the `class` attribute of the `<p>` tag for each question paragraph is now set to `question`. No additional formatting code is present in the question paragraphs. More importantly, the style of the paragraph is set in one place—the style sheet. So, if you want to change the appearance of the question paragraphs, you change the `p.question` style in the style sheet. This reveals how style sheets make it possible to separate formatting code from Web page content, and ultimately improve the structure of Web pages.

This brings us to the question of the day—what is a style sheet? A *style sheet* is a collection of formatting rules for a Web page. Style sheets consist of individual styles that apply to parts of a Web page. You can specify a style sheet directly within a Web page using the `<style>` tag, as the FAQ page demonstrated, or in a separate document that is referenced by a Web page. You can also apply styles individually throughout a Web page.

The formal name for style sheets is *cascading style sheets* (CSS), which refers to the manner in which styles cascade down from one HTML tag to another. This means that if you apply a style sheet to a tag that has child tags, the styles will apply to both the parent and child tags, cascading down from the parent to the children. Furthermore, if you specify a style for a tag, such as the `<p>` paragraph tag, the style will apply to all paragraphs. However, you can still use the class approach shown earlier in the FAQ example to override general styles with a specific style for a certain class of tags.

Don't worry at this point if style sheets seem a little complicated. I've thrown a lot at you quickly to immerse you in style sheets so you can see them in context. Let's take a short step back to reconsider the significance of style sheets and why you need to add them to your Web design knowledge base. Keep in mind that you've been liberally using HTML formatting tags to dress up your Web pages so they have more impact. Style sheets are designed to replace these HTML formatting tags (`<font>`, `<big>`, `<small>`, and so on) with a more unified approach to styling Web pages. Not only is it a good idea to start using style sheets instead of HTML formatting tags, but it's also eventually going to be a necessity.

Use style sheets not because you love them, but because you hate HTML formatting tags. Maybe *hate* is too strong a word, but the reality is that HTML formatting tags are going away.

The W3C has already ruled that most HTML formatting tags are obsolete, meaning that at some point browsers may stop supporting them. This actually isn't a likely scenario when you consider how many Web pages rely on such tags, but you could take it as a warning sign that style sheets represent the future of Web page formatting. HTML formatting tags won't be phased out in browsers any time soon, but style sheets are quickly becoming the standard for formatting Web pages.

The Essentials of Style

You've already learned a great deal about style sheets, even if it felt like a cyclone hit you. In this section, I want to take things more slowly and lay the ground rules for style sheets, which will prove invaluable as you progress. Let's begin with the structure of a style. Look at this example of a style that is used to format a heading:

```
h1 {font-weight:bold; font-size:14pt; color:orange }
```

In this example, a style is created for the `<h1>` tag, setting the font weight, size, and color for the heading. The `font-weight`, `font-size`, and `color` names in the style are style properties. Each style property is separated from its respective value by a colon (:), and individual properties within a style are separated by semicolons (;). All of the style properties are enclosed in braces ({}), which are preceded by the name of the tag that the style applies to.

The `<h1>` style is an example of a style that is declared in a style sheet using the `<style>` tag, as the following code demonstrates:

```
<style>
  h1 { font-weight:bold; font-size:14pt; color:orange }
</style>
```

The style section of a Web page must be included in the head of the page, as the following code shows:

```
<head>
  <title>A Stylish Web Page</title>

  <style>
    h1 { font-weight:bold; font-size:14pt; color:orange }
  </style>
</head>
```

As you can see, this code shows how a style sheet is created for a single Web page. You will learn later in the chapter about creating a style sheet in a separate file to use in multiple Web pages.

It's also possible to create styles directly in HTML code without using a formal style sheet (<style> tag). Following is an example of how to apply a style directly to a piece of HTML code:

```
<h1 style="font-weight:bold; font-size:14pt; color:orange">
Part I
</h1>
```

In this code, the same style that you previously saw is created and applied to a specific instance of the <h1> tag. The difference between the two style approaches is that the first created a style as part of a style sheet that applies to all <h1> tags. The second approach created a style that applied only to the specific instance of the <h1> tag. In the latter example, any other <h1> tags in the Web page would be unaffected by the style because the style only applies to that particular <h1> tag. In coding the two different tags, the primary difference is that one uses <style> tags and the properties are enclosed in braces, but the other is an attribute of the tag being styled and its properties are enclosed in quotes. How the style properties are described remains the same.

Although the standard technique used to describe styles is to create a listing of style property/value pairs, you can group some style properties together. Here is an example of how to describe a font by grouping font style properties:

```
h1 { font:bold 14pt "Helvetica" }
```

In this example, the font style for the <h1> tag is created using a single property name (font) and several property values listed one after the next. The only required values for the font property are the font size and font family. Keep in mind that this code is equivalent to the following code, which specifies each font property individually:

```
h1 { font-weight:bold; font-size:14pt; font-family:"Helvetica" }
```

It's easy to see how the compact approach to defining font properties is easier to read and understand than spelling out each property individually. Don't forget that you can still use other style properties in addition to the font property, as in the following code:

```
h1 { font:bold 14pt "Helvetica"; color:orange }
```

In this example, the text color for the <h1> tag is set, in addition to the font styles. At this point I could go on and on about how to create different types of styles, but that's the focus of the next chapter. Right now it's more important to learn the specifics of how styles are applied to Web pages.

Applying Styles to Web Pages

Although styles are powerful and enable you to describe how Web content is formatted for viewing, they wouldn't be much use without a way to describe how to use them on Web pages. In other words, it's important to have a way of pointing out the Web page content affected by each style you create. You've already seen two approaches that can be used to apply styles to Web content. Now we're going to explore each of the other options available to you in applying styles to your Web pages.

Internal Style Sheets

When you create a style or set of styles and enclose it within the `<style>` tag in the head of a Web page, you are basically saying that the styles apply to the page as a whole. This collection of styles within a Web page is known as an *internal style sheet*, because it's defined directly within the page that it styles. Internal style sheets are always created using the `<style>` tag, and they must appear in the head of a Web page. Individual styles in an internal style sheet apply to the entire Web page, but they do not affect any other Web pages. Following is an example of an internal style sheet that is correctly specified:

```
<head>
  <title>Inc. The Game of Business - FAQ</title>

  <style>
    h3 { background:green; color:white; font-style:italic;
    font-weight:bold }
    p.question { color:green; font-style:italic;
    font-weight:bold }
  </style>
</head>
```

As you may have guessed, this is the internal style sheet for the *Inc. The Game of Business* FAQ Web page that you saw earlier. Actually, this style sheet is more interesting than the first one. In addition to including additional formatting for the `<p>` tag, it includes a style for the `<h3>` tag, used in the Web page to divide the questions and answers into groups. Notice that the background style is set, which determines the background color of all `<h3>` tags in the page. Figure 11-2 shows the resulting Web page as seen in Internet Explorer.

This internal style sheet is a good example of how such style sheets fit into the overall structure of Web pages. Specifically, it shows how an internal style sheet is formatted with the `<style>` tag that appears in the head of the page beneath the familiar `<title>` tag.

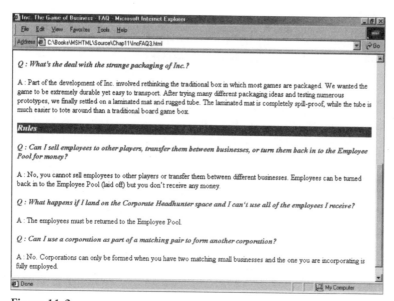

Figure 11-2.

The Inc. The Game of Business FAQ page relies on an internal style sheet to format portions of its text content.

External Style Sheets

Like internal style sheets, external style sheets define styles that you apply to a Web page. However, external style sheets are contained in separate files, apart from the Web page that they are used for. The primary advantage to using external style sheets is that you can apply styles to multiple Web pages. For example, if you create a Web site and you want all the pages to look similar, you could create an external style sheet that describes styles for the different tags used in the pages. These styles would specify the font, color, and other formatting details of the Web pages. The pages themselves wouldn't contain any style information except a reference to the style sheet.

External style sheets typically help you organize your Web pages, because they allow you to describe styles in one place and apply them to multiple Web pages. If you decide to change the style of a Web site, you simply change the style sheet. This is much more efficient than going to each page to update the styles. But if you only want to apply styles to a single Web page, then you might as well stick with an internal style sheet.

The code for external style sheets is no different than that for internal style sheets. For example, following is the code for an external style sheet that defines the same styles you saw in the previous section in an internal style sheet:

```
h3 { background:green; color:white; font-style:italic;
font-weight:bold }
p.question { color:green; font-style:italic; font-weight:bold }
```

This code must appear in a file named with a .css file extension, the standard extension used for cascading style sheets. Assuming that you place this code in a file named IncStyles.css, use the following code to reference the style sheet from a Web page:

```
<link rel="stylesheet" type="text/css" href="IncStyles.css">
```

Hold on—the `<link>` tag doesn't sound familiar. That's right, the `<link>` tag is something you haven't encountered so far. But it's not hard to use. The `<link>` tag is used to reference the .css style sheet, and associate it with a Web page. The `rel` attribute simply says that the link references a style sheet to be applied to the document. The `type` attribute specifies the type of link content, in this case a cascading style sheet. The `href` attribute is the most important element for this discussion because it identifies the file name of the external style sheet. When you reference your own style sheets, the `href` attribute is the only attribute you need to change.

Note

The `<link>` tag is an all-purpose tag used to reference different kinds of external files from a Web page.

Just as internal style sheets must appear in the head of a document, the reference to an external style sheet must also appear there. This is an example of how a `<link>` tag is placed in the head of the FAQ Web page you've been working with:

```
<head>
  <title>Inc. The Game of Business - FAQ</title>

  <link rel="stylesheet" type="text/css" href="IncStyles.css">
</head>
```

The best way to understand this code is to visualize the external style sheet being placed in the Web page where the `<link>` tag appears.

Classes of Styles

Styles are surprisingly flexible in how they can be applied to different portions of a Web page. In addition to applying a style to all instances of a given tag in a page, you can also establish a *style class* that applies to a class of tags. A class of tags is simply a subset of a particular tag. For example, you could organize the paragraphs in the FAQ Web page according to question paragraphs and answer paragraphs. Using style classes, you could create a different class for each type of paragraph. Following is an example of how to create a style class for a question paragraph:

```
p.question { color:green; font-style:italic; font-weight:bold }
```

The code shows that a style class is created by specifying the style as the tag name (p) followed by a period, and then the class name, question. This means that all `<p>` tags of class question will have the specified style. To identify a paragraph as a question paragraph, you use the class attribute of the `<p>` tag to identify the name of the class:

```
<p class="question">
Q : Can I sell employees to other players, transfer them
between businesses, or turn them back in to the Employee Pool
for money?
</p>
```

In this code, the class of the paragraph is set to question using the class attribute, which means that the p.question style will be used to style the paragraph when it's displayed in a Web browser. Keep in mind that any other paragraphs coded with the `<p>` tag will not have the style applied unless they specify the same class information.

Styling Individual Tags

Like class styles, which allow you to style a class of tags, style sheets support a means of styling individual tags. The technique is known as *individual styles* and involves assigning a special identifier to a tag that uniquely identifies the tag in the Web page. This identifier is then used in the style sheet to create a style that applies only to the tag. Here's an example of how to create a style that applies only to the copyright information on the FAQ Web page:

```
p#copyright { text-align:center; font-size:8pt }
```

This code shows how an individual style is created by specifying the style as the tag name (p) followed by a number symbol (#), and then the unique identifier for the tag, copyright. To apply the individual style to a tag, you use the id attribute of the tag to specify the unique identifier, as the following code demonstrates:

```
<p id="copyright">Inc. The Game of Business
(c)1998 Gas Hound Games</p>
```

In this code, the id attribute of the `<p>` tag is used to specify the unique identifier for the individual style. Figure 11-3 on the next page shows the resulting Web page containing this individual style; pay close attention to the copyright notice near the bottom of the browser window.

Note

In addition to allowing you to style individual tags, the unique identifier used with an individual style is also important when it comes to scripting a Web page using a scripting language such as JavaScript or VBScript. You will learn how to script Web pages in Chapter 14, "Dynamic HTML."

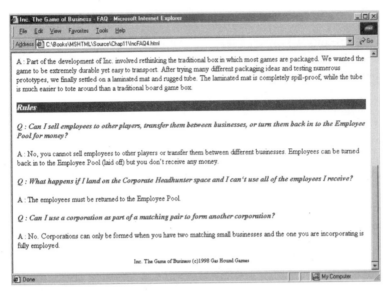

Figure 11-3.
An individual style is applied to the copyright notice on this Web page.

Local Styles

Although style sheets provide the most organized approach to applying styles to Web pages, it's possible to apply styles to tags on an individual basis throughout the HTML code for a Web page. This kind of style is known as a *local style*. Local styles are coded in Web pages using the `style` attribute, which is supported by most HTML tags. When using the `style` attribute, you can specify styles in the same way that you specify them in style sheets, except you enclose them in quotation marks instead of braces. Following is an example of applying a local style to a heading:

```
<h3 style="background:green; color:white; font-style:italic;
font-weight:bold">Rules</h3>
```

This is actually the same style you saw in the previous external style sheet, except in this case it's applied to a specific `<h3>` tag, instead of all `<h3>` tags. Local styles allow you to style individual tags, which can be useful in situations where you want to establish a unique style for a specific tag. It's still perfectly fine to have a style sheet for the same Web page. In this case, the local style will override any styles in the style sheet that apply to the same tag.

Linking with Style

Have you had enough styles? Of course not! I'd like to show you one other interesting technique related to the application of styles. I'm referring to *link styles*, styles that apply specifically to hyperlinked text in a Web page. Link styles are similar to other styles in that they declare specific style information, but they apply only to hyperlinks. You can apply styles to the unique aspect of a hyperlink known as a state. Study the hyperlink states that correspond to link styles:

- link—the link has not been visited
- visited—the link has been visited
- active—the link has just been clicked
- hover—the mouse pointer is hovering over the link

You create a style for one of these hyperlink states by specifying the tag name (a) followed by a colon (:), followed by the name of the hyperlink state. For all link states, the tag name is a, because hyperlinks are defined using the <a> tag. Following is an example of how to set a style for the hover state:

```
a:hover { background:green; color:white }
```

This code shows how simple it is to set a style for a hyperlink state. Follow the same pattern for the other hyperlink states: a:link, a:visited, and a:active. Link styles are powerful because they affect all of the hyperlinks on a Web page. Figure 11-4 shows the effect of the hover link style, as the mouse pointer is held over an e-mail hyperlink.

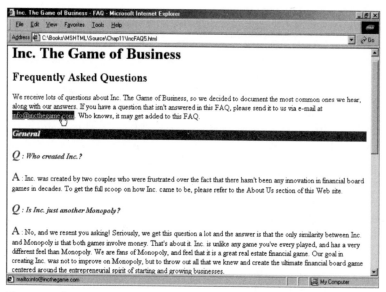

Figure 11-4.
Link styles allow you to set styles for the different states of a hyperlink.

Styles and Custom Style Tags

Based upon what you've learned throughout this book, there is no doubt that HTML is a rich markup language that provides a great deal of control over how information is organized and displayed in Web browsers. Even so, HTML is not without its shortcomings. Later in the book in Part V, "Leveraging XML," you will learn how the eXtensible Markup Language (XML) is remedying some of the problems found in HTML.

As you will see, one of the benefits of XML is that it allows you to create custom tags. This is useful in describing information in more detail than just marking it up with a trusty <p> tag. Although XML provides the ultimate in flexibility by allowing you to create custom markup languages of your own, you can extend HTML without using XML by applying styles.

Custom style tags are special HTML tags that you use to identify and format content in your Web pages according to your own rules. Custom style tags are not custom in the sense that you get to make up your own tag names. Instead, you use one of two generic tag names, div or span, and then customize them with attributes. The benefit is that they allow you to carefully structure your Web pages according to the meaning of the content, which goes a long way toward separating the formatting of your pages from the content. If you recall, this is a desirable goal in all Web pages.

Custom style tags also make it easier to use style sheets with your Web pages, because the content is organized according to specific tags. So, although custom style tags have structural and organizational benefits, they are also significant in styling your Web pages. Styles and custom style tags may not get you into the National Gallery, but they can certainly help you create more organized and visually appealing Web pages.

Before launching into the creation and use of custom style tags, you need to understand the difference between the two main types of HTML tags: block-level tags and inline tags. *Block-level tags* usually start a new line in a Web page, and often contain other tags. The best example of a block-level tag is the <p> tag, which contains text content as well as other tags. Other examples of block-level tags include the <body>, <table>, and heading tags <h1>, <h2>, and so on. *Inline tags* are tags that usually do not start a new line in a Web page, and can only contain text or other inline tags. Inline tags differ from block-level tags in that they are typically both more concise and apply to smaller pieces of content. Examples of inline tags include the <b>, <i>, <font>, and <img> tags.

The significance of block-level and inline tags here is that you must determine whether a custom HTML tag is either a block-level tag or an inline tag when you create it. The <div> tag is used to create custom block-level tags, and the <span> tag is used to create custom inline tags. The next two sections will show you how to create custom block-level and inline tags.

Creating Custom Style Tags

Custom HTML tags affect style sheets because you can use them to apply styles to a Web page in a controlled manner. For example, you can create several custom style tags that have their own styles—using these tags throughout a Web page achieves a high degree of both organization and formatting, while still separating formatting code and content.

Using `<div>` to Create Custom Block-Level Tags

You recently learned that one of the uses of the `<div>` tag is to create custom block-level tags. I don't mean that the tag name itself is custom; the `<div>` tag name is used for all custom block-level tags. The custom aspect of the `<div>` tag comes into play when you classify a specific type of `<div>` tag. This might be confusing, so let's look at a practical example. Following is the style code for a custom block-level tag that you could use to represent a question in the FAQ Web page:

```
div.question { color:green; font-style:italic;
font-weight:bold }
```

This code creates a style for a custom question tag. The style is specified by using the `div` tag name followed by a period, and followed next by the name of the custom style tag, `question`. Keep in mind that this doesn't mean you've created a custom style tag named `<question>`; instead, you've created a custom classification of the `<div>` tag named `question`. The bottom line is that you have a custom style tag that you can use to mark up questions in an FAQ Web page. More important is that the questions will be styled according to the `div.question` style in the style sheet.

Notice that the style code for the custom style tag is similar to that of the earlier example of creating a style class. But style classes require an existing HTML tag such as the `<p>` paragraph tag. The `<div>` tag is more generic and can be used to mark up virtually any content, not necessarily just paragraphs.

Creating Custom Inline Tags with `<span>`

Just as the `<div>` tag allows you to create custom block-level tags, the `<span>` tag allows you to create custom inline tags. If you recall, inline tags are used to mark up smaller sections of content, and don't allow you to nest block-level tags within them. Inline tags are typically used to mark up individual words or phrases. For example, the `<b>` tag is used to bold a section of text, and typically doesn't apply to more than a few words. Custom inline tags are created in the same manner as custom block-level tags, except that you use the `span` tag name instead of `div`. The following example demonstrates how to create a simple custom inline tag:

```
span.qna { font-size:150% }
```

In this example, a custom style tag is created that has the class name qna, which stands for *Question and Answer*. The qna tag is used to mark up the letters Q and A that appear in the questions and answers in the FAQ Web page. More specifically, the font size of the text enclosed by the custom tag increases to 150 percent. This makes the text larger, which improves the appearance of the FAQ page, as you will see in the next section.

Putting Custom Style Tags to Work

You now understand that a custom style tag created with the generic <div> or <span> tags is really just a style class associated with one of the two generic tags. You use these custom style tags in the same manner that you used style tags earlier in the chapter—by specifying the name of the style class in the class attribute of the appropriate tag, <div> or <span>. Study this example to clear up any confusion about how custom style tags are used:

```
<div class="question">
<span class="qna">Q</span> : What happens if I land on the
Corporate Headhunter space and I can't use all of the
employees I receive?
</div>
<p>
<span class="qna">A</span> : The employees must be returned
to the Employee Pool.
</p>
```

In this example, the custom question style class is used with the <div> tag to mark up the question paragraph. Even though you're using the <div> tag to carry out the coding specifics of the custom style tag, the net effect is that a Web browser considers the question style class to be its own unique tag. Contrast this code to the answer paragraph that appears just after the question paragraph, which is still marked up using the traditional HTML <p> tag. Along with adding more meaning to the question paragraph, the custom question tag also applies the appropriate style to the question paragraph.

This code also demonstrates inline custom tags by specifying the qna style class with the <span> tag. In this case, the <span> tag is used to mark up the individual Q and A letters in the FAQ content, which has the result of presenting them in a larger font when displayed. Again, the benefit of this tag is not just that it applies a style to the inline content, but that it also adds meaning to the content. In other words, you can read the code and immediately see that the Q and A letters are related to questions and answers because they are marked up with the qna custom style tag. Figure 11-5 shows the FAQ Web page as it appears with these custom style tags applied.

Custom style tags go beyond simply providing a better method of applying styles to Web content. They also help identify content in a Web page for use within scripting languages such as JavaScript and VBScript, which you will learn about in Chapter 14, "Dynamic HTML."

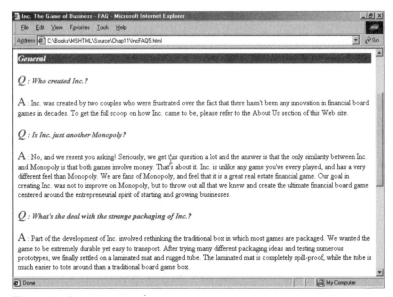

Figure 11-5.
Custom style tags can be used to improve the structure of Web pages and apply styles to Web content more effectively.

Conclusion

Even if you don't find yourself perusing the latest copy of *In Style* magazine when you pass the magazine rack at the grocery store, you can appreciate the role style sheets play in Web pages. In addition to helping separate formatting code from Web page content, style sheets dramatically improve the organization of Web pages and provide a clean approach to formatting Web content for display in a Web browser. Also, style sheets support a richer set of formatting styles than you could ever achieve purely through HTML formatting tags. Although you were introduced to a few in this chapter, you will learn a great deal more about these formatting styles in the next chapter.

This chapter began by introducing you to style sheets and describing what a style sheet does. You then worked through a quick tutorial on how to create and use style sheets to format Web pages. You learned several ways to apply styles to Web pages, including both style sheets and individual styles. You wrapped up the chapter by learning how to use the <div> and <span> tags to create custom style tags that can be used to identify the meaning of Web content, as well as to apply styles to it.

Chapter 12

Using Styles to Format Text

This probably explains why we seldom get teary-eyed while working at our computers. A great deal of research has gone into making computer screens easier on the eye. Much of this research focuses on fonts and how they can help people read computer screens with the same efficiency as the printed page. Microsoft's ClearType technology emerged from this research and is used in the Microsoft Reader eBook software. But, you don't have to go to the same lengths to make your Web pages more readable; you can use a variety of cascading style sheets to alter the appearance of text.

This chapter presents the different styles used to format text with cascading style sheets (CSS) styles. You'll learn interesting ways to enhance your Web pages, and gain a better appreciation of styles. Previously, you saw a few text formatting styles, but not their possible values. This chapter takes a closer look at text formatting styles and how to use them.

Assessing Cascading Style Sheets Text Styles

In the previous chapter, I introduced you to the basics of cascading style sheets and how to apply styles to Web page content. But you didn't spend much time learning style details. A significant goal of CSS is to carefully format the appearance of text. Not surprisingly, you can use several different text-related styles. CSS has no formal organization of text styles, so I've used the following general categories:

- **Font styles** set the font for text
- **Dress styles** set the foreground color, background color, and background image of text
- **Space styles** control the spacing of text

- **Alignment styles** position text on a page
- **Other styles** perform text formatting tasks that don't fit into the other categories

These categories are sufficient to organize CSS text styles and clarify their role in text formatting. In other words, I created these categories to provide structure to the CSS text styles. The remainder of this chapter explores each category and how to use it.

Working with Font Styles

If you've ever heard of Courier, Arial, Times New Roman, or Wingdings, then you probably have some experience with fonts. If not, fonts aren't difficult to understand. A *font* establishes, sometimes dramatically, the appearance of text. You can use several different font style properties to fine-tune the appearance of your text. Table 12-1 shows these properties and the elements they format.

Table 12-1.   Font Style Properties

Property	Characteristic
font	Style, variant, weight, size, and family of a font as a single property
font-style	Style of a font
font-weight	Thickness of a font
font-size	Size of a font
font-family	Family of a font
font-variant	Normal or small caps

You can specify several font styles at once using the font property. It doesn't allow you to describe a font in more detail than the other properties. Instead, it serves as a convenience property to describe a font using a single property. For example, the font property allows you to list values for each of the individual font properties as a single property value, thereby eliminating the need to use the individual font properties. You will learn how to use the font property to group font styles in a later section.

Setting Individual Font Properties

You can use most of the font style properties to set individual aspects of a font such as its size or weight.

Note

If you don't specify a style property, the default setting will be applied.

The font-style property sets the style of a font to normal or italic. The default setting for the font-style property is normal, resulting in a font without any special style. Following is an example of how to use the font-style property:

```
<p style="font-style:italic">This is italic text.</p>
```

This code sets the font style for a short paragraph of text to italic, which means that all the text in the paragraph will be displayed in italics.

The font-weight property sets the weight, or thickness, of a font, which can be set to any one of the following values: normallight, boldbolder,100,200,300,400, 500, 600, 700, 800, or 900.

The default value of the font-weight property is normal, which results in a font with a normal weight. Here is an example of how to use the font-weight property:

```
<p style="font-weight:bold">This is bold text.</p>
```

This code sets a paragraph of text so that it appears in a bold font.

The values 100 through 900 set the font weight based on 100 being very light and 900 being very bold. A value of 400 results in normal, and a value of 700 is equal to bold. Not all fonts can be weighted across this entire range, so the browser will select the next most appropriate weight.

The font-size property sets the size of a font, and can be specified in several different units: points (pt), inches (in), centimeters (cm), or pixels (px). The sky is the limit in selecting font sizes. Following are a few examples of how to use the font-size property:

```
<p style="font-size:12pt">This is 12 point text.</p>
<p style="font-size:0.75in">This is 0.75 inch text.</p>
<p style="font-size:20px">This is 20 pixel text.</p>
```

Note

When you use a font in a word processor such as Microsoft Word, the font size is expressed as a number such as 12 or 14. This number specifies the font size in points. So, a value of 12 is a 12-point font.

Each of these examples sets the font size using a different unit. The first line of code specifies the size in points, the second line uses inches, and the last line expresses the font size in pixels. No unit is better than the others, but being consistent helps eliminate confusion.

The most important font style property is font-family, which sets the family, or *face*, of a font. For example, Times New Roman, Courier, and Helvetica are all font faces. Following are a few examples of how to use the font-family property:

```
<p style="font-family:Courier">This is Courier text.</p>
<p style="font-family:Helvetica">This is Helvetica text.</p>
<p style="font-family:Arial">This is Arial text.</p>
```

These examples show how you can use different font names with the `font-family` property to set the family of a font for several paragraphs of text. When you choose a font whose name consists of several words, such as Times New Roman, you must enclose the name in quotes, like this:

```
<p style="font-family:'Times New Roman'">This is Times New Roman text.</p>
```

It's important to understand that there are no guarantees that a user will have a particular font installed on his or her system. If you specify a font that isn't available, Web browsers will find the best match. If you're thorough and want to make a contingency font plan, you can identify several fonts that serve as alternates if the main font isn't available. Following is an example of specifying a backup font using the `font-family` property:

```
<p style="font-family:Courier, Arial">This is Courier text that
will display as Arial if the Courier font isn't available.</p>
```

In this example, the Courier font is the primary font, which means that it will be used if it's available. If it can't be found, the Arial font will be applied to the paragraph. You can list additional fonts if you want more backup fonts. Just be sure to separate the font names with commas.

Use the `font-variant` property to set a font so that the text is displayed in small caps. The only values for the `font-variant` property are `normal` (the default value) or `small-caps`. Following is an example of how to use the `font-variant` property:

```
<p style="font-variant:small-caps">This is small-caps text.</p>
```

A small-cap font displays all of the characters in uppercase, but not as large as normal uppercase characters. This code establishes a small-cap font for a paragraph of text; all of the characters in the paragraph will be displayed as small uppercase characters, regardless of their case in the code.

Setting Font Properties as a Group

If you've ever benefited from a group discount at a retail establishment, you might appreciate the capability of grouping several font properties in a single property. The `font` property allows you to specify a complete font by listing the different individual parts of a font after the `font` property name. Following is an example of how to use the `font` property:

```
<p style="font:italic bold small-caps 12pt Courier">This is
italic, bold, small-caps, 12 point, Courier text.</p>
```

This example code shows how you can specify several font property values as part of the single `font` property. The `font` property is a convenience property, and has no significant style features of its own. The `font` property does have some rules, though. The order in which property values are coded is important. With the exception of the font-family value, any single value can be specified for the font property; the value for font-family must always be preceded by the value for font-size. To ensure correct handling of the value parameters when multiple values are coded, specify the values in this order: font-style, font-variant, font-weight, font-size, and font-family. If the browser cannot find a match for one of the values, or if it can't correctly resolve the coded parameters, it does its best to generate reasonable text. But there are no messages sent regarding any inability to completely adhere to the coded parameters.

Putting the Font Styles Together

I've shown you many code snippets that demonstrate how to use font style properties, but you've yet to see any results. Voilà! Here is the code for a Font Styles Web page that combines each of the previous font style examples into a single page:

```
<html>
<head>
  <title>Font Styles Example Page</title>
</head>

<body style="background-color:white">
  <h1>Font Styles Example Page</h1>
  <p style="font-style:italic">This is italic text.</p>
  <p style="font-weight:bold">This is bold text.</p>
  <p style="font-variant:small-caps">This is small-caps
  text.</p>
  <p style="font-size:12pt">This is 12 point text.</p>
  <p style="font-size:0.75in">This is 0.75 inch text.</p>
  <p style="font-size:20px">This is 20 pixel text.</p>
  <p style="font-family:Courier">This is Courier text.</p>
  <p style="font-family:Helvetica">This is Helvetica text.</p>
  <p style="font-family:Arial">This is Arial text.</p>
  <p style="font-family:Courier, Arial">This is Courier text
  that will display as Arial if the Courier font isn't
  available.</p>
  <p style="font:italic bold small-caps 12pt Courier">This is
  italic, bold, small-caps, 12 point, Courier text.</p>
</body>
</html>
```

Although the Font Styles page isn't designed to simulate the layout of a real Web page, it nonetheless helps you visualize the application of each font style property. Figure 12-1 shows the Font Styles Web page example as viewed in Internet Explorer.

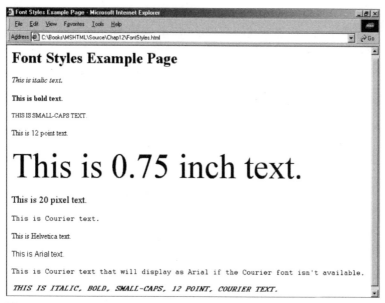

Figure 12-1.
The Font Styles Web page example demonstrates how to use font styles.

Dressing Up Text with Style

It wasn't much more than a decade ago that a color monitor was a luxury for most computer users. Now we all take for granted the rainbow of colors on our screens. I propose a Color Appreciation Day to celebrate how far we've come in a few short years. If you're not into that, then appreciate color on your own terms. Use a few style properties today—inject some color into your Web pages! Following are several CSS style properties that control the foreground and background colors, as well as set images as backgrounds:

- `color` sets the foreground color of text
- `background-color` sets the background color for text
- `background-image` sets the background image for text
- `background-repeat` determines how the background image for text is drawn
- `background` sets the background color, image, and repeat for text as a single property

The `color` property sets the foreground color of text, and accepts a standard color name as its value. The following standard colors are supported by the `color` property:

- black
- blue
- olive
- lime

- white
- yellow
- maroon
- fuchsia

- red
- gray
- purple
- aqua

- green
- navy
- teal
- silver

Following is an example of how to use the `color` property:

```
<p style="color:red">This is red text.</p>
```

This code displays a paragraph of red text. You can also use custom colors in addition to standard colors. (To learn more about custom colors, see Appendix C, "Using Custom Colors.")

The `background` properties in the property list are used to alter the background that appears behind text. The `background-color` property sets the background color for the paragraph. Following is an example of how to use the `background-color` property:

```
<p style="color:yellow; background-color:gray">This is yellow
text with a gray background.</p>
```

This code formats the style of a paragraph so that the text is yellow on a gray background, which provides a decent amount of contrast. Contrast is important because a page can be difficult to read without it.

The `background-image` property displays an image behind text. The image is stored in a file using the GIF, PNG, or JPEG image format. To specify the file for the background image, enter the property value using the following form:

```
background-image:url(ImageFile)
```

When using the `background-image` property, replace the text *ImageFile* with the name of the actual image file. Following is an example of how to use the `background-image` property to set a background image for a paragraph of text:

```
<p style="color:black; background-image:url(Lattice.gif)">This
is black text with a lattice image background.</p>
```

In this example, the background image of the paragraph is set to the image file Lattice.gif. By default, the background image is tiled, or repeated, to fill the entire background of a paragraph or other Web element. The `background-repeat` property can alter the manner in which a background image is tiled. It can be set to one of the following values: `repeat`, `repeat-x`, `repeat-y`, and `no-repeat`. Obviously, the default value of the `background-repeat` property is `repeat`. The `no-repeat` value displays the background image only once. The `repeat-x` and `repeat-y` values duplicate an image only in the X or Y direction, respectively. Following is an example of how to use the `background-repeat` property to ensure the background image is not repeated:

```
<p style="color:black; background-image:url(Lattice.gif);
background-repeat:no-repeat">This is black text with a
non-repeating lattice image background.</p>
```

In this code, the `background-repeat` property is set to `no-repeat` so that the background image isn't tiled. The image will appear only once behind the paragraph text.

Note

It's possible to set both the `background-color` and `background-image` style properties. The background image is then displayed over the background color. The background color will show through if there are any transparent areas within the background image.

The `background` property is used to specify the different background properties as a single property. Following is an example of how to use the `background` property to combine several background properties:

```
<p style="color:maroon; background:url(Brick.gif) repeat">This
is maroon text with a repeating brick image
background.<br><br><br><br></p>
```

This code shows how to use the `background` property to combine several background properties and simplify the code for applying background styles.

To get a feel for how the color and background-related properties affect the appearance of a real Web page, take a look at the following code for the Dress Styles Web page example:

```
<html>
<head>
  <title>Dress Styles Example Page</title>
</head>

<body style="background-color:white">
  <h1>Dress Styles Example Page</h1>
  <p style="color:red">This is red text.</p>
  <p style="color:yellow; background-color:gray">This is yellow
  text with a gray background.</p>
  <p style="color:black;
  background-image:url(Lattice.gif)">This is black text with a
  lattice image background.</p>
  <p style="color:black; background-image:url(Lattice.gif);
  background-repeat:no-repeat">This is black text with a
  non-repeating lattice image background.</p>
  <p style="color:maroon; background:url(Brick.gif)
  repeat">This is maroon text with a repeating brick image
  background.<br><br><br><br></p>
</body>
</html>
```

This Web page contains the color and background style code samples that you've seen throughout this section. Figure 12-2 on the next page shows the Dress Styles Web page example as viewed in Internet Explorer.

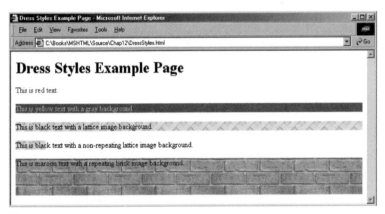

Figure 12-2.
The Dress Styles Web page example demonstrates how to use color and background styles to dress up Web content.

Altering the Spacing of Text

Have you ever seen a Web page where the letters in a group of words are spaced out? It looks like someone manually inserted additional space between the letters, right? Let me clue you in—you can use a style property to control the amount of space between characters of text. I should point out that using the keyboard's space bar to inject the extra space does work, but the style approach is more powerful and elegant. Don't be too critical of yourself if you thought the space bar was the ultimate solution to all of your spacing needs. Just prepare to embrace styles as a better approach to controlling the spacing in your Web pages.

You can also use a style property to control the amount of space that appears before any text on the first line of a paragraph of text—the indentation of a paragraph. Following are the two style properties that alter the character spacing and indentation of text:

- `letter-spacing` adjusts the spacing between text characters
- `text-indent` sets the amount of indentation for the first line of text in a paragraph

Both of these properties can be specified in units you are now familiar with: points (`pt`), inches (`in`), centimeters (`cm`), or pixels (`px`). Keep in mind that the amount of space identified by these units determines the spacing between characters—relative to *normal* spacing—when you're using the `letter-spacing` property, and the width of the indentation of a paragraph when used with the `text-indent` property. Following are several examples of how to set the letter spacing of paragraphs with this property:

```
<p style="letter-spacing:0">The letters in this sentence are
separated normally.</p>
<p style="letter-spacing:4px">The letters in this sentence are
separated by normal spacing plus 4 pixels.</p>
<p style="letter-spacing:0.25cm">The letters in this sentence
are separated by normal spacing plus 0.25 cm.</p>
```

Notice that the first example uses a value of zero for letter-spacing, which is the default value for the property. By comparing the letter spacing of the other examples, you can get an idea how other values will affect the spacing.

Note

To tighten the spacing between characters, set the letter-spacing property to a negative value.

Following are a couple of examples of using the text-indent property to indent paragraphs of text:

```
<p style="text-indent:0">This paragraph has a normal text
indent.</p>
<p style="text-indent:0.5in">This paragraph has a text indent
of 0.5 inches.</p>
```

The first use of the text-indent property contains the default property value of zero, which results in a paragraph with no indentation. The second example indents the text one-half inch.

You're no doubt curious about how these letter spacing and text indent examples look in a real Web page. The following code for the Space Styles Web page example shows these styles in the context of a complete Web page:

```
<html>
<head>
  <title>Space Styles Example Page</title>
</head>

<body style="background-color:white">
  <h1>Space Styles Example Page</h1>
  <p style="letter-spacing:0">The letters in this sentence are
  separated normally.</p>
  <p style="letter-spacing:4px">The letters in this sentence
  are separated by normal spacing plus 4 pixels.</p>
  <p style="letter-spacing:0.25cm">The letters in this sentence
  are separated by normal spacing plus 0.25 cm.</p>
  <p style="text-indent:0">This paragraph has a normal text
  indent.</p>
  <p style="text-indent:0.5in">This paragraph has a text indent
  of 0.5 inches.</p>
</body>
</html>
```

This Web page uses the letter spacing and text indent style code that you've learned about in this section. Figure 12-3 on the next page shows the Space Styles Web page example as viewed in Internet Explorer.

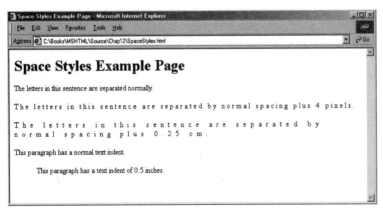

Figure 12-3.
The Space Styles Web page example demonstrates how to control the spacing of text.

Using Styles for Text Alignment

Just as spacing is important to obtain a desired text appearance, alignment is also a key element. You can't understand alignment without knowing how margins affect a text element. The following style properties determine the alignment and margins of text:

- `text-align` positions text
- `margin-top` sets the top margin of text
- `margin-right` sets the right margin of text
- `margin-bottom` sets the bottom margin of text
- `margin-left` sets the left margin of text
- `margin` sets the top, right, bottom, and left margins of text as a single property

The next two sections demonstrate how to use these properties to control the alignment and margins of text.

Aligning Text

It's easy to align text on a Web page with the `text-align` property's `left`, `right`, and `center` values. Following are a few examples of these property values:

```
<p style="text-align:left">This paragraph is left-
aligned.</p>
<p style="text-align:right">This paragraph is right-
aligned.</p>
<p style="text-align:center">This paragraph is centered.</p>
```

This code is straightforward in that the `text-align` style property is set to different values to align the paragraph differently in each example.

Adjusting the Margins

I mentioned earlier that margins affect the alignment of text. This is because they limit the area where text can appear. For example, if you set a 1-inch margin along the left side of a page, text can't appear in that margin. So, left-aligned text will appear at the margin as opposed to along the left edge of the page. Following is an example of setting the left and right margins for a paragraph of text using the margin-left and margin-right properties:

```
<p style="background-color:silver; margin-left:25px;
margin-right:25%">This paragraph has a left margin of 25 pixels
and a right margin of 25%.</p>
```

In this code, why have I ignored my own advice against mixing units when specifying the size of style properties? I just wanted to demonstrate the use of two different units without showing you two different examples. The interesting thing about this code is that the right margin is specified as a percentage. When you specify a margin as a percentage—25 percent in this case—it applies to the dimension of the entire Web page. This approach allows margins to shrink and grow in relation to the size of a Web page, instead of committing them to a specific value.

In addition to the margin-left and margin-right properties that set the side margins, the margin-top and margin-bottom properties set the top and bottom margins for a paragraph. Following is an example of setting the top margin for a paragraph:

```
<p style="background-color:silver; margin-top:40px">This
paragraph has a top margin of 40 pixels.</p>
```

In this example, the top margin is set to 40 pixels, which means that above the paragraph, there will be an invisible border 40 pixels high.

Most of the time you will use the individual margin properties to set margins one at a time. However, you might want to set several margin properties at once, which is where the margin property comes into play. The margin property can be used in three different ways, distinguishable by how many pieces of information you list for the property's values:

- If one size value is specified, that size applies to all four margins.
- If two size values are specified, the first applies to the top and bottom margins, and the second applies to the left and right margins.
- If all four size values are specified, they apply to the top, right, bottom, and left margins, in that order.

To understand how the margin property works, look at the following example, which sets all of the margins for a paragraph to a single value:

```
<p style="background-color:silver; margin:10%">This paragraph
has a margin of 10% on all sides.</p>
```

In this example, all of the margins are set to 10 percent, thanks to the margin property. Keep in mind that this margin style is equivalent to margins of 10%, 10%, 10%, and 10%.

Putting the Text Alignment Styles Together

Like the text styles you've learned about so far, the text alignment styles make more sense once you see them in action. The following code shows how the text alignment styles appear within the context of a Web page:

```
<html>
<head>
  <title>Alignment Styles Example Page</title>
</head>

<body style="background-color:white">
  <h1>Alignment Styles Example Page</h1>
  <p style="text-align:left">This paragraph is left-
  aligned.</p>
  <p style="text-align:right">This paragraph is right-
  aligned.</p>
  <p style="text-align:center">This paragraph is centered.</p>
  <p style="background-color:silver; margin-left:25px;
  margin-right:25%">This paragraph has a left margin of 25
  pixels and a right margin of 25%.</p>
  <p style="background-color:silver; margin-top:40px">This
  paragraph has a top margin of 40 pixels.</p>
  <p style="background-color:silver; margin:10%">This paragraph
  has a margin of 10% on all sides.</p>
</body>
</html>
```

The Alignment Styles Web page includes all of the text alignment example code that you've learned about. Of course, the benefit to having the code in a Web page is that you can view the page to see the effect of the styles. Figure 12-4 shows the Alignment Styles Web page as viewed in Internet Explorer.

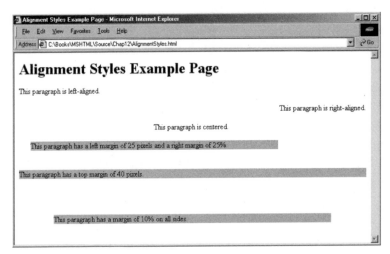

Figure 12-4.
The Alignment Styles Web page demonstrates how to align paragraphs of text.

Digging Into the Bag of Style Tricks

I mentioned earlier in the chapter that some text styles don't fit into any single category. These rogue styles are interesting; so let's see how they might affect your text formatting plans. Consider the following styles for your bag of text formatting tricks:

- `text-decoration` sets the highlight of text
- `text-transform` sets the case of text to lowercase or uppercase
- `cursor` sets the mouse pointer icon to be used when you let the mouse pointer hover over the paragraph

The `text-decoration` style property does exactly what its name implies—it decorates text. Use it to set the highlight of text to one of the following values: `underline`, `overline`, or `line-through`. Following are a few examples that demonstrate how to use the `text-decoration` style:

```
<p style="text-decoration:underline">This text is
underlined.</p>
<p style="text-decoration:overline">This text is overlined.</p>
<p style="text-decoration:line-through">This text is struck
out.</p>
```

These examples are straightforward, showing how to apply each of the different text decoration values to a paragraph.

You might find the `text-transform` property a little more interesting, because you can change text to lowercase or uppercase without having to retype all of the text by hand. If you ever need to display text in all lowercase or uppercase, the `text-transform` property makes it easy. The values you can use with the `text-transform` property are: `none`, `lowercase`, `uppercase`, and `capitalize`. The `none` value is the default value, because it doesn't alter text in any way. The `capitalize` value capitalizes the first letter of every word in a paragraph. Following are a few examples of how to use the `text-transform` property:

```
<p style="text-transform:none">This text is completely
normal.</p>
<p style="text-transform:lowercase">This text is all
lowercase.</p>
<p style="text-transform:uppercase">This text is all
uppercase.</p>
<p style="text-transform:capitalize">This text is all
capitalized.</p>
```

These examples demonstrate how to use each of the `text-transform` property values to alter the case of paragraphs.

The last property is without a doubt the trickiest in this section. The `cursor` property is used to change the appearance of the mouse pointer when the mouse pointer is dragged over that paragraph of text. When using the `cursor` property, set the mouse pointer to any of the standard cursor values shown in the list on the next page.

- default
- text
- hand
- crosshair
- wait
- help
- move
- n-resize
- ne-resize
- e-resize
- se-resize
- s-resize
- sw-resize
- w-resize
- nw-resize

Note

Web browsers will eventually support custom cursors, so you won't continue to be stuck using standard cursors for this property.

Each of these cursor values identifies a different cursor icon. For example, in Windows, the `wait` cursor corresponds to the hourglass that you often see when a program is busy. Following is an example of setting the `wait` cursor for a paragraph:

```
<p style="cursor:wait">This text changes the mouse pointer to
an hourglass when you drag the mouse pointer over it.</p>
```

Note

In this context, a cursor and a mouse pointer are actually the same thing.

In this example, the `wait` cursor value is used to specify the hourglass mouse pointer for the paragraph. The end result is that the mouse pointer will change to the hourglass when you drag it over the paragraph. As neat as it may be to alter the appearance of the mouse pointer, I encourage you to resist the temptation to change the `cursor` style property except in situations where it would make the Web page more meaningful or effective.

I'm cautioning you about the use of the `cursor` property because most standard cursors are used to convey information to the user. For example, the presence of the hourglass mouse pointer should only mean that a program is busy, so the user is accustomed to waiting for it to change. If you don't use the `cursor` property carefully, you could confuse the user by displaying a familiar cursor out of context. On the other hand, if your goal is to trick visitors to enter your Web site with a practical joke, feel free to use the `cursor` property at will!

This section covered several *trick* style properties. To get a better feel for how these properties function within a complete Web page, check out the following code:

```
<html>
<head>
  <title>Trick Styles Example Page</title>
</head>

<body style="background-color:white">
  <h1>Trick Styles Example Page</h1>
  <p style="text-decoration:underline">This text is
  underlined.</p>
```

```
<p style="text-decoration:overline">This text is
overlined.</p>
<p style="text-decoration:line-through">This text is struck
out.</p>
<p style="text-transform:none">This text is completely
normal.</p>
<p style="text-transform:lowercase">This text is all lowercase.</p>
<p style="text-transform:uppercase">This text is all uppercase.</p>
<p style="text-transform:capitalize">This text is all capitalized.</p>
<p style="cursor:wait">This text changes the mouse pointer to
an hourglass when you drag the mouse pointer over it.</p>
</body>
</html>
```

The Trick Styles Web page pulls together all the code you've seen throughout this section into a complete page. Figure 12-5 shows the Trick Styles Web page example as viewed in Internet Explorer.

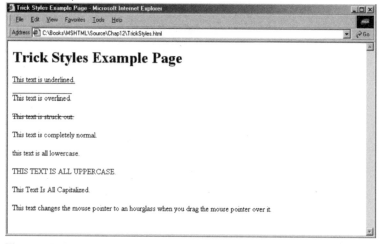

Figure 12-5.
The Trick Styles Web page example demonstrates how to apply a few neat formatting styles to text.

Conclusion

Just as *The Empire Strikes Back* deepened the plot of the *Star Wars* saga and laid the groundwork for a third and final installment in the classic space movie trilogy, this chapter serves a similar purpose in your ongoing quest for style sheet knowledge. Fortunately, your quest is not about good vs. evil, or Luke Skywalker vs. Darth Vader, but instead it's about improving the appearance of your Web pages. This chapter guided you through the details of using style properties to format text in a variety of different ways. You found out that several style properties are available for altering the size, appearance, color, and spacing of text, among other things.

This chapter began by quickly assessing the different categories of text styles. You then learned about font styles, and how to fine-tune the specific fonts used to display text. You learned about the style properties that allow you to alter the color and background of text. Then we addressed text spacing, the art of carefully controlling th indentation of paragraphs and the space between letters of text. The chapter concluded by revealing a few interesting style properties that you may find handy every once in a while.

You are now equipped to move on to the third and final style episode of this saga in the next chapter, "Using Styles for Web Page Positioning."

Chapter 13

Using Styles for Web Page Positioning

Web fact for the day

Apple co-founder Steve Wozniak earned money while in college by selling *blue boxes* to other students. A blue box is an electronic device people attach to a pay telephone to make free phone calls.

In case you're wondering, blue boxes are illegal. But with the popularity of mobile phones and 10-cent minutes, not many people are concerned about saving money at pay phones these days. In this chapter, I won't be teaching you how to make free phone calls, but I will show you how to create a different kind of blue box. A legal one, that is, which can be any color you want. It is the border, or box, you draw around Web content. Borders are only one of the style sheet features related to positioning page content that you will learn about.

Whereas the previous chapter, "Using Styles to Format Text," focused on formatting individual pieces of Web content, in this chapter you arrange them on a page. I'll describe several style properties that are used to control the positioning and layout of Web content such as text and images. By the time you finish this chapter, you will have rounded out your knowledge of style sheets and should be prepared to tackle virtually any Web page style issue.

The Basics of Positioning with Style

As you learned in the previous chapter, cascading style sheets (CSS) support a wide range of styles used to format text in a variety of ways. In addition to these formatting styles, several other styles affect the way that Web content is positioned on a page. These extremely flexible styles are important because you can use them to organize the layout of Web content. One critical concept before we launch into the properties: to successfully apply the positioning style properties, you have to think of each element on a Web page as if it had an invisible box around it. These boxes serve as boundaries for each image and paragraph of text on a page, identifying how much space an element occupies and the position of the element relative to other elements.

When an element is used within another element—a paragraph of text within the <body> tag, for example—the element's boundary is contained within the boundary of the parent element. Figure 13-1 shows a Web page you've seen several times throughout this book. I drew the boundaries of the major elements so that you can see exactly how each element is positioned on the page.

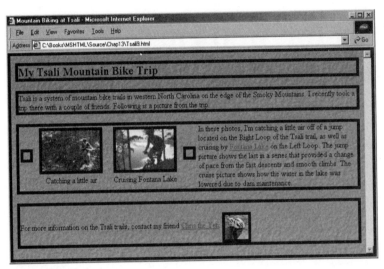

Figure 13-1.
The boundaries of each major Web element are clearly shown in this modified version of the familiar Tsali mountain bike Web page.

The positioning style properties manipulate the boundaries for elements on a page, which is useful when you produce a page according to a specified layout. Prior to style sheets, most Web designers relied on tables to organize their Web pages. The two fundamental approaches to positioning Web content using the now-popular CSS are *relative positioning* and *absolute positioning*. Relative positioning specifies the position of an element, text or image, based on its normal position. Absolute positioning, on the other hand, specifies the position of an element with respect to the parent element.

Consider an image that appears in the body of a Web page, just after a paragraph of text. With relative positioning, changing the position of the image will position it with respect to its original location after the paragraph. However, with absolute positioning, the image will be positioned with respect to the body of the page because the <body> tag is the parent element of the image.

Note

Relative positioning is the default positioning approach used by HTML.

Figure 13-2 shows an example of a simple Web page that describes a backyard pond, including a couple of images. This is a good Web page to use as an example to illustrate how relative and absolute positioning differ from one another.

Figure 13-2.
The backyard pond Web page includes two images that are positioned normally after a paragraph of text.

In this figure, two images are positioned normally following a paragraph of text (assuming the screen is wide enough), simply because they appear after the paragraph of text in HTML. This is the standard HTML approach to laying out elements on a page. Figure 13-3 on the next page shows how the page changes when you specify that the top of the second image, the big fish, is to be placed 100 pixels lower than its normal position.

Things get more interesting when you change the pond image so that it's placed using absolute positioning. More specifically, the image is positioned so that it appears 25 pixels to the right of the left edge and 0 pixels below the top edge of the page. When using absolute positioning, you position an element with respect to its parent—in this case, the body of the Web page. Therefore, the image is positioned with respect to the entire page. Figure 13-4, also on the next page, shows the result of shifting the pond image 25 pixels to the right, and 0 pixels below, the edges of the page.

As you can see in the figure, the image is positioned with respect to the upper left corner of the Web page. The interesting thing about the resulting page is that the image appears on top of the paragraph of text. This reveals the power of the positioning style properties, and that you must be careful when using them.

Also interesting, because the first image is now positioned using absolute positioning, is that it no longer factors into the relative positioning of the second image. The second image slides over as if no other image preceded it. This again points out that the positioning styles properties are quite flexible, but that they must be used with care. Let's move on and learn how they work.

Figure 13-3.
The big fish image in the backyard pond Web page is positioned 100 pixels lower than its original position by using relative positioning.

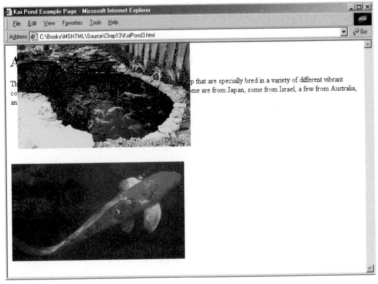

Figure 13-4.
The pond image in the backyard pond Web page is positioned 25 pixels to the right, and 0 pixels below, the edges of the entire Web page by using absolute positioning.

Using Relative and Absolute Positioning

You might be surprised to know that you need only one main style property to carry out both relative and absolute positioning in CSS. However, a few support properties are required to specify the position of an element using either of these approaches. Following are the style properties for relative and absolute positioning:

- `position` declares the type of positioning used for an element (`relative` or `absolute`)
- `top` specifies the top offset of an element's position
- `right` specifies the right offset of an element's position
- `bottom` specifies the bottom offset of an element's position
- `left` specifies the left offset of an element's position

The `position` style property is used to specify whether an element uses relative or absolute positioning, and can be set to one of the following values: `relative` or `absolute`. When using the `position` property, you must also specify the placement of the element by using one or more of the `top`, `right`, `bottom`, or `left` properties. These properties specify the position of the element based on whether the type of positioning used is relative or absolute. The values for these four properties can be specified in points (`pt`), inches (`in`), centimeters (`cm`), or pixels (`px`). Following is an example of setting the relative position of an image:

```
<img style="position:relative; left:0px; top:100px"
src="Fish2.jpg">
```

Although it isn't obvious from the code, this is the example you saw in Figure 13-3, where the fish image was moved down 100 pixels by using relative positioning. Figure 13-4 showed how absolute positioning affects images on a page. Following is the code for that example, which positioned an image 25 pixels over, and 0 pixels down, from the upper left corner of the page:

```
<img style="position:absolute; left:25px; top:0px"
src="Pond1.jpg">
```

Understand that when you use absolute positioning, an element no longer affects the layout of other items on the same page. Think of an absolutely positioned element as floating independently over the other elements on a page, as opposed to being placed next to them. In the next section you will learn how to set the layering of elements so that you control how they appear when they overlap.

Note

You can position elements so that text flows around them, but only by using relative positioning. With absolute positioning, the positioned element essentially floats over the rest of the page independently of the other elements.

Managing Overlapping Elements

You don't need to tinker much with the positioning style properties to figure out that you can move elements around so that they overlap each other. This is a new capability that styles add to Web design; you can come up with interesting designs based upon layered elements. Any time an element overlaps another element, it's important to control which element appears on top. The z-index property, which sets the z-index of an element, is the style property designed to do just that.

The *z-index* of an element determines how the element is displayed with respect to any elements it overlaps. The layering of elements is effectively a third dimension (Z) added to the two dimensions (X and Y) displayed on the screen. Pretend that each element on your page is a sticky note that you stuck on your computer screen. If a red sticky note overlaps a yellow note, the red note has a higher z-index than the yellow one. If you stick a blue note on top of the red one, the blue note will have a z-index greater than either of the other notes. In HTML, the z-index determines which element is drawn on top of other elements.

When you set the z-index of an element, you specify it as a number. This number has meaning only with respect to other elements that you've set. In other words, setting the z-index for a single element doesn't have any effect. But if you set it for several elements, the elements with the higher numbers will appear on top of the elements with lower z-index values.

Note

The z-index of an element is always specified relative to the parent of the element. This results in the element always appearing on a layer above its parent, regardless of how high you set the parent's z-index.

Following is an example of how differing z-index values for two overlapping images are set so that one of the images is displayed on top of the other:

```
<img style="position:relative; left:50px; top:-50px; z-index=1"
src="Pond1.jpg">
<img style="position:relative; left:-200px; top:0px; z-index=2"
src="Fish2.jpg">
```

The results of this code are shown in Figure 13-5. As you can see in the figure, by setting the left property to a negative value, the fish image is forced to overlap the pond image. But the fish image is displayed on top of the pond image because it has a higher z-index. Keep in mind that it's also possible to set the z-index of text to make a paragraph appear on top of an image. Following is a line of code for the paragraph of text in the example that sets the z-index of the paragraph higher than that of the images:

```
<p style="z-index=3">
```

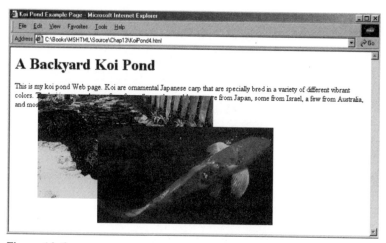

Figure 13-5.
By assigning it a higher z-index value, the overlapped fish image appears on top of the pond image.

Just to show how easy it is to change the z-index of elements to get different results, check out the following code for the images:

```
<img style="position:relative; left:50px; top:-50px; z-index=2"
src="Pond1.jpg">
<img style="position:relative; left:-200px; top:0px; z-index=1"
src="Fish2.jpg">
```

This code reverses the z-index values for the images, which should cause the pond image to appear on top of the fish image. But the paragraph still has a higher z-index than both images, so it should appears as the highest element. Figure 13-6 shows the resulting Web page for this example.

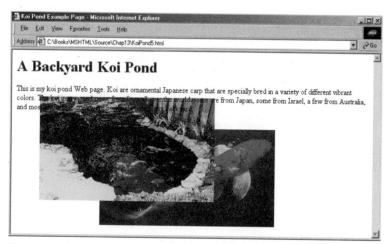

Figure 13-6.
The paragraph of text has the highest z-index, followed by the pond image, and finally the fish image.

If you look closely at this figure you can see where the text of the paragraph is visible over the top of the pond image. Also, notice that the pond image is now shown on top of the fish image, which is consistent with the modified z-indexes.

Tweaking the Appearance of Elements

Several position-related style properties control how an element is displayed, altering the size, visibility, and border of elements. Following are these style properties:

- width sets the width of an element
- height sets the height of an element
- display shows or hides an element
- border-width sets the border width of an element
- border-style sets the border style of an element
- border-color sets the border color of an element
- border sets the border styles of an element as a single property

The next few sections introduce you to these style properties, and how you can use them to control the size, visibility, and border of elements.

Changing the Size of Elements

You can set the width and height of an element with the width and height style properties. They accept familiar units as values: points, inches, centimeters, or pixels. When you change the width or height of a paragraph of text, you can hide part of the text if you size the paragraph smaller. When you resize an image, the browser will do its best to scale it to fit the new dimensions. Following is an example of reducing the size of an image:

```
<img style="width:200px; position:relative; top:-0.75in;
left:-0.5in" src="Fish2.jpg">
```

The results of this code are shown in Figure 13.7.

Note

It's usually better to resize an image using an image-editing tool which will decrease the size of the image file. Also, most image-editing tools are better than Web browsers at scaling images while maintaining their quality.

You also can change the width and height of paragraphs, which then wrap according to the new paragraph size. Here is an example of how to alter the width of a paragraph using the width style property:

```
<p style="width:375px">
```

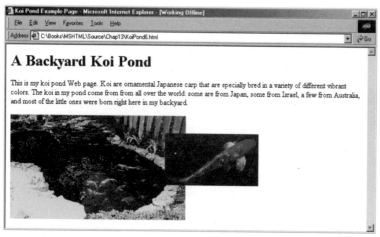

Figure 13-7.
The width style property allows you to reduce (or enlarge) images with ease.

If you apply this code to the main paragraph in the backyard pond Web page, you'll see the page as shown in Figure 13.8.

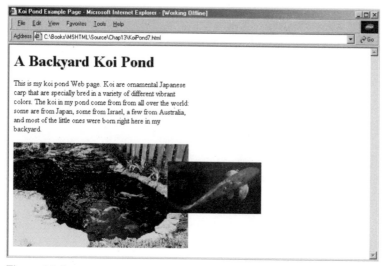

Figure 13-8.
The width style property is valuable for setting the size of paragraphs.

Notice in this figure that the width property overrides the default width of the paragraph, effectively matching the paragraph width with the width of the pond image. The ability of the width and height properties to control the size of paragraphs of text can be quite handy.

Note

In addition to the units mentioned previously, the `width` and `height` properties can also be specified as percentages for elements that are placed with absolute positioning.

Showing and Hiding Elements

If I showed you a blank Web page and told you that several images were positioned on the page, you probably wouldn't believe me. If I made a compelling argument for the concept of invisible elements, would you have faith that the images are there even though you couldn't see them? The truth is that you can't know whether my blank page contains images or not. Just trust me for now; you can hide any element in a Web page, making it completely invisible when the page is displayed in a Web browser.

The `display` style property controls the visibility of elements, and can be set to any of the following values:

- `none` hides an element
- `block` displays an element as a block-level element
- `inline` displays an element as an inline element
- `list-item` displays an element as a list item

As you might have guessed, the `display` style has a default value of either `block` or `inline`, depending upon whether the element in question is a block-level or inline element. To hide an element, set the `display` style to `none`, as the following code demonstrates:

```
<img style="display:none" src="Fish2.jpg">
```

The results of this code are shown in Figure 13-9.

You're probably curious as to why you'd ever want to hide an element so that it's never displayed. For traditional Web pages, there is no reason. However, there are situations—such as when creating dynamic Web pages with scripts—where it's helpful to have hidden information. You will learn all about scripting and dynamic Web pages in Part IV of the book, "Adding Interactivity to Your Pages."

Giving Your Elements a Border

Earlier in the chapter I mentioned that it's helpful to think of HTML elements as having invisible boxes around them. Although imagining invisible boundaries is a good way to visualize the positioning and layout of elements on a page, you might want to make these boundaries visible for some elements. For any element, it's possible to establish a border—basically an outline along the boundary of the element. Borders can be useful for outlining elements, but they can be a visual annoyance if you overdo it and put borders around everything.

Figure 13-9.
An example of the display *style being used to hide the fish image.*

Next are the style properties for borders:

- border-width sets the width of the border for an element
- border-style sets the style of the border for an element
- border-color sets the color of the border for an element
- border sets the border properties for an element as a single property

The border-width property specifies the width of a border as any of the following standard values: thin, medium, or thick. You can also define the width of a border as a numeric value in units of pixels, points, centimeters, or inches.

The border-style property sets the style of the border to one of the following values: none, solid, double, dashed, dotted, groove, ridge, inset, or outset. Each of these border styles applies a different effect to the border, with the simplest styles being the solid and double styles. The default value of the border-style property is none, for no border at all.

The border-color style specifies the color of the border, and is set to one of the standard colors that you learned in the previous chapter. You can also set the color to a custom color. To learn more about custom colors and how they are specified, refer to Appendix C, "Using Custom Colors."

The last of the border style properties is border, which combines the three border properties into a single property. It's a convenience property, but it's useful in creating more concise borders. Following is an example of how to create a border around the paragraph of text in the backyard pond Web page:

```
<p style="width:375px; border:medium solid navy">
```

Borders can also be drawn around images. Look at this code showing how different borders are specified for the two images in the backyard pond Web page:

```
<img style="border:thick double navy" src="Pond1.jpg">
<img style="width:200px; position:relative; top:-0.75in;
left:-0.5in; border:medium dashed green" src="Fish2.jpg">
```

Figure 13-10 shows the backyard pond Web page with its three new borders.

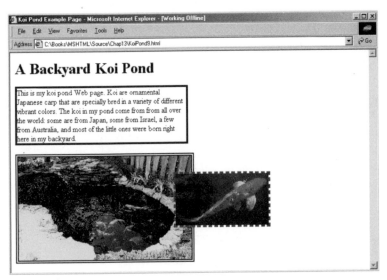

Figure 13-10.
The border style is used to add borders to the elements in the backyard pond page.

As the figure shows, borders are a powerful means of clearly identifying elements on a page. When used properly, borders can serve an important visual and organizational role on Web pages.

Controlling Space on a Page

When you think about it, positioning elements is simply controlling space on a Web page. Not surprisingly, most positioning style properties directly affect the space around elements. Some give you more control over the spacing of elements than others. Following are the style properties used to fine-tune the spacing of elements on a page:

- `margin`—sets the margins of an element
- `padding`—sets the padding of an element
- `vertical-align`—aligns an element vertically with other elements

The `margin` property should sound familiar because you ran across it in the previous chapter. If you recall, the margins are used to constrain the area where text can appear in a paragraph. Margins don't just apply to paragraphs, however. Set the `margin` property for any element, and it serves to add space next to the element. In addition to the `margin` property, you can set individual margins for each side of an element using the `margin-left`, `margin-right`, `margin-top`, and `margin-bottom` properties.

Padding works like a margin, applying to the inside of an element as opposed to the outside. The inside and outside of an element refer to the invisible element boundary mentioned earlier in the chapter. A margin adds space around the outside of the boundary, which means that margin is displayed according to the parent element's style. Padding appears within the boundary of an element, and therefore appears in the same style as the element.

As an example, an element with a red background that's displayed in a `<body>` tag with a white background results in red padding for the element and a margin for the element with a white background. Likewise, if you specify a border for the element, the padding will appear inside of the border and the margin will appear outside.

The `padding` property style is specified using a numeric measurement expressed in one of the now-familiar units. Following is an example of setting the padding for the paragraph in the backyard pond Web page:

```
<p style="width:375px; border:medium solid navy; padding:25px">
```

The results of this code are shown in Figure 13-11. As the figure reveals, the padding for the paragraph results in extra space appearing within the boundary of the paragraph element.

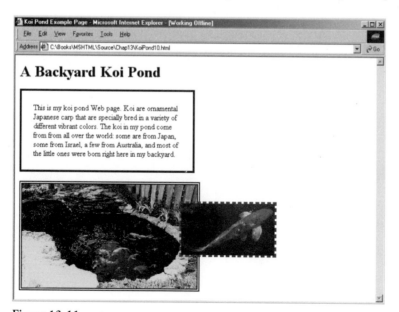

Figure 13-11.
The `padding` style is used to add space around the text in a paragraph, but within the boundary of the paragraph element.

The vertical-align property aligns elements with each other vertically. It's often useful for aligning images of different sizes that wouldn't be aligned vertically without help. When you specify a value for the vertical-align property, you're specifying how an element is aligned with its parent, or in some cases the current line of elements on the page. To align several images, place them within the same parent element, and set their vertical alignments to the same value. Following are the values that can be used with the vertical-align property:

- top—aligns the top of an element with the current line
- middle—aligns the middle of an element with the middle of the parent
- bottom—aligns the bottom of an element with the current line
- text-top—aligns the top of an element with the top of the parent
- baseline—aligns the baseline of an element with the baseline of the parent
- text-bottom—aligns the bottom of an element with the bottom of the parent
- sub—aligns an element as a subscript of the parent
- super—aligns an element as a superscript of the parent

Most of these property values make sense based on their descriptions, but a few require additional explanation. The top and bottom property values align elements according to the current line of a page, the location on the page where the elements naturally appear. Consider that elements on a page are naturally arranged from left to right, and then top to bottom, to understand the concept of the *current line*. If you place a number of images on a page, they will appear from left to right across the page. When there isn't enough room, the next images are displayed on a new line below the previous images. The top and bottom property values align elements according to this invisible line.

The baseline value aligns an element with respect to its baseline and its parent's baseline. For images, the baseline is the same as the bottom of the image. The baseline of an element only has meaning when you're dealing with text. The baseline is the bottom of a line of text, excluding any letters that reach down below the others, such as *g* or *y*.

Following is an example of how to use the vertical-align property to align the tops of the two images in the backyard pond Web page:

```
<img src="Pond1.jpg">
<img style="width:200px; vertical-align:top" src="Fish2.jpg">
```

In this example, the results of this code are shown in Figure 13-12. This figure reveals that you can align images vertically with surprisingly little code.

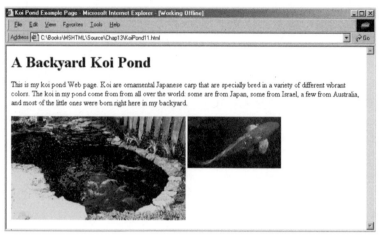

Figure 13-12.
The vertical-align style is used to align the two images along their top edges.

Controlling the Flow of Text

In the previous section I discussed the concept of the *current line*, an invisible line used to place elements on a page. It deals with the flow of elements on a page and comes into play as elements are arranged next to each other across and down the page. Part of the flow of elements is the flow of text on a page. When you mix text with other elements such as images, it's important to control how the text flows around the other elements. Here are a few style properties that make this possible:

- float—determines how text flows around an element
- clear—stops the flow of text around an element
- overflow—controls the overflow of text when an element is too small to contain all of the text

  The next few sections explore these style properties in more detail.

Flowing Text Around Other Elements

To control how text flows around an element, set the float style property of the element. It can be set to either of the following values: left or right. These values determine where to position an element with respect to flowing text. So, setting the float property to left results in an element positioned to the left of flowing text. Following is an example of how the float property is used to flow text between the two images in the backyard pond Web page:

```
<p>
<img style="float:left" src="Pond1.jpg">
<img style="width:200px; vertical-align:top; float:right"
src="Fish2.jpg">
This is my koi pond Web page. Koi are ornamental Japanese carp
that are specially bred in a variety of different vibrant
colors. The koi in my pond come from all over the world:
some are from Japan, some from Israel, a few from Australia,
and most of the little ones were born right here in my
backyard.
</p>
```

The results of this code are shown in Figure 13-13. As you can see in the figure, the pond image is positioned to the left of the flowing text, the fish image to the right. You don't need to set the float property for the paragraph of text.

Stopping the Flow of Text

Just as the float property controls the flow of text around elements, you can prevent text from flowing next to an element. The clear style property is used to stop the flow of text, and can be set to none, left, right, or both. The default value for the clear property is none, indicating that text is to continue flowing normally. The left value denotes that text is to stop flowing around an element until the left side of the page is clear. Likewise, the right value means that text is to stop flowing around an element until the right side is clear. The both value indicates that text is to stop flowing until both sides of the page are clear of elements.

Figure 13-13.
The float *style is used to set the way text flows around the two images in the backyard pond Web page.*

Thy Text Overfloweth

Earlier in the chapter you learned that you can change the size of an element using the `width` and `height` properties, but keep in mind that making it too small might prevent you from seeing all of it. The text that doesn't fit within the paragraph is known as *overflow text*, and can be dealt with in several ways.

The `overflow` property style handles overflow text, and can be set to `visible`, `hidden`, or `scroll`. `Visible` automatically enlarges the element so that the overflow text will fit within it; this is the default setting for the `overflow` property. The `hidden` value leaves the element the same size, allowing the overflow text to remain hidden from view. Perhaps the most interesting is `scroll`, which adds scroll bars to the element so that you can move around and see the text in the element.

A Complete Positional Style Example

You've seen most of the property styles discussed in this chapter in isolation. The point of the examples wasn't to demonstrate good layout strategies, but to show you how the different positioning property styles work. Now it's time to pull together what you've learned and create a final version of the backyard pond Web page that has a nice visual layout. Study this code for the complete page, which also includes some new content:

```html
<html>
<head>
  <title>Koi Pond Example Page</title>

  <style>
    img.left { float:left }
    img.right { float:right }
    p { padding:20px; width:625px; border:medium double navy }
  </style>
</head>

<body bgcolor="white">
  <h1>A Backyard Koi Pond</h1>
  <p>
  <img class="left" src="Pond1.jpg">
  This is my koi pond Web page. Koi are ornamental Japanese
  carp that are specially bred in a variety of different
  vibrant colors. The koi in my pond come from all
  over the world: some are from Japan, some from
  Israel, a few from Australia, and most of the little
  ones were born right here in my backyard.
  </p>
  <p>
  <img class="right" src="Pond2.jpg">
  This is another view of the pond that shows how the
  fish like to congregate in one end while eating. As
```

```
with people, they like to socialize at mealtime. Of
course, they are more aggressive eaters than most
people I know.
</p>
<p>
<img class="left" src="Fish1.jpg">
This picture shows a feeding frenzy of koi of all
sizes and colors. Notice the orange fish in the
picture--his name is Big Ern. I've had him for several
years, and he's one of the friendlier fish in the
pond. He likes to splash about while eating--I suppose
you could call him a rowdy eater.
</p>
<p>
<img class="right" src="Fish2.jpg">
Here's a close-up of Big Ern, the rowdy eater.
</p>
</body>
</html>
```

I'll admit that this is one of the longer pages that you've seen in this book, but the extra code demonstrates how the positional style properties affect the layout of the page. Look at the code; you'll notice that the positional style properties are specified in a style sheet, rather than as local styles. This dramatically simplifies the code for the page, and also makes it easier to maintain. Figure 13-14 shows the final backyard pond Web page as viewed in Internet Explorer.

Figure 13-14.
The completed backyard pond Web page uses several positional style properties in its layout.

Although you can't see all of the content for this page in the figure, it gives you an idea of how the positional style properties are used to control the position of elements on the page. Granted, by most standards this is a simple layout, yet you should be able to use the general layout of this page as a starting point for applying the positional style properties to your own Web pages.

Conclusion

This chapter concludes a trilogy of chapters focusing on styles and their application to Web content. You should now have some perspective on how the positional style properties fit into the overall scheme of styles. Like the style properties you learned in the previous two chapters, the positional style properties can be used either locally or in style sheets. They give you a surprising amount of control over how elements are positioned on a Web page. It comes at the cost of having to carefully think through your page layouts so that you properly apply the positional style properties.

You began this chapter by learning the basics of how styles fit into the positioning of elements on a Web page. You learned about relative and absolute positioning, and the different ways they affect the positioning of elements. You then found out how to control the layering of overlapped elements.

Several style properties were introduced, which relate to the appearance of elements, including properties that control an element's size, visibility, and borders. You then learned how to determine the spacing in and around elements. Next we tackled the flow of text, and you studied how to control the flow of text around elements. The chapter concluded by pulling together much of what you learned in a complete example Web page.

Part 4

Adding Interactivity
to Your Pages

Chapter 14

Dynamic HTML

I think the moral of this story is that the old adage, "bigger is better," doesn't always hold true. Okay, for proud Texans, this does apply to steak and cowboy hats. But when it comes to today's computers, the best things often come in compact packages. Not only that, but simplicity often rules over complexity for computer systems. In the past, it was expected that you needed complex, heavy-duty programming tools to create interactive software applications, not to mention substantial knowledge of intricate programming languages. But the recent advent of Web scripting allows you to create interactive Web pages with relative ease.

This chapter will explore the technologies involved in Web scripting, and will show you how to use them to add interactivity to your Web pages. You will find out that the merger of HTML and other Web tools make up what's known as DHTML, which stands for Dynamic HTML. You will also create some of the most interesting Web pages covered in the entire book.

DHTML Basics

DHTML is a grouping of technologies used to create interactive Web pages. But first you must understand what constitutes an interactive Web page. Interactivity implies that you can do something to a page and have it respond to your actions. For example, you might click a button to change the appearance of an image on the page, or maybe drag the mouse over a piece of text to change the color of the letters. Interactive Web pages can also carry out more advanced tasks such as retrieving and displaying information from a database.

DHTML is not a special version of HTML, or even a version of HTML at all. Instead, it consists of a combination of the following three Web technologies:

- HTML
- Cascading Style Sheets (CSS)
- Web scripting

The practical implication of this combination is that it allows you to change the HTML code for a Web page after the page has been loaded and displayed in a Web browser. In other words, the HTML code for a Web page is no longer etched in stone when you create the page. Using DHTML, you can interact with the user and alter the content of a page at any time. Specifically, you can use Web script code to alter the styles of Web content based upon user interactions such as clicking or dragging the mouse. You can also directly change the content of Web pages by using script code.

The Least You Need to Know About Scripts

Scripts are small programs embedded directly in Web pages. In DHTML, they are used to access styles and content of elements in a Web page. To develop your own custom scripts, you'll need to use a scripting language such as JavaScript or VBScript. Instead of teaching you a scripting language—which would be definitely beyond the scope of this chapter—I'll bestow upon you some short scripts that you can reuse in your own Web pages. Script programming isn't terribly hard to learn, but I'd wait to tackle it until after you get comfortable with HTML.

Scripting Languages

The two main scripting languages in use today are JavaScript and VBScript. Netscape originally developed JavaScript as a scripting version of the popular Java programming language created by Sun Microsystems. Likewise, Microsoft created VBScript as a scripting version of their popular Visual Basic programming language. JavaScript and VBScript do essentially the same tasks in developing script code, so the selection of a language has more to do with your background than the language itself. In other words, if you've used BASIC, you may find VBScript easier to learn. The one downside to VBScript is that it's only supported in Internet Explorer; JavaScript is supported in several browsers.

In this chapter you will use JavaScript to create DHTML Web pages. Again, don't worry about the details of each script; I will point out the important parts to give you a feel for how they work. You may be surprised at how simple some scripts can be. If you happen to have any experience with the Java or C++ programming languages, you'll find JavaScript somewhat familiar.

Using Scripts in Web Pages

As you might guess, there's a special HTML tag used to add scripts to Web pages. The `<script>` tag encapsulates scripting code. Some older Web browsers don't support scripts, so you have to perform a little trick when including script code in the `<script>` tag. Just enclose the script code inside an HTML comment, as the following example demonstrates:

```
<script language="JavaScript">
<!-- Hide the script from old browsers
alert("Hello!");
// Stop hiding the script -->
</script>
```

In this code segment, the `<!--` code that signifies the start of a comment is used just before the single line of script code. Following the script code is the `-->` code which ends the comment. The script code displays an alert message of `Hello!` as shown in Figure 14-1.

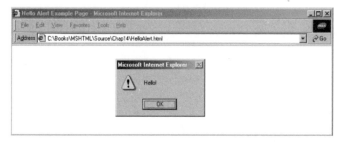

Figure 14-1.
The Hello Alert Example Web page shows how to create a simple script that displays an alert message.

In addition to appearing in the `<script>` tag, you can also take advantage of scripting code directly in the attributes of traditional HTML tags. You will learn how to do this in the next section, which introduces you to event handling.

Responding to Events

The primary way that a DHTML Web page provides interactivity is by responding to actions taken by the user. For example, if the user clicks the mouse button or presses a key on the keyboard, the page might respond by changing the appearance of text on the page. A user interaction such as a mouse click or key press is known as an *event*. The process of a script taking action based upon an event is known as *event handling*. You associate event-handling script code with elements on a Web page using special attributes. Following are some of the commonly used event attributes that come in handy in DHTML, and when they occur:

- `onload`—Browser loads the element
- `onkeydown`—User presses a key
- `onkeyup`—User releases a key

- onclick—User clicks the element with the left mouse button
- ondblclick—User double-clicks the element with the left mouse button
- onmousedown—User presses either mouse button while the mouse pointer is over the element
- onmouseup—User releases either mouse button while the mouse pointer is over the element
- onmouseover—User moves the mouse pointer into the boundaries of the element
- onmousemove—User moves the mouse pointer while the pointer is over the element
- onmouseout—User moves the mouse pointer out of the boundaries of the element

As you can see, you use event attributes to handle common user input events such as mouse clicks and key presses. You associate script code with an event by assigning the event attribute to the script code, like this:

```
<h2 onclick="this.style.color = 'blue';">
I turn blue when clicked.
</h2>
```

In this example, you assign script code to the onclick event attribute, which means that the code runs in response to the user clicking the left mouse button on the text. The script code sets the color of the text to blue. So, interactivity is added to normally bland text by changing the color of the text in response to a mouse click.

Getting to Know the Document Object Model

In the script event example in the previous section, you saw what will happen when the user initiates this script code with the click of the mouse button:

```
this.style.color = 'blue';
```

It's easy to see that the color style property of the text is being set, but the code is a little strange looking because it has a few pieces of information you haven't seen before. The color style property is preceded by the code this.style., specifying that the color is for this text element. The style part of this code identifies the style attribute in which the color property is typically used. For example, the following code clarifies how a color style property is usually set using CSS:

```
style="color:blue"
```

Of course, this code applies to HTML content; the previous code applies to scripts. You know why the color property in the script code is preceded by the word style, but you may not have known that the word this means that a script applies to the current element. By appending the style.color code to this, you are saying that you want to set the color property of the style attribute for the given text element. If it's confusing, keep in mind that script code is capable of manipulating any part of a Web page. Therefore you must clearly identify the element to which an attribute or property applies.

Exposing the pieces of content on a Web page as objects that can be referenced in script code is performed in a Web browser by the Document Object Model, or DOM. The DOM essentially creates a programmatic interface around all of the content in a Web page, making it possible for any part to be accessed and modified with script code.

The DOM consists of a hierarchy of objects that describe every bit of content in a Web page. When referencing content in script code, you identify the hierarchy of DOM objects by separating each object with a period (.). That's why I punctuated the words `this`, `style`, and `color` with periods in the previous example. `Color` is part of the `style` object; `style` is part of the `this` object.

To give you an example of how to reference an object using the DOM, take a look at the following example code:

```
alert(window.location);
```

This code shows how to display the URL of the current Web page in an alert window. The word `location` specifies a property of the `window` object that stores the URL of the current Web page. Figure 14-2 shows the results of this Web page.

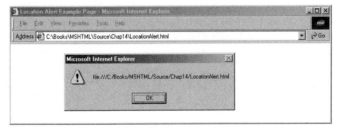

Figure 14-2.
The Location Alert Example Web page shows how to display the URL of the current Web page in an alert window.

Your head is probably spinning from all this talk of objects and the Document Object Model, so I won't go into more detail. I don't expect you to become a DOM expert in the span of a few minutes. My main goal is to lay down a few ground rules so that when you see scripts during the remainder of the chapter, you won't totally be in the dark.

Working with Dynamic Styles

As you know, CSS styles make it possible to fine-tune the appearance of Web pages in powerful and interesting ways. In Chapter 12, you learned how to apply styles that perform slick formatting on text. However, those styles were fixed, not interactive, once you finished the code for the page. Now you're going to learn how to use CSS styles to create dynamic style effects.

Earlier in this chapter you learned that you can handle events that are created in response to user interactions such as mouse clicks and key presses. Event attributes represent perhaps the easiest way to add dynamic styles to Web pages. Following is an example of how to change the color of a piece of text when the user clicks it with the mouse.

```
<h3 onclick="this.style.color = 'red';">Click me, I dare
you!</h3>
```

This code is similar to the example you saw earlier in the chapter, but I wanted to show it to you again now that you have a better understanding of script code. Following is a more dramatic example showing how to apply a dynamic style whenever the mouse pointer is dragged over text:

```
<div onmouseover="this.style.fontSize = '20pt';
this.style.color = 'green'">
Drag the mouse over me to see me get larger and turn green
with envy.</div>
```

In this example the font size of the text increases to a 20-point font, and the color is changed to green. This code is interesting because the changing of the font size increases the amount of space that the text occupies.

To better understand how dynamic styles work, take a look at the following code. It includes the two style examples you just saw, along with another awesome dynamic style:

```
<html> .
<head>
  <title>Dynamic Styles Example Page</title>

  <script language="JavaScript">
  <!-- Hide the script from old browsers
  function StartRainbow() {
    window.setInterval("Rainbow()", 100);
  }

  function Rainbow() {
    if (rainbow.style.color == 'red')
      rainbow.style.color = 'green';
    else if (rainbow.style.color == 'green')
      rainbow.style.color = 'blue';
    else if (rainbow.style.color == 'blue')
      rainbow.style.color = 'yellow';
    else if (rainbow.style.color == 'yellow')
      rainbow.style.color = 'orange';
    else if (rainbow.style.color == 'orange')
      rainbow.style.color = 'purple';
    else
      rainbow.style.color = 'red';
  }
```

```
    // Stop hiding the script -->
    </script>
</head>

<body style="background-color:white" onload="StartRainbow()">
    <h1>Dynamic Styles Example Page</h1>

    <h3 onclick="this.style.color = 'red';">Click me, I dare
    you!</h3>
    <div onmouseover="this.style.fontSize = '20pt';
    this.style.color = 'green'">
    Drag the mouse over me to see me get larger and turn green
    with envy.</div>
    <div id="rainbow">
    This text appears in a rainbow of colors.
    </div>
</body>
</html>
```

This Web page is admittedly quite ambitious given your limited knowledge of scripting. However, the script code isn't too hard to understand, and can always be copied and pasted into your pages without understanding every detail.

In addition to the two style examples you worked through earlier, this page includes a dynamic style that yields an animated rainbow effect. Near the bottom of the code you'll notice a <div> tag with its id attribute set to "rainbow". The script code in the head of the page uses this identifier to reference the <div> text and change its color every 1/10 of a second. Two *script functions*—small self-contained scripts—are defined in the <script> tag for the page.

The StartRainbow() function sets a timer for the page that calls the other function, Rainbow(), every 1/10 of a second (100 milliseconds). The Rainbow( ) function checks the current color of the text, and then sets it to another color. If you picture this code running every 1/10 of a second, you can visualize the animated rainbow effect. The script code begins, thanks to the onload event attribute in the <body> tag, set so that the StartRainbow() function runs when the page is loaded.

Note

One neat thing about the script code in the Dynamic Styles Example Web page is that you can cut and paste it into your own Web pages and apply it to virtually any text. All you do is set the id of the text element to "rainbow". You also need to make sure that you paste the script code into the head of the Web page.

Figure 14-3 shows the Dynamic Styles Example Web page when it's first being loaded in Internet Explorer.

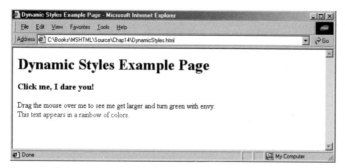

Figure 14-3.
The Dynamic Styles Example Web page demonstrates several different techniques for using dynamic styles.

When you click the first line of text, it changes to the color red. When you drag the mouse pointer over the second line of text, it becomes larger and turns green. The animated rainbow effect on the third line of text is somewhat hard to capture in a figure. So, Figure 14-4 shows the Dynamic Styles page after I clicked, dragged, and otherwise interacted with the page.

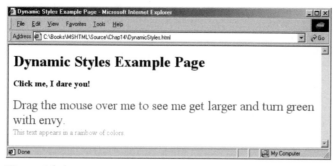

Figure 14-4.
After clicking and dragging the mouse pointer over text in the Dynamic Styles Example Web page, you can see the changes in the appearance of the text.

Manipulating Dynamic Content

Just as dynamic styles allow you to alter the style of Web content based on user interactions or script code, you can also change the content of elements on a Web page. For example, you can change the text in a paragraph or even change the source file of an image. For images, the key to changing the content is the `src` attribute. Following is an example of how to change the source of an image when the mouse pointer moves over the image:

```
<img src="Candles.jpg"
onmouseover="this.src = 'CandlesHilite.jpg';"
onmouseout="this.src = 'Candles.jpg';">
```

This code demonstrates how to change an image when the mouse pointer moves over and out of the image boundary. Notice that the code `this.src` is used to access and set the `src` attribute of the image element.

To alter the content of text elements, you set the `innerText` attribute as opposed to the `src` attribute used for images. Following is an example of an entertaining little paragraph that's altered dynamically:

```
<p style="font-size:14pt" onmouseover="this.innerText = 'Stop
it!';" onmouseout="this.innerText = 'Thank you.';">
I dare you to drag the mouse here.
</p>
```

In this example the content of the paragraph changes when you move the mouse pointer into or out of the boundary of the paragraph. The `this.innerText` reference is used to set the content for the paragraph.

To get a feel for how these dynamic content examples fit into the context of a real Web page, take a look at the following code:

```
<html>
<head>
  <title>Dynamic Content Example Page</title>
</head>

<body style="background-color:white">
  <h1>Dynamic Content Example Page</h1>

  <p>
  <img src="Candles.jpg"
  onmouseover="this.src = 'CandlesHilite.jpg';"
  onmouseout="this.src = 'Candles.jpg';">
  Drag the mouse over the candles to see them flare up.
  </p>

  <p style="font-size:14pt" onmouseover="this.innerText = 'Stop
  it!';" onmouseout="this.innerText = 'Thank you.';">
  I dare you to drag the mouse here.
  </p>
</body>
</html>
```

This code describes a page named Dynamic Content that includes the two examples you just saw. Figure 14-5 shows what this Web page looks like when opened in Internet Explorer.

If you drag the mouse pointer over the image, the candles appear to flare up as shown in Figure 14-6.

Likewise, if you drag the mouse pointer over the second paragraph of text, the text changes. Figure 14-7 shows how the text in the paragraph changes in response to dragging the mouse pointer over it.

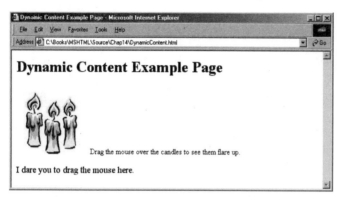

Figure 14-5.
The Dynamic Content Example Web page displays an image of candles and a paragraph of text when it's first opened.

Figure 14-6.
When you drag the mouse pointer over the image, the candles appear to flare up.

Figure 14-7.
When you drag the mouse pointer over the paragraph of text, the text changes.

Fun with Dynamic Positioning

If you really want to add excitement to your Web pages with DHTML, how about dynamically altering the position of elements? That's right, it's possible to use script code and CSS style properties to change the position of elements so that they animate and move around on the page.

If you recall from Chapter 13, you can use CSS styles to position images and text so that they appear in an exact location on the page. This type of positioning is known as *absolute positioning*. If you position an element using absolute positioning, you can easily alter its position on the page using script code. Following is an example of an image that's positioned using absolute positioning:

```
<img id="glider" style="position:absolute; top:100px; left:0"
src="IncRat.jpg">
```

This image uses absolute positioning, and will be displayed at a position 100 pixels down from its parent element on the left edge of the parent. If the parent is the body of the Web page, the image will appear 100 pixels down from the top of the page along the left edge of the page. Notice that the image has its id attribute set to "glider". The id attribute is necessary so that script code can access the image and alter its position. Following is a Web page named Gliding Image Example that contains script code that animates this image by making it appear to glide across the page:

```
<html>
<head>
  <title>Gliding Image Example Page</title>

  <script language="JavaScript">
  <!-- Hide the script from old browsers
  function StartGlide() {
    window.setInterval("Glide()", 50);
  }

  function Glide() {
    glider.style.pixelLeft += 5;
    if (glider.style.pixelLeft >= document.body.offsetWidth)
      glider.style.pixelLeft = 0;
  }
  // Stop hiding the script -->
  </script>
</head>

<body style="background-color:black" onload="StartGlide()">
  <p>
  <h1 style="color:white; text-align:center">Gliding Image
  Example Page</h1>
```

```
    <h3 style="color:white; text-align:center">Watch out for the
    rat!</h3>
    </p>
    <img id="glider" style="position:absolute; top:100px; left:0"
    src="IncRat.jpg">
</body>
</html>
```

This code is structured like the code in the Dynamic Styles Example Web page from earlier in the chapter. For example, the script code in this page sets up an interval timer that runs a script function over and over. The script function increments the pixelLeft property of the image, causing it to move across the page from left to right. Figure 14-8 captures the image during its glide across the page.

Figure 14-8.
The Gliding Image Example Web page shows how to dynamically alter the position of an image by using script code and CSS style properties.

I've admittedly glossed over some details in the Gliding Image Example Web page, but it's another example of script code that you can reuse in pages of your own. In this case it allows you to move content around dynamically.

Getting Practical with DHTML

Throughout the chapter I've shown you how to do some neat things with DHTML; you can now spice up your Web pages with a bit of interactivity. However, most of the examples are aesthetic or cute interactive effects, as opposed to practical uses to improve the functionality of your pages. The next two sections remedy this with a couple of example Web pages using DHTML to carry out practical problems. Keep in mind that the examples would be virtually impossible to create without DHTML or another more complicated custom programming solution.

Displaying an Animated Ad Banner

As you may know, many Web sites make their money from advertising. The ad-based business model of most of these Web sites has been questioned following the Great Dot-Com Fallout of 2000, but the fact remains that ads play an important role on the Web. You may not be able to put ads on your Web pages to obtain millions of dollars in venture capital, but you may find other uses for advertising that can still add value to your Web pages.

As I'm sure you've seen, most online ads appear as horizontal images known as *ad banners*, usually sized about 468 by 60 pixels. Although you could easily slap an ad banner on a Web page with an `<img>` tag, why not use DHTML to create an animated ad banner that rotates between several different images? Using a little script code, you can create an animated ad banner without much effort. Take a look at the following code for the Ad Banner Example Web page, which demonstrates how to create a DHTML ad banner:

```
<html>
<head>
  <title>Ad Banner Example Page</title>

  <script language="JavaScript">
  <!-- Hide the script from old browsers
  var bannerNum = 1;

  function linkBanner() {
    window.alert("You just clicked Ad Banner " + bannerNum +
    ".");
  }

  function rotateBanner() {
    if (++bannerNum > 3)
      bannerNum = 1;
    banner.src = "Banner" + bannerNum + ".jpg";
    window.setTimeout('rotateBanner();', 3000);
  }
  // Stop hiding the script -->
  </script>
</head>

<body style="background-color:white"
onLoad="window.setTimeout('rotateBanner();', 3000);">
  <h1>Ad Banner Example Page</h1>

  <p style="text-align:center">
  <a href="javascript:linkBanner();">
  <img id="banner" style="border:none" src="Banner1.jpg">
  </a>
  </p>
</body>
</html>
```

Not surprisingly, the Ad Banner Example Web page uses the same `<img>` tag that you saw earlier in this section. The page rotates through three different ad banner images, stored in image files named Banner1.jpg, Banner2.jpg, and Banner3.jpg. If you want to add additional ad images, modify the following line of code in the `rotateBanner()` script function:

```
if (++bannerNum > 3)
```

This code checks to see if the number of the banner that's displayed is greater than 3. If so, the next line of code sets the current banner number back to 1:

```
bannerNum = 1;
```

If you want to expand the number of ad banner images to 5, for example, you change the `if` code to:

```
if (++bannerNum > 5)
```

Hey, you're now a script programmer! Seriously, you've learned some of the details about the inner workings of scripts, and more importantly, you've learned how to modify scripts to suit your own purposes.

Figure 14-9 shows the Ad Banner page as it first appears on opening in Internet Explorer.

Figure 14-9.
The Ad Banner Example Web page begins by displaying the first ad banner image.

The timer in the Ad Banner Example Web page is set so that the ad banners rotate every 3 seconds (3000 milliseconds). After waiting approximately 3 seconds, the ad banner changes to the second image, as shown in Figure 14-10.

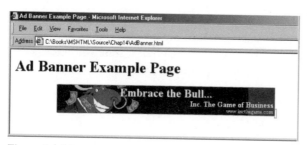

Figure 14-10.
After approximately 3 seconds, the second ad banner image is displayed on the Ad Banner Example Web page.

If you click an ad banner image, an alert message displays the number of the current banner. Figure 14-11 shows the alert message for the third ad banner.

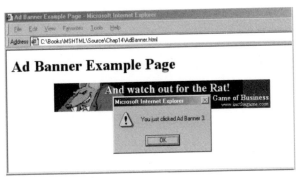

Figure 14-11.
Clicking an ad banner image displays an alert message indicating the number of the current banner.

One interesting aspect of the Ad Banner Example Web page is what happens when an ad banner image is clicked. Keep in mind that the whole point of ad banners is to provide a link to another Web site. The `linkBanner()` script function displays an alert message in response to a click on an ad banner. For a real ad banner, you would probably change this code so that a link is followed to the URL of a different page. Following is what this script code might look like:

```
if (bannerNum == 1)
   window.location = 'http://www.incthegame.com/about.htm';
else if (bannerNum == 2)
   window.location = 'http://www.incthegame.com/game.htm';
else if (bannerNum == 3)
   window.location = 'http://www.incthegame.com/rules.htm';
```

The URLs shown in this code are for my financial board game Web site, and relate to the ad banner images in the Ad Banner Example page. Substitute your own URLs when creating animated ad banners.

Displaying Random Quotes

The Quotable Quotes Example Web page displays a randomly selected quote, and is a good example of how to vary the appearance of a Web page so that it looks different when visited repeatedly. The code for the Quotable Quotes Example Web page follows.

```
<html>
<head>
   <title>Quotable Quotes Example Page</title>
```

```
<script language="JavaScript">
<!-- Hide the script from old browsers
function getQuote() {
  // Create the arrays
  quotes = new Array(8);
  sources = new Array(8);

  // Initialize the arrays with quotes
  quotes[0] = "When I was a boy of 14, my father was so " +
  "ignorant...but when I got to be 21, I was astonished " +
  "at how much he had learned in 7 years.";
  sources[0] = "Mark Twain";
  quotes[1] = "Everybody is ignorant. Only on different " +
  "subjects.";
  sources[1] = "Will Rogers";
  quotes[2] = "I have every sympathy with the American " +
  "who was so horrified by what he had read of the " +
  "effects of smoking that he gave up reading.";
  sources[2] = "Lord Conesford";
  quotes[3] = "The trouble with being punctual is that " +
  "nobody's there to appreciate it.";
  sources[3] = "Franklin P. Jones";
  quotes[4] = "The most likely way for the world to be " +
  "destroyed, most experts agree, is by accident. That's " +
  "where we come in; we're computer professionals. We " +
  "cause accidents.";
  sources[4] = "Nathaniel Borenstein";
  quotes[5] = "They say such nice things about people at " +
  "their funerals that it makes me sad that I'm going to " +
  "miss mine by just a few days.";
  sources[5] = "Garrison Keilor";
  quotes[6] = "Have you ever noticed? Anybody going " +
  "slower than you is an idiot, and anyone going faster " +
  "than you is a maniac.";
  sources[6] = "George Carlin";
  quotes[7] = "What's another word for thesaurus?";
  sources[7] = "Steven Wright";

  // Get a random index into the arrays
  i = Math.floor(Math.random() * quotes.length);

  // Write out the quote as HTML
  document.write("<dl>\n");
  document.write("<dt>" + "\"<i>" + quotes[i] + "</i>\"\n");
  document.write("<dd>" + "- " + sources[i] + "\n");
  document.write("<dl>\n");
}
// Stop hiding the script -->
</script>
</head>
```

```
<body style="background-color:white">
  <h1>Quotable Quotes Example Page</h1>

  <p>
  Following is a random quotable quote. To see a new quote just
  reload this page.
  <br>
  <script language="JavaScript">
  <!-- Hide the script from old browsers
  getQuote();
  // Stop hiding the script -->
  </script>
  </p>
</body>
</html>
```

I apologize for the length of this code, but if you look carefully you'll see that a lot of the code consists of the eight quotes available for display on the page. Once you get past the shock of the code size, the script code for the page is relatively simple to understand.

After creating an array, or list, of quotes and their sources, the getQuote() script function picks a random number and uses it to select a quote to be displayed. The quote is formatted on the page by the HTML code that is generated by the getQuote() function. Notice that the standard document.write() function is used to generate the HTML code that formats the quote. This script function is powerful because, using it, you can dynamically generate HTML code at any point in a Web page.

Figure 14-12 shows the Quotable Quotes Example Web page as it appears in Internet Explorer. To view a different quote, simply click the Refresh button in your Web browser, and the page reloads.

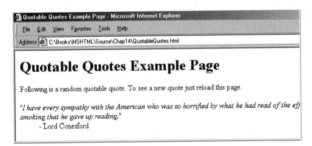

Figure 14-12.
The Quotable Quotes Example Web page displays a randomly selected quote.

Keep in mind that you can easily modify the Quotable Quotes Example Web page to include your own quotes or other Web content that you want to display randomly. You can also increase the number of quotes available for display by adding more entries in the quotes and sources arrays in the code. I realize that some of this script code might be intimidating. Just understand that the best way to learn how to use DHTML is to take something that works and experiment with making modifications to it. If you use the

Quotable Quotes page as a starting point, I guarantee you will be able to alter the script and create your own interesting variation on the idea without much trouble. And if you make mistakes along the way, so be it. Any time you learn something new, you're likely to make mistakes. Experiment and have fun with DHTML.

Conclusion

You hear stories about people who learned how to swim after being thrown into deep water— the sink-or-swim method. Apparently the fear of death can enhance the ability to learn new things. Okay, maybe I'm exaggerating a bit. Probably only a few people ever truly faced death while learning how to swim, but you get the idea. This chapter took a similar approach to teaching you about DHTML. Instead of spending a lot of time building layer upon layer of DHTML knowledge, I laid a few ground rules and then jumped into the details of coding DHTML Web pages. I realize that this approach is challenging, but I could easily fill a whole book on just DHTML. In fact, several other authors already have. This book is really about HTML; I just wanted to introduce you to the basics of DHTML by showing you some neat examples of DHTML Web pages.

This chapter began by explaining the big picture of DHTML and how it relates to HTML. From there you learned about scripting and how to incorporate script code into Web pages. With just enough scripting knowledge to get you into trouble, you found out about dynamic styles, dynamic content, and dynamic positioning. Finally, the chapter concluded by showing you interesting Web pages that also carry out practical tasks, thanks to DHTML.

Chapter 15

Creating Special Effects

Although moving from the United States to Australia would be expensive, you would see interesting visual effects on your computer monitor. But there is an easier way. You could add special effects to your Web pages by altering the appearance of images and text. And you could use animation to transition between different elements on a Web page, or even an entire page.

This chapter will introduce you to some of the interesting features added to Internet Explorer in version 5.5 that make it possible to carry out all kinds of special visual effects. Of course, some of these effects require the help of DHTML, so the scripting skills you picked up in the previous chapter will come in handy. This chapter also will show you how to create an interactive slide show Web page that relies on special effects to transition from one slide to the next.

The Basics of Special Effects

When I speak of special effects on Web pages, I'm not talking about the kind of special effects used in the movies. Although Web page special effects can result in slick looking Web pages, they aren't going to rival the visual effects cooked up in Hollywood. Fortunately, people don't expect your Web pages to be as flashy or realistic as a movie. Even so, you'll find that a few special effects placed here and there can significantly improve the appearance or even the functionality of your Web pages.

Recall that Microsoft introduced a variety of special effects features with Internet Explorer 5.5, which make it possible to dramatically alter the appearance of both text and images. In many cases, this is done through animation. What previously required a Java applet or miles of script code can now be accomplished with a special effect coded as a Cascading Style Sheets (CSS) property. However, some special effects do also require a small amount of script code. The special effects made possible by Internet Explorer are divided into two major types: visual filters and transitions.

Note

A Java applet is a special program developed using a programming language called Java. Java applets are designed so that they can be run on a Web page. Developing Java applets requires a fair amount of programming experience, so they are a little beyond the scope of this book.

A *visual filter* is an extended CSS property that allows you to alter the appearance of an element on a Web page. Examples of the kinds of effects you can achieve with visual filters in both text and images are shadows, embossing, engraving, and blurring. Like a visual filter, a *transition* affects the appearance of Web content, but it uses animation to reveal a change in the content. For example, if you use scripting code to change the source of an image element, you could use a transition to have the image fade into view. Of course, changing the source of an element on a page requires script code, which is why some special effects require a small amount of scripting.

Even though scripting code is required to use some special effects, I think you'll generally find the Internet Explorer special effects to be easy to use. The next section will get you started with special effects by introducing you to visual filters.

Working with Visual Filters

You now know that a visual filter is used to alter the appearance of Web content. Practically speaking, you set a special visual filter style property for an image or block of text. Like other CSS properties, visual filter properties are applied to elements using the `style` attribute. However, visual filter style properties are a little different from other CSS properties because they accept additional parameters that control the filter. To see what I'm talking about, check out the following example, which shows how to set a visual filter style property for a paragraph of text:

```
<p style="width:100%;
filter:progid:DXImageTransform.Microsoft.FilterName()">
This text is being filtered.
</p>
```

As you can see, you set the `width` of the paragraph to `100` percent. Then you apply the filter using the style property `filter:progid:DXImageTransform.Microsoft.FilterName()`. This isn't an actual style property but it does show the general form that the visual filter properties follow. To use a real visual filter, you replace the *FilterName* part of the code with the name of the filter. Most of the filters also require special parameters that determine the specific functionality of the filter; this information is entered inside of the parentheses that follow the filter name.

Note

You typically set the width or height of an element when applying a visual filter. This is necessary because visual filters require that an element have a predetermined size, as opposed to letting the browser figure it out. It's okay to specify the width or height as a percentage, but it must be specified for visual filters to work.

Following is an example of how to apply a glow visual filter to a paragraph of text:

```
<p style="width:100%; font-size:20pt;
filter:progid:DXImageTransform.Microsoft.Glow(Color=red,
Strength=1)">
This text is glowing in red.
</p>
```

In this example, the filter name is Glow. The parameters Color and Strength are specified inside of the parentheses. The Color parameter determines the color of the glow that is to appear around the text, and the Strength parameter establishes the intensity of the glow. You can use the same technique with all of the visual filters undertaken in this chapter. Following is a list of these filters:

- Shadow
- Drop Shadow
- Emboss
- Engrave
- Glow
- Blur
- BasicImage

You will learn about each of these visual filters in more detail in the next few sections, where you will also see practical examples of how to use each filter in Web pages.

The Shadow and Drop Shadow Filters

The Shadow and Drop Shadow filters add shadow effects to Web content. The Shadow filter creates a solid silhouette of the content and then casts the silhouette in a given direction so that it looks like a shadow behind the content. You can specify the color of the shadow, as well as the direction it's cast. The parameters used to fine-tune the Shadow filter are Color and Direction.

The `Color` parameter accepts a standard CSS color name; the `Direction` parameter is a number that stipulates the direction of the shadow in degrees. The `Direction` parameter must be specified in 45 degree increments, which means that it can be any of the following values: 0, 45, 90, 135, 180, 225, 270, or 315. Following is an example of how to use the Shadow filter to create a green shadow that is offset in the direction of 90 degrees (3 o'clock):

```
<p style="width:100%; font:20pt;
filter:progid:DXImageTransform.Microsoft.Shadow(Color=green,
Direction=90)">
This text has a green shadow that is cast at a 90 degree angle.
</p>
```

The Drop Shadow filter creates a shadow that's offset from the content, whereas the Shadow filter casts a shadow that originates from the content. Use the following parameters to control how drop shadows are created:

- `Color`
- `OffX`
- `OffY`
- `Positive`

The `Color` parameter sets the color of the drop shadow; the `OffX` and `OffY` parameters specify the offset of the shadow from the content, in pixels. The `Positive` parameter is a little trickier to visualize because it determines what part of the content you use to produce the shadow. If you set the parameter to `true` the shadow is created from the non-transparent parts of the content. With a value of `false`, the shadow is made from the transparent portions. Changing the value of the `Positive` parameter influences the appearance of the drop shadow significantly. Following is an example of creating an orange drop shadow with the `Positive` parameter set to `true`:

```
<p style="width:100%; font:20pt;
filter:progid:DXImageTransform.Microsoft.DropShadow(
Color=orange, OffX=3, OffY=3, Positive=true)">
This text has an orange drop shadow.
</p>
```

To show you how the other value of the `Positive` parameter can be used, following is another example that creates a red drop shadow, with `Positive` set to `false`:

```
<p style="width:100%; font:20pt;
filter:progid:DXImageTransform.Microsoft.DropShadow(
Color=red, OffX=3, OffY=3, Positive=false)">
This text has a red drop shadow cast on its background.
</p>
```

Figure 15-1 on the next page shows all three of these examples within the context of a single Web page. You may need to study the figure carefully to see the differences in how the filters affect the content.

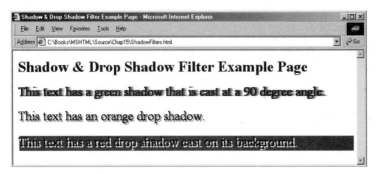

Figure 15-1.

The Shadow and Drop Shadow filters allow you to add shadow effects around Web content.

The Emboss and Engrave Filters

Use the Emboss and Engrave filters to apply an embossed or engraved texture to Web content. Neither of these filters relies on any parameters, which means you can't customize the filters in any way. Therefore, we can jump straight into an example of how to use the Emboss filter:

```
<img src="Sparky.jpg" alt="Embossed"
style="filter:progid:DXImageTransform.Microsoft.Emboss()">
```

This code shows how to apply the Emboss visual filter to an image. The Engrave filter is just as easy to use, as the following code demonstrates:

```
<img src="Sparky.jpg" alt="Engraved"
style="filter:progid:DXImageTransform.Microsoft.Engrave()">
```

To make it easier to see the effects in action, both of these examples are combined in a single Web page shown in Figure 15-2.

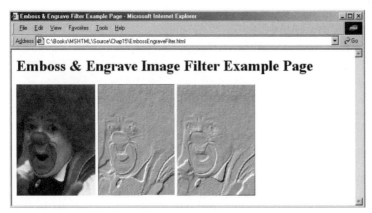

Figure 15-2.

The Emboss and Engrave filters allow you to give images an embossed or engraved appearance.

The Glow Filter

The Glow filter adds a glow effect around the outside edges of Web content. The filter allows you to control the color and strength of the glow effect using the `Color` and `Strength` parameters.

The `Color` parameter sets the color of the glow effect, and the `Strength` parameter establishs the strength of the effect. The following example shows how to create a weak red glow effect:

```
<p style="width:100%; font-size:20pt;
filter:progid:DXImageTransform.Microsoft.Glow(Color=red,
Strength=1)">
This text is glowing in red.
</p>
```

You can even kick it up a notch. Check out this example creating a blue glow with a higher intensity:

```
<p style="width:100%; font-size:20pt;
filter:progid:DXImageTransform.Microsoft.Glow(Color=blue,
Strength=3)">
This text is glowing in blue with more strength.
</p>
```

To really add some punch with the Glow filter, take a look at the following code:

```
<p style="width:100%; font-size:20pt;
filter:progid:DXImageTransform.Microsoft.Glow(Color=green,
Strength=5)">
This text is glowing in green with a lot more strength.
</p>
```

This code creates a green glow effect with a relatively high strength. To see how the strengths affect the appearance of the glow effects, check out the Web page that includes all three examples in Figure 15-3.

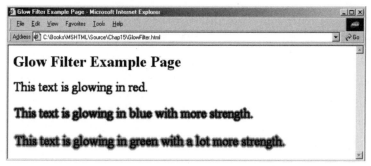

Figure 15-3.
The Glow filter allows you to add a colorful glow around Web content.

The Blur Filter

Of course, you can use the Blur filter to blur the appearance of Web content. Although I don't encourage blurring too much of the content on your Web pages, the Blur filter can be used in special situations to add a unique feel to a page. Or, you can blur everything and give people who visit your Web pages headaches.

Use the `PixelRadius` parameter to control the degree to which content is blurred by the Blur filter. The *pixel radius* is the radius of the area around a pixel that is blurred. In simpler terms, the pixel radius determines how blurry the Blur filter makes the content. The `PixelRadius` parameter is specified as a number in the range 1.0 to 100.0, with 1.0 resulting in a tiny bit of blur and 100.0 maxing out the blurring effect. Following is an example of creating a blur effect with a minimal amount of blurring:

```
<div style="width:100%; font-size:24pt;
filter:progid:DXImageTransform.Microsoft.Blur(
PixelRadius=1.5)">
This text is a little blurry.
</div>
```

> **Note**
>
> Realistically, values in the range 1.0 to 10.0 for the `PixelRadius` parameter are usually sufficient for most of your blurring needs.

To get a stronger blur effect, raise the value of the `PixelRadius` parameter, like this:

```
<div style="width:100%; font-size:24pt;
filter:progid:DXImageTransform.Microsoft.Blur(
PixelRadius=3.0)">
This text is blurrier.
</div>
```

Here is code that uses yet a higher value for the `PixelRadius` parameter, resulting in a considerable amount of blurring:

```
<div style="width:100%; font-size:24pt;
filter:progid:DXImageTransform.Microsoft.Blur(
PixelRadius=5.0)">
This text is extremely blurry.
</div>
```

Figure 15-4 shows what these blur examples look like when viewed in Internet Explorer.

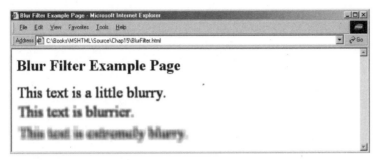

Figure 15-4.
The Blur filter allows you to alter Web content so that it appears blurry.

The Basic Image Filter

The Basic Image filter is different from the previous visual filters you've seen; it applies only to images. It also supports several different sub-effects, which are carried out using the following parameters:

- Mirror
- Rotation
- Invert
- XRay
- Opacity

The Mirror parameter is used to reverse the appearance of an image, and is applied by setting it to 1; a value of 0 results in no mirroring. Following is an example of how you can create a mirror image using the Mirror parameter with the BasicImage filter:

```
<img src="Sparky.jpg" alt="Mirrored"
style="filter:progid:DXImageTransform.Microsoft.BasicImage(
Mirror=1)">
```

The Rotation parameter allows you to rotate an image in 90 degree increments. The values 0, 1, 2, and 3 correspond to 0, 90, 180, and 270 degrees. So, to rotate an image by 180 degrees, set the Rotation parameter to 2, as in the following code:

```
<img src="Sparky.jpg" alt="Rotated"
style="filter:progid:DXImageTransform.Microsoft.BasicImage(
Rotation=2)">
```

You use the Invert parameter to invert the colors in an image, resulting in a negative of the image. Turn it on by setting the Invert parameter to 1, or turn it off by setting it to 0. Following is an example of code that inverts an image using the Invert parameter:

```
<img src="Sparky.jpg" alt="Inverted"
style="filter:progid:DXImageTransform.Microsoft.BasicImage(
Invert=1)">
```

Use the XRay parameter to create a version of an image that looks much like an x-ray. The effect is somewhat like a black-and-white version of the invert effect. You turn on the x-ray effect by setting the XRay parameter to 1, or turn it off by setting it to 0. The following code demonstrates how to use the XRay parameter:

```
<img src="Sparky.jpg" alt="XRayed"
style="filter:progid:DXImageTransform.Microsoft.BasicImage(
XRay=1)">
```

The last of the Basic Images sub-effects, the Opacity parameter, changes the transparency of an image. By default, all images are completely opaque. However, you can use the Opacity parameter to make any image appear to have a degree of transparency. The Opacity parameter is specified as a number in the range 0.0 to 1.0, where 0.0 is completely transparent and 1.0 is completely opaque, which is the default setting. Following is an example of how to use the Opacity parameter:

```
<img src="Sparky.jpg" alt="Transparent"
style="filter:progid:DXImageTransform.Microsoft.BasicImage(
Opacity=0.25)">
```

Check out Figure 15-5 to see how the different parameters of the BasicImage filter affect a real image. It shows the previous code snippets in the context of a Web page.

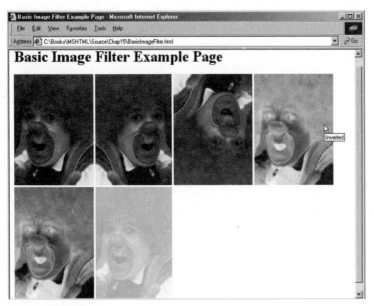

Figure 15-5.
You can use the Basic Image filter to apply visual effects such as mirroring, rotating, and inverting the image, to name a few.

Animating Content Changes with Transitions

If you watch much television you'll recognize common tricks used to tie together scenes on television shows. For example, it's fairly common for both television shows and movies to use a blurry effect to transition to a dream sequence. Many shows and movies fade a scene out as it's ending, and fade in new scenes. Another commonly used effect is the wipe effect that rolls a new scene across the screen to replace the previous one. All of these effects are transitions because they form the changeover from one scene to another.

In the Web page special effects covered here, transitions are special property styles used to bridge the transition between changing content on a Web page. Although Web page transitions aren't quite as flexible as television show or movie transitions, they provide an interesting approach to adding visual sizzle to your Web pages. One situation where transitions could prove useful is in banner ads that change every few seconds. Because one image is constantly being replaced by another, banners present the perfect opportunity to apply a transition effect such as a fade or wipe.

Transitions involve a little help from script code, so they are somewhat trickier to use than visual filters. However, I'll provide you with some reusable script code that you'll find applicable to many different transitions. First, you need to learn how to apply transitions to Web content by using special CSS styles. You'll be glad to know that applying transition styles is virtually identical to applying visual filter styles—each transition has its own name along with parameters that determine how it functions. Following is an example of how to create a fade transition effect for an image:

```
<img id="image" src="Sparky.jpg" onclick="doTransition()"
style="filter:progid:DXImageTransform.Microsoft.Fade(
Duration=2, Overlap=1.0)">
```

It's not important at this point that you understand the parameters of the Fade transition. Instead, focus on the structure of the code required to make the transition work properly. In addition to the src attribute for the image and the style attribute for the transition, you'll notice that the id and onclick attributes are specified. Based on what you learned in the previous chapter, you can probably guess that the id and onclick attributes are involved in the script code for the transition. In fact, the id attribute is used to identify the image for the script. The onclick attribute identifies the script function utilized when the user clicks the image. In other words, this transition is set up so that it's carried out in response to the user clicking the image.

With the transition style applied to the image, you need script code to change the image and apply the transition. Following is the script code for the doTransition() function, which applies the filter to the image:

```
<script language="JavaScript">
var transitioned = 0;
function doTransition() {
  image.filters[0].Apply();
```

```
  if (transitioned) {
    transitioned = 0;
    image.src="Sparky.jpg";
  }
  else {
    transitioned = 1;
    image.src="Ernest.jpg";
  }
  image.filters[0].Play();
}
</script>
```

I realize that you only have one brief chapter of scripting knowledge under your belt, so I don't expect you to immediately understand this code. The good news is that you don't really have to because the code will work with any transition. The parts of the code you need to understand are those where the different images are set. To transition between other images, you'll need to change the code that sets the images. Beyond that, I recommend simply cutting and pasting this code into your own Web pages and not worrying for the moment about how it works. Just make sure that you place the code in the head of the page, where script code is generally placed.

Note

If you'd like to learn more about JavaScript and creating scripts of your own, by all means go for it. Script programming can be fun, and will give you an incredible amount of control over your Web pages. It's just beyond the scope of this chapter to digress into a lengthy discussion of scripting.

Now that you have an idea about how transitions are applied to Web content, you're ready to find out exactly what transitions are available. Following are the most interesting transitions supported in Internet Explorer 5.5:

- RandomDissolve
- Fade
- Strips
- Wheel
- Barn
- Blinds
- CheckerBoard
- GradientWipe
- RadialWipe

The next several sections will introduce you to these transitions and show you how to use them to create a transition between two images. Note that all of the transitions have a Duration parameter that determines the duration of the animated transition effect, in seconds. For example, if you use a Fade transition to fade out an image, the `Duration` parameter determines how long the fade lasts. The `Duration` parameter is one parameter that you need to set for all transitions regardless of any other parameters that they may use.

The RandomDissolve Transition

The RandomDissolve transition reveals changed content in a Web page by randomly adding pixels from the new content to the display. This transition doesn't include any special parameters other than the `Duration` parameter, so it's easy to use. The following code demonstrates how to use the RandomDissolve transition:

```
<img id="image" src="Sparky.jpg" onclick="doTransition()"
style="filter:progid:DXImageTransform.Microsoft.RandomDissolve(
Duration=1)">
```

If you place this code in a Web page and throw in the general script code that you saw earlier in the chapter, you'll have a Web page that successfully uses a random dissolve effect as a transition between two images. Figure 15-6 shows this page as the transition is taking place.

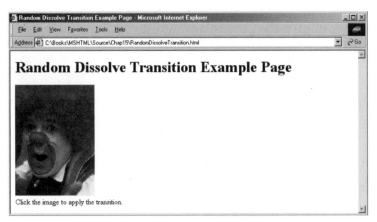

Figure 15-6.
The RandomDissolve transition is used to animate Web content by making the individual pixels of the old content appear to dissolve.

The Fade Transition

The Fade transition reveals changed content by fading out the original content, and optionally fading in new content at the same time. This transition uses a parameter named `Overlap` to determine how much the old and new content overlap as the fade progresses. More specifically, the value of this parameter is a number in the range 0.0 to 1.0 that specifies the fraction of the transition time that the old and new content overlap. So, a value of 0.0 means that there's no overlap (meaning that the original image completely fades out before the new image begins to fade in), and a value of 1.0 indicates that the content completely overlaps throughout the fade. Following is an example of using the Fade transition with an image:

```
<img id="image" src="Sparky.jpg" onclick="doTransition()"
style="filter:progid:DXImageTransform.Microsoft.Fade(
Duration=2, Overlap=1.0)">
```

Figure 15-7 shows the results of this transition as the image changes from Sparky the Clown to Ernest the Salamander.

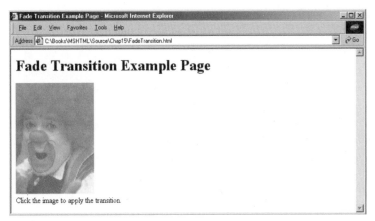

Figure 15-7.
The Fade transition is used to animate Web content by making the old content fade out and the new content fade in.

The Strips Transition

The Strips transition reveals new content by peeling away the old content in successive strips. The result is something of a diagonal wipe whose direction is specified by the `Motion` parameter. This parameter can be set to one of the following values, which determine the direction of the wipe: `leftdown`, `leftup`, `rightdown`, or `rightup`. Following is an example of how to use the Strips transition:

```
<img id="image" src="Sparky.jpg" onclick="doTransition()"
style="filter:progid:DXImageTransform.Microsoft.Strips(
Duration=1.5, Motion=rightdown)">
```

Figure 15-8 shows the results of applying the Strips transition to two images.

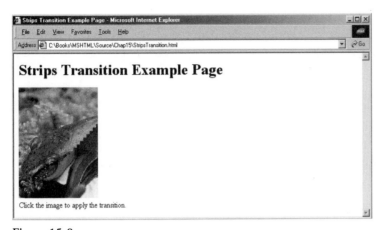

Figure 15-8.
The Strips transition is used to animate Web content by diagonally peeling away the old content to reveal the new.

The Wheel Transition

The Wheel transition reveals changed content in a Web page by rotating angular *spokes* of the old content to reveal the new. The `Spokes` parameter stipulates how many of these spokes are used in the transition, and is set to a number. The following code shows how to use the Wheel transition:

```
<img id="image" src="Sparky.jpg" onclick="doTransition()"
style="filter:progid:DXImageTransform.Microsoft.Wheel(
Duration=3, Spokes=6)">
```

The results of this transition code are shown in Figure 15-9.

The Barn Transition

The Barn transition definitely gets credit for being the transition with the cutest name. The name comes from the fact that the transition looks kind of like a barn door swinging open or closed to reveal the new content. This transition relies on two parameters to control these virtual barn doors: `Motion` and `Orientation`. Set the `Motion` parameter to either `in` or `out`, to determine whether the barn door is opening or closing. Set the `Orientation` parameter to either `horizontal` or `vertical` to determine whether the door opens up and down or left and right, respectively. Following is an example that demonstrates the use of the Barn transition:

```
<img id="image" src="Sparky.jpg" onclick="doTransition()"
style="filter:progid:DXImageTransform.Microsoft.Barn(
Duration=2, Motion=in, Orientation=horizontal)">
```

Figure 15-10 shows the results of viewing this transition in action in Internet Explorer.

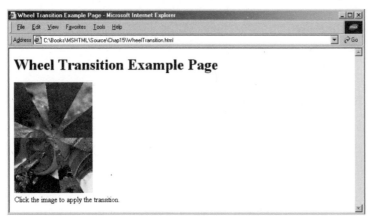

Figure 15-9.
*The Wheel transition is used to animate Web content by rotating the old content as a series of **spokes** to reveal the new content.*

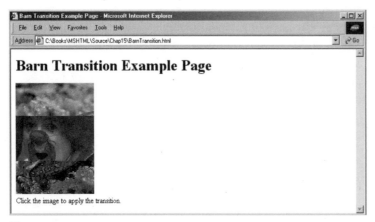

Figure 15-10.
*Use the Barn transition to animate Web content by opening or closing a **barn door** to reveal the new content.*

The Blinds Transition

I doubt you're surprised that the Blinds transition shows new content in a page by using an animation that resembles the opening or closing of window blinds. It relies on two parameters to control the animated blind effect: Bands and Direction. The Bands parameter establishes how many bands (blind pieces) are used. The `Direction` parameter specifies the direction the blinds are moving, and can be one of the following values: `up`, `down`, `left`, or `right`. Following is an example of how you can use the Blinds transition:

```
<img id="image" src="Sparky.jpg" onclick="doTransition()"
style="filter:progid:DXImageTransform.Microsoft.Blinds(
Duration=1, Bands=10, Direction=right)">
```

The results of this transition code are shown in Figure 15-11.

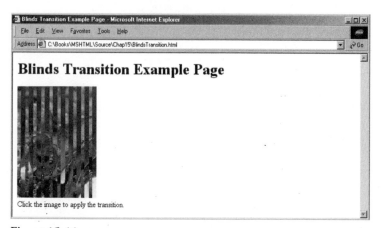

Figure 15-11.
You can use the Blinds transition to animate Web content in a way that resembles the opening or closing of window blinds.

The Checker Board Transition

The Checker Board transition reveals changed content in a Web page by simultaneously uncovering multiple rectangular areas of the new content in a pattern that resembles a checkerboard. You can use the `Direction` parameter of this transition to determine the direction in which the checkerboard effect moves. It can have any of the following values: `up`, `down`, `left`, or `right`. Use the SquaresX and SquaresY parameters to determine how many squares appear on the checkerboard in the X and Y directions. Following is an example of using the CheckerBoard transition:

```
<img id="image" src="Sparky.jpg" onclick="doTransition()"
style="filter:progid:DXImageTransform.Microsoft.CheckerBoard(
Duration=2, Direction=down, SquaresX=5, SquaresY=8)">
```

Figure 15-12 on the next page shows the checkerboard transition effect in action.

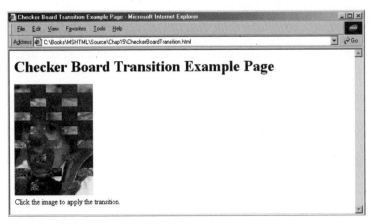

Figure 15-12.
You can use the Checker Board transition to animate Web content by simultaneously uncovering multiple rectangular areas of the new content in a pattern that resembles a checkerboard.

The Gradient Wipe Transition

The Gradient Wipe transition shows new content in a page by moving a gradient band across the original content. A gradient effect involves a smooth transition from one color to another, or from one set of colors to another set of colors. A rainbow is a good example of a natural gradient effect. The Gradient Wipe transition results in a smooth wipe that slides across the old content to reveal the new content. The GradientSize parameter is a number in the range 0.0 to 1.0 that determines the size of the gradient band as a fraction of the content size. The WipeStyle parameter is set to 0 or 1, and establishes whether the transition is applied horizontally (0) or vertically (1). The Motion parameter is set to forward or reverse, and determines the direction that the band travels based upon the WipeStyle parameter. Following is an example that shows how to create a Gradient Wipe transition:

```
<img id="image" src="Sparky.jpg" onclick="doTransition()"
style="filter:progid:DXImageTransform.Microsoft.GradientWipe(
Duration=2, GradientSize=0.25, Motion=forward, WipeStyle=0)">
```

The resulting transition effect of this code is shown in Figure 15-13.

The Radial Wipe Transition

The Radial Wipe transition reveals changed content by wiping around the content radially. The radial wipe transition effect looks somewhat like the second hand sweeping around the face of a clock. The WipeStyle parameter determines the specific kind of radial wipe used, and can be set to one of the following values: `clock`, `wedge`, or `radial`. Following is an example of how to apply this transition to an image:

```
<img id="image" src="Sparky.jpg" onclick="doTransition()"
style="filter:progid:DXImageTransform.Microsoft.RadialWipe(
Duration=4, WipeStyle=wedge)">
```

Figure 15-14 shows the resulting radial wipe transition effect created in this code.

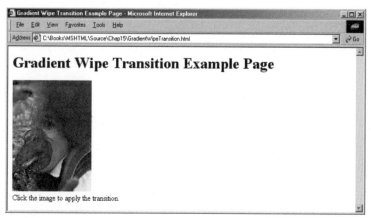

Figure 15-13.
You can use the Gradient Wipe transition to animate Web content by moving a gradient band across the original content.

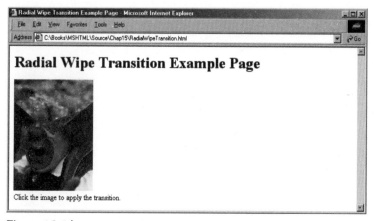

Figure 15-14.
Use the Radial Wipe transition to animate Web content by wiping around the content radially.

Putting on a Slide Show

Now that you understand how to use transitions, it's time to examine them in a more interesting Web page. When you think about it, transitions would work great in a Web page for an online slide show. You could use a transition to add interest as the user flips from slide to slide. Although a slide show Web page would need script code to flip through the slide images, the transition effects would still primarily be carried out using style properties. I could go on and on about this hypothetical slide show Web page, but I'd rather just show you the real thing. Following is the complete HTML code for a slide show Web page using the Fade transition when moving from slide to slide:

```
<html>
<head>
  <title>Slide Show Example Page</title>

  <script language="JavaScript">
  var transitioning = 0;
  var imageNum = 2;
  function nextImage() {
    if (transitioning == 0) {
      transitioning = 1;
      image.filters.item(0).Apply();
      image.src = "Pond" + imageNum + ".jpg";
      image.filters.item(0).Play();
      if (++imageNum > 5)
        imageNum = 1;
    }
  }
  </script>

  <script language="JavaScript" for="image" event="onfilterchange">
  transitioning = 0;
  </script>
</head>

<body style="background-color:white">
  <h1 style="text-align:center">My Backyard Pond</h1>

  <p style="text-align:center">
  <img id="image" src="Pond1.jpg"
  style="filter:progid:DXImageTransform.Microsoft.Fade(
  Duration=2)"
  onclick="nextImage()">
  <br>
  Click the image to view the next image in the slide show.
  </p>
</body>
</html>
```

You probably noticed that this page relies on some script code that looks a little complicated. The script code takes care of moving through the slides each time the user clicks the current slide image. The code also associated the transition with the image so that it's applied properly. To understand the transition aspects, focus on the code that sets the transition style property:

```
<img id="image" src="Pond1.jpg"
style="filter:progid:DXImageTransform.Microsoft.Fade(
Duration=2)"
onclick="nextImage()">
```

As you can see, this code is similar to what you've seen several times throughout this chapter when working with transitions. Once the Fade transition is set up for the image, the nextImage() script function handles the rest of the details for the slide show. Figure 15-15 shows one of the slides in the slide show.

Figure 15-15.
The Slide Show Web page demonstrates how to use transitions to provide a smooth move between images in a Web-based slide show.

Creating Interpage Transitions

In addition to normal transitions applying to individual pieces of content within a Web page—such as images or paragraphs of text—*interpage transitions* apply to an entire page as it's being loaded or exited. Just as the curtain draws and closes in a stage performance, you can use interpage transitions to apply transition effects to a Web page during its opening and closing.

When a page opens and when the page closes, you can use the special <meta> tag to specify an interpage transition. Following is an example of how to stipulate a RadialWipe opening transition for a Web page using the <meta> tag:

```
<meta http-equiv="Page-Enter"
content="progid:DXImageTransform.Microsoft.RadialWipe(
Duration=4)">
```

Notice in this code that there's an attribute named http-equiv set to "Page-Enter". This identifies the transition as applying to the opening of the Web page, as opposed to its closing. The transition is then specified using the content attribute, which sets up the transition almost exactly as you've seen it stipulated in the style attribute. To transition to the closing of a Web page, you use similar code. In fact, the only change is the value of the http-equiv attribute, which must be set to "Page-Exit". Following is example code that establishes a RandomDissolve transition for the closing of a Web page:

```
<meta http-equiv="Page-Exit"
content="progid:DXImageTransform.Microsoft.RandomDissolve(
Duration=2.5)">
```

Of course, the best way to get a feel for using interpage transitions is to see them at work in the context of a real Web page. A great example page for this is a title page for the Slide Show Web page you saw in the previous section. Following is the complete code for the Show Title Web page, which serves as a slick title page for the Slide Show Web page:

```
<html>
<head>
  <title>Show Title Example Page</title>

  <meta http-equiv="Page-Enter"
  content="progid:DXImageTransform.Microsoft.RadialWipe(
  Duration=4)">

  <meta http-equiv="Page-Exit"
  content="progid:DXImageTransform.Microsoft.RandomDissolve(
  Duration=2.5)">
</head>

<body style="background-color:white">
  <p style="text-align:center">
  <a href="SlideShow.html">
  <img id="title" src="LargePond.jpg">
  </a>
  </p>
  <h1 style="text-align:center">My Backyard Pond Slide
  Show</h1>
</body>
</html>
```

As the code reveals, this is a simple Web page containing a single image and a line of text. However, it contains both opening and closing interpage transitions, adding significant interest to the page. Figure 15-16 shows the page being opened in Internet Explorer and the Radial Wipe transition effect taking place.

268

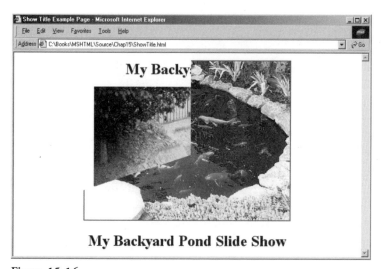

Figure 15-16.
The Show Title Web page uses the Radial Wipe transition when the page is opened.

Likewise, the Random Dissolve transition takes place when you click the image on the title page to enter the slide show. Figure 15-17 shows this interpage transition at work, as the Show Title page changes to the Slide Show page.

Figure 15-17.
The Show Title Web page uses the Random Dissolve transition when the page is closed.

Conclusion

Don't plan on packing your bags and heading to Hollywood to become a special effects expert after reading this chapter. But even though the special effects introduced in Internet Explorer 5.5 aren't quite up to Hollywood standards, they are quite effective in the context of Web pages. In fact, this chapter only presented a sampling of the fun visual filters and transitions that are available for use. If you enjoyed learning about using these special effects, I encourage you to explore them further on your own and find even more fascinating possibilities.

This chapter began by laying the groundwork for special effects in Internet Explorer, and how to create them with extended CSS styles. You moved on to visual filters, and how to use them to alter the appearance of Web content. You tackled transitions, which offer a cool technique for animating changes of Web content. You then put your new special effects skills to practical use by developing a slide show Web page. The chapter concluded by showing you how to use interpage transitions, applying animated transition effects to entire Web pages.

Chapter 16

Assessing the Capabilities of a Client

Web fact for the day

The Los Angeles Police Department uses a special computer program to help them solve murders; it's called HITMAN, which stands for HomIcide Tracking Management Automation Network.

Just as HITMAN helps the LAPD track and assess the behavior of criminals, you can use special Dynamic HTML (DHTML) features to assess the behavior of people who visit your Web pages. Or, at least you can determine information about the computers of users who view your Web pages. But don't worry about feeling like a police detective; you're not planning to make an arrest. The information you gather will personalize and improve the experience for those who visit your Web site. For example, you can tailor the size and quality of your site's images to the capabilities of the viewer's monitor. So what if this chapter about clients doesn't have the same intrigue as the HITMAN criminal tracking system? You'll end up with some powerful techniques for improving the experience of visitors to your Web site.

You will explore *client capabilities*—the exposure of information about a user's computer—so that you can custom-tailor your pages to that visitor. You might also use this information to statistically track the technical capabilities of your average visitor's computer. Regardless of how you use the information, you'll find it interesting. This chapter shows how to retrieve the client capabilities of visitors to your Web pages, and gives a practical example of how to use the information in a real Web page.

What Are Client Capabilities?

I used to be a competitive amateur skateboarder, and I would often travel to skateboard parks for contests. Any time I arrived at a new park and approached one of the ramps, I recognized the look I got from other skaters. It was the look that said, "How good is this guy?" For a brief moment, I enjoyed a certain mystique because no one knew if I was a

271

beginner, an expert, or—accurately for me—somewhere in between. I'm sure the *assessment look* is common in other sports and in business situations.

I mention this experience because it relates to how you perceive people who visit your Web sites. Granted, you aren't concerned with how skilled they are as Web surfers, but you do benefit from having information about the capabilities of their computer systems. Fortunately, you don't have to rely solely on a look.

Internet Explorer includes several properties known as *client capabilities*, which determine certain characteristics of a user's computer system. Recall that a Web browser is known as a client, which is why the user's computer capabilities are called client capabilities. The properties that provide access to client capabilities are DHTML properties, so you must access them through scripting code. This isn't a problem, however, because you are now a Web scripting expert, right? Okay, maybe not, but you definitely know enough to learn how to use client capabilities.

Client capabilities provide access to information such as the size of a user's computer screen, along with other things like the type of processor and operating system being used. Although you probably won't be tweaking your Web pages to accommodate different processors, you might take into consideration the screen size for some pages. As an example, to display a large image that takes up the majority of a Web page, you would want the image to fill the screen but not require the user to scroll around to see it all. However, there's a problem; people with different sized monitors sometimes have their screens set to different resolutions. Fortunately, the majority of people have their resolution set to a common size, which makes the problem of varying resolutions not quite so significant.

Note

Client capabilities define 'screen size' in terms of the number of pixels that can be displayed horizontally and vertically, making the term synonymous with 'screen resolution.' Monitor size is the diagonal dimension of a monitor's display area, and is a fixed value, generally expressed in inches.

For example, the majority of computers use a 15" or 17" monitor with a screen size or *screen resolution* of 800 x 600, which means that the screen is 800 pixels wide and 600 pixels tall. Some people still use smaller monitors with 640 x 480 resolution, and also some people use larger monitors that easily support resolutions of 1600 x 1200, or even higher. Obviously, an image can appear to be sized quite differently, depending on the resolution of your screen. Therefore, in some situations it makes sense to offer several images tailored to different screen sizes. You will learn how later in the chapter. For now, let's delve into the relationship between client capabilities and Internet Explorer.

Client Capabilities and Internet Explorer

I mentioned that Internet Explorer provides access to client capabilities through a series of DHTML properties. These properties are readily available through scripting code and can be used to control the manner in which a Web page presents information to users based upon their system capabilities. Table 16.1 lists the most important properties that provide access to client capabilities through Internet Explorer 5.5 or later.

Table 16-1.   Internet Explorer's Client Capability

Property Name	Information Obtained	Accessed As
cpuClass	System's CPU type	window.navigator.cpuClass
platform	Name of the operating system	window.navigator.platform
width	Total screen width, in pixels	window.screen.width
height	Total screen height, in pixels	window.screen.height
availWidth	Available screen width, excluding the Windows task bar, in pixels	window.screen.availWidth
availHeight	Available screen height, excluding the Windows task bar, in pixels	window.screen.availHeight
colorDepth	Color depth of the screen, in bits per pixel	window.screen.colorDepth

Note

The colorDepth property in the table informs you how many bits of information are used to describe a pixel of color. To understand, a 1-bit pixel can only be one of two colors: generally black or white. The more bits used to represent colors, the more colors you have available, and the better looking your graphics. The minimum color depth for most computers—8 bits of color—results in 256 different colors. Higher end graphics cards use color depths up to 32 bits, resulting in 4,294,967,296 different colors. That should suffice even for the set designer of Robin Williams's movie, *What Dreams May Come*.

Notice that the properties in the table provide access to information such as the CPU type and the name of the computing platform of a system. The first column in the table is the name of the property; the last shows how the property is accessed from scripting code. For example, if you want to display the CPU capabilities using an alert box, you use the cpuClass property:

```
alert("CPU : " + window.navigator.cpuClass);
```

For another example of how client capabilities can be accessed from within a real Web page, check out the following code for the Screen Size Web page:

```html
<html>
<head>
  <title>Screen Size Example Page</title>

  <script language="JavaScript">
  <!--
  alert("Screen Size : " + window.screen.width +
    "x" + window.screen.height);
  -->
  </script>
</head>

<body style="background-color:white">
  <h1>Screen Size Example Page</h1>
</body>
</html>
```

This Web page includes a script in the head, which displays the screen size. Figure 16-1 shows the Web page as viewed in Internet Explorer 5.5.

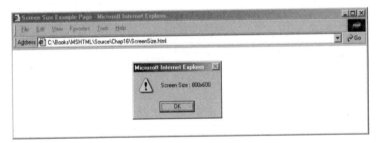

Figure 16-1.
The Screen Size Web page displays an alert box containing the size of your screen, in pixels.

The figure reveals how the screen size of the user's monitor appears in an alert box, thanks to the width and height client capability properties. Although this use of an alert box is okay, you might want to format the client capabilities on a page so that it's easier to read. That's the topic of the next section.

Obtaining Client Capabilities

Although most users know what kind of CPU, platform, and screen they have, it's still useful to develop a Web page that displays the client capabilities in a nice format. The following code for the Client Capabilities Web page demonstrates how this is carried out:

```html
<html>
<head>
  <title>Client Capabilities Example Page</title>
```

```
</head>

<body style="background-color:white">
  <h1>Client Capabilities Example Page</h1>

  <p>
  Following are the capabilities of your computer:
  <ul>
  <li id="cpu"></li>
  <li id="platform"></li>
  <li id="screenSize"></li>
  <li id="availableSize"></li>
  <li id="colorDepth"></li>
  </ul>
  </p>

  <script language="JavaScript">
  <!--
  cpu.innerText = "CPU : " + window.navigator.cpuClass;
  platform.innerText = "Platform : " +
    window.navigator.platform;
  screenSize.innerText = "Screen Size : " +
    window.screen.width + "x" + window.screen.height;
  availableSize.innerText = "Available Size : " +
    window.screen.availWidth + "x" + window.screen.availHeight;
  colorDepth.innerText = "Color Depth : " +
    window.screen.colorDepth + " bits per pixel";
  -->
  </script>
</body>
</html>
```

Unlike the earlier Screen Size example page, the script code doesn't appear in the head of the document. Because the script code references HTML elements with specific IDs, it must appear below the elements in the code. So the script code is placed just after the list of items. Each item in the list is given a different ID so that it can be uniquely identified in the script code. For example, the color-depth list item is created like this:

```
<li id="colorDepth"></li>
```

With the unique ID set for the item, you access it from within the script code:

```
colorDepth.innerText = "Color Depth : " +
  window.screen.colorDepth + " bits per pixel";
```

Note

To view or change the color depth of your screen in Microsoft Windows, right click anywhere on the desktop and select Properties from the popup menu. In the Display Properties dialog box, click the Settings tab. Near the lower left corner of the window is the Colors setting for the display. Click this to change the color depth of the screen.

The neat thing about this script code is that it sets the text for the list item. In other words, the code creates a piece of text that describes the color depth capabilities of the user's system, and then assigns it to the colorDepth list item. The standard innerText property is what makes this possible, as you can see in the code. All of the other client capabilities are retrieved and displayed in a similar manner. Figure 16-2 shows the Client Capabilities Web page as viewed in Internet Explorer.

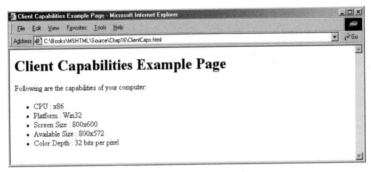

Figure 16-2.
The Client Capabilities Web page displays several important pieces of information regarding the capabilities of your computer.

As you can see in the figure, the Client Capabilities Web page displays pertinent information about your system's capabilities in a nicely formatted list. At this point you may be thinking that it's neat finding out about your system, but asking what's the practical application for such information? The next section shows you how to put client capabilities to use in enhancing your Web pages based on a user's screen size (resolution).

Reacting to Client Capabilities

Determining the system capabilities of the visitors to your Web site might be useful if you just want to keep track of what hardware your average user has, but that's not enough to justify hassling with client capabilities data. However, you might consider some practical reasons to incorporate client capabilities into the design of your Web pages.

Say you want to display an image that fills most of the browser window without requiring the user to scroll around to see it. Because the size of screen varies considerably, you pretty much have to commit to one image size that looks good, and then hope for the best on smaller or larger screens. Or you can peek at the user's screen size using the client capability properties and display a different-sized image for each screen size.

This technique of altering the content of a Web page based on the capabilities of the user's system is a great way to improve the *feel* of your Web pages and ultimately make them look better. To pull off the example I just described, you create several images of different sizes appropriate for different standard screen sizes. Following are the screen sizes you might consider supporting with unique images:

- 640 x 480
- 800 x 600
- 1024 x 768
- 1152 x 864
- 1280 x 1024
- 1600 x 1200

Am I recommending that you create six images for the title page of your Web site so that every one of these screen sizes is supported? No. In fact, it's only necessary to target three of these screen sizes to cover the majority of visitors to your site. It's safe to assume that most Web users have one of the following three screen sizes: 800 x 600, 1024 x 768, or 1152 x 864. Keep in mind that even if a few people with a different screen size visit your site, you'll still be displaying an image that's targeted to a reasonably similar screen size. For example, you might create a custom image for the 1152 x 864 screen size, and someone else might view your page on a screen that is 1280 x 1024. The page still looks good; it just has a little extra space around the image.

So, I'm suggesting that you create three images for a title Web page that targets the following screen sizes: 800 x 600, 1024 x 768, and 1152 x 864. Understand that the screen size does not translate directly into viewable browser area. In other words, the amount of room available for displaying an image on a Web page is considerably smaller than the overall screen size. This is because most browsers have menu bars and toolbars, not to mention the status bar and scroll bars.

With this in mind, create the images smaller than the target screen size by a consistent percentage. This percentage may vary based on whether or not you plan to display elements such as title and caption text along with the image. For the purpose of an example Web page, I opted to go with the following three image sizes: 440 by 330, 600 by 450, and 800 by 600. It's important to understand that there aren't really any rules when it comes to determining these image sizes. Experiment with different screen sizes and see what looks good, but try to maintain a 4:3 ratio of width to height. Determining a good look for a Web page is more an art than a science.

To choose the size of the image that will be displayed on the Web page, you check the available screen size using the client capability properties. The available screen size is the total screen size, except that it accounts for whether or not a task bar takes up space on the screen. For example, most Windows systems include a task bar along the bottom of the screen. Once you know the available screen size, you can set the image for the page accordingly. Following is the code for the Title Image Web page, which shows exactly how this task is carried out:

```
<html>
<head>
  <title>Title Image Example Page</title>
</head>

<body style="background-color:white">
  <p style="text-align:center">
  <img id="title" src="">
  </p>
  <h1 style="text-align:center">My Backyard Pond Web Site</h1>

  <script language="JavaScript">
  <!--
  if (window.screen.availwidth >= 825 &&
    window.screen.availheight >= 750)
    title.src="Pond800.jpg";
  else if (window.screen.availwidth >= 625 &&
    window.screen.availheight >= 600)
    title.src="Pond600.jpg";
  else
    title.src="Pond440.jpg";
  -->
  </script>
</body>
</html>
```

This code shows how a couple of simple if-else statements determine which image to display. I realize that you probably aren't a scripting expert, but if you study this script code, you'll understand how it works. The if-else statements check to see if the user's available screen size is larger than the minimum amount required for a given image size. If so, the ID in the <img> tag loads that image. If not, a smaller screen size is checked. If that one fails too, the smallest image is displayed. So, the code attempts to use each of the images from largest to smallest.

The images used for the Title Image example are pond images, each sized according to the three resolutions I chose. To make the page easier to see in action, I indicated the size of each image in the lower right corner. Figure 16-3 shows what the page looks like when you view it on an 800 x 600 screen.

As you can see, the 440 by 330 image fits nicely on the page and allows room for the title text. However, this image would be way too small on a larger screen such as one set to 1152 x 864. Figure 16-4 shows the same page viewed on an 1152 x 864 screen, but with an 800 by 600 image.

Figure 16-3.
The Title Image Web page figures out the best size title image to display based upon the available screen size.

Figure 16-4.
If you change the resolution (size) of your screen, the Title Image Web page will display a different sized title image.

This figure shows how the Title Image page automatically selects a larger image given the larger size of the screen. In this case, the 800 by 600 image fills the page nicely and provides a better quality image thanks to the higher resolution of the screen. The result is that visitors to this Web page will view an image sized according to the capabilities of their system, dramatically improving the appeal of the Web page.

Conclusion

Just as World Series of Poker champion Hieu "Tony" Ma carefully studies the skills and strategy of his opponents at the poker table, you can assess the capabilities of the computers that people use to view your Web pages. Unlike a poker game, determining the capabilities of your visitors' computer systems has no adversarial element, but it can be useful in terms of improving the appearance of your Web pages. These capabilities are client capabilities and consist of information about the CPU, platform, and screen size of users' computers.

This chapter began by introducing you to the concept of client capabilities and why they are important to Web design. You learned about the client capability properties made available as of Internet Explorer 5.5. From there, you saw an example Web page that demonstrated how to view the different client capabilities of a user's computer. The chapter concluded by showing you a practical use of client capabilities to display a custom-sized title image on a Web page based upon the screen size of the user's computer.

Part 5

Leveraging XML

Chapter 17

Understanding XML

Web fact for the day

Individuals, not businesses, create most of the electronic information on the Web. E-mail messages alone account for 500 times the information in all the Web pages combined.

Even without using a calculator, it's easy to compute that there's a great deal of information floating around out there on the Internet. Not surprisingly, little of this information is structured in a meaningful way, other than simply being formatted for easy viewing. The lack of context for masses of information about everything from abalone to ZIP codes sometimes makes it difficult to find what you're looking for. Granted, search engines do a good job of dealing with the chaos of the Web's colossal information overload, but for most of us, organization and structure would be more popular than Julia Roberts on Oscar night; fortunately, the industry is rapidly adopting the technology that aims to provide both.

I'm referring to XML, which stands for eXtensible Markup Language. Like HTML, it allows you to use tags to create Web pages and other documents. In addition, XML is designed to be completely open-ended; you can create your own tags to give pages unique meaning. This isn't possible with HTML. You will learn in this chapter that XML introduces a whole new way of thinking about the Web and electronic information in general. It is sure to challenge and broaden your perspective on Web pages.

What is XML?

In addition to being another lovable acronym, XML is a groundbreaking technology that aims to completely change the way information is structured on the Web. The fundamental principle behind XML is the ability to create custom tags that can be used to describe any kind of information. To understand a custom tag, consider some of the commonly used tags in HTML: `<html>`, `<body>`, `<p>`, and `<img>`. These tags are all defined in the HTML language and have specific meanings for Web pages.

But what if you wanted to include something in a Web page that doesn't necessarily match one of the HTML standard tags? For example, what if you wanted to include a joke? Of course, you could code the joke text any number of ways using standard HTML tags such as `<i>` or `<b>` to italicize or bold the words, but neither of these tags carries any meaning. Wouldn't it be neat to have a `<joke>` tag that has no other purpose than marking up jokes? XML makes this, and much more, possible.

At this point you're probably wondering why in the world anyone would want a special tag for jokes in a Web page. That's a good question because, as I said, nothing is stopping you from using standard HTML tags for jokes on a Web page. However, standard HTML tags do little to convey the meaning of the content that they mark up. A `<joke>` tag, on the other hand, states that the content it highlights is a joke; it describes the meaning of the content. But I still haven't answered the question: Why does it matter whether or not you know the meaning of the content?

You've no doubt used a search engine to look for information on the Web. Imagine that you are compiling a list of jokes for your next family gathering or Oscar ceremony, and you want to search the Web for some real knee-slappers. The obvious approach would be to search on the word joke, which would find some joke sites. Yet this method would probably never find the jokes that individuals have placed on their Web pages— because there is nothing for the search engines to find.

Keep in mind that search engines look for important words, also known as *keywords*, so Web developers must be diligent about embedding the right words in their pages. If you've simply put a few jokes on your personal Web page, it's doubtful you'll take the time to add the word *joke* as one of your keywords.

What if every joke on the Web was coded with our new `<joke>` tag? Instead of searching for inconsistent and often misused keywords, search engines would search for the `<joke>` tag. Presto! A list of all the jokes on the Web. Step aside, Steve Martin. This works because the jokes are now tagged based upon their meaning, making it possible to perform more intelligent searches. Here you have the main premise of XML—adding context to content.

The advantages of XML extend far beyond search engines, but they do come to mind as the most obvious and immediate beneficiaries of a Web with XML-based pages. XML is in vogue now as a means of shuttling information back and forth between Web-based applications such as online stores. XML has already proven to be a highly efficient and simple means of storing and transferring information between different kinds of computing systems, both on and off the Web.

XML and HTML

Now that you have a basic understanding of what XML is and what it can do, you're probably wondering how XML relates to HTML. Is XML a newer, more advanced version of HTML? The answer is a resounding *no*! XML is not a *version* of HTML at all. If anything, HTML is a version of XML. To understand this, you have to grasp how XML works.

XML defines other markup languages by laying the groundwork for creating tags and attributes and describing the structure of documents of a given type. You use HTML to develop a Web page, a type of XML document. It would be accurate to say that HTML is an application of XML. More specifically, HTML is considered an *XML vocabulary*.

Note

An XML vocabulary is a language that describes a document of a certain type. For example, HTML is an XML vocabulary used to describe Web pages. Many XML vocabularies are in use today. In addition to HTML, a few examples include VML (Vector Markup Language) for two-dimensional graphics and MathML (Mathematical Markup Language) for mathematical equations.

Is your head spinning from my description of HTML as a markup language created from XML? All I can say is that I warned you at the beginning of the chapter that XML would challenge the way you view Web pages and information in general. The best way to grasp the idea of XML is to take a step back and assess the role of HTML and what it's used for. HTML is merely a big group of tags that evolved over the last few years to meet the needs of the Web community. The `<img>` tag wasn't always a part of HTML. It wasn't until graphical browsers became available that the `<img>` tag was added, making it possible to add graphical images to Web pages. You have to accept the fact that HTML is not a constant that's never changed.

So why shouldn't it be possible to mark up all information with tags, not just Web pages? That's where XML enters the picture; it provides a means of marking up any information with a set of customized tags.

Note

As you know, I hate to muddy things, but I must point out that, technically speaking, HTML isn't a true XML markup language. You will learn in the next section that XML imposes strict structural requirements on Web pages and other documents it creates. HTML currently doesn't meet these requirements, so there's a special version of HTML known as XHTML that serves as a true XML markup language. You will learn about XHTML in Chapter 19, "XHTML: XML Meets HTML."

You might have noticed that I've used the word *document* several times when referring to XML content. I'm not advocating that you stop using the term Web page, but when it comes to XML you'll find that *document* often does a better job of describing XML content, both Web and otherwise. This is because XML requires that you think in terms of the meaning of the content.

The term Web page conjures up an image of a page displayed in a browser, but the term HTML document simply refers to content marked up with HTML. Although a Web page is in fact an HTML document, a distinction between the two emerges as you learn about other XML markup languages and their documents. Although it may be simple in theory, the big picture of XML is actually an elusive concept. The biggest challenge for most people is figuring out how they can use it. XML is usually described in such general terms that it's hard to pinpoint its practical implications. Sure, I mentioned the search engine example, but you may have guessed that my dream XML search engine doesn't exist yet.

Another irony of XML is that you can't do much with it by itself. Unlike HTML, which solves a specific problem, XML is not a solution by itself. Instead, it lays the ground rules for solving problems. To understand this, consider the fact that there is no such thing as a generic XML Web browser. A Web browser is inherently an HTML-based program, and it can't process the content of XML documents for display. More importantly, XML doesn't even specify what content should look like when displayed, which is also why a generic XML browser isn't possible.

Note

Although it isn't possible to browse generic XML code, it is possible to apply styles to XML code so that content can be viewed in a Web browser. You will learn how to do this in the next chapter, "Styling XML with XSL."

Please forgive me if this discussion of XML and HTML seems abstract. Trust me, I don't stay up late at night pondering the meaning of life in terms of XML. The fact of the matter is that XML involves a significant shift in how you think about Web pages, which is why it's necessary to hit you with theory and clarify exactly how XML and HTML relate to one another. I promise to put away the pipe and leather chair now so we can get down to the business of putting XML to use in your Web pages.

Getting to Know XML

Now that you understand the theoretical implications of XML, it's time to learn the language structure of XML. Let me repeat that the XML language is a generic language used to describe other markup languages such as HTML. Knowing this, you'll find XML to be extremely general and open-ended. It's not until you begin working with specific XML vocabularies that the true power of XML comes into full view. So as you learn about XML, try to think how it might affect the HTML markup you've used thus far.

The first thing to understand about XML is that it makes a clear distinction between markup and content. *Markup* consists of the tags and attributes used to describe information in an XML document; *content* is the information itself. In the following example of HTML code, can you guess which parts are markup and which are content?

```
<p>Let's sing a lament, the world isn't round it's <i>twisted
and bent</i>.</p>
```

In this HTML code, the `<p>`, `<i>`, `</i>`, and `</p>` tags are all markup; the remaining sentence text is content. Here, the markup is used to describe the appearance of the content, which is typical of HTML code. XML markup is often more descriptive and doesn't necessarily have anything to do with the appearance of content. Following is an example of a hypothetical XML document:

```
<question answer="true">The world's termites outweigh the
world's humans ten to one. True or False?</question>
```

In this code, a hypothetical question-and-answer XML vocabulary is used to mark up content for a True/False question. Notice that the question is marked up using the `<question>` tag; the answer is specified by the `answer` attribute. None of this markup has anything to do with the appearance of the content, and instead focuses on its meaning. However, the markup is instantly familiar because it's formatted in a way similar to HTML.

Although I've talked in terms of tags when describing the creation of XML documents, the actual structure is determined by elements. An *element* is a discrete piece of information within an XML document, typically corresponding to a tag or set of tags. For example, in the question markup you just saw, there is an element named `question` that is marked in the document by using the `<question>` and `</question>` tags. It's helpful to think in terms of elements when you're analyzing an XML vocabulary, instead of thinking in terms of tags. Another way to explain elements is to say that they describe the structure of XML documents.

An element can have both start and end tags, as in the `question` element, or a single empty tag. An HTML example of an element with both start and end tags is the p paragraph element, which has both the `<p>` and `</p>` tags. An HTML element with a single empty tag is the `img` image element, which has only the `<img/>` tag. Notice that I closed the empty `<img/>` tag with a forward slash (/) before the closing angle bracket (>). This is important in XML; all empty tags must have a closing slash. This is the first of several picky XML coding conventions that you might as well get used to.

XML elements are capable of containing content, child elements, or both. Content in XML is often referred to as *character data,* to indicate that it consists of characters of text. When an element contains child elements, or subordinate items, it means that they're nested within the element. Although this may sound complex, you are already experienced with nested elements. In fact, you just saw an example of HTML code that included both nested child elements and character data. Here is the sentence I just showed you:

```
<p>Let's sing a lament, the world isn't round it's <i>twisted
and bent</i>.</p>
```

In this code, the p element contains the i element as a child element, along with the character data for part of the sentence. The i element also contains the character data *twisted and bent*. When you look at examples such as this, it becomes apparent that XML is not as complicated as it sounds.

Note

XML is a very formal language, so it helps to get used to terms like *character data*. I've made an effort to dress down XML as much as possible, but some of the formality is still necessary to explain things accurately.

The XML language consists of several components that describe the makeup of different parts of a document. Following are the major XML components:

- Element tags
- Entity references
- Comments
- Processing instructions
- Document type declarations

Don't worry if these components sound technical, because you're about to see that they're actually easy to understand. Their significance is that they describe the fundamental structure of the XML language, dictating the makeup of all XML documents. With a solid understanding of these components, you'll be able to read and understand the overall structure of any XML document, not to mention gain a new perspective on HTML.

Because I'm the kind of guy who loves to get in over my head when I learn new things, I'm going to use a similar approach here by explaining the XML components in the context of a real XML document. Don't worry if the document doesn't make sense immediately, because it will soon enough. The document I'm talking about uses a special XML vocabulary to mark up an audio collection. You would use a document like this to catalog all your CDs and tapes. Following is the audio collection XML document:

```
<?xml version="1.0"?>
<!DOCTYPE audiocollection SYSTEM "AudioCollection.dtd">

<audiocollection>
  <! This is the Rock section of the collection. -->
  <audio type="rock" review="5" year="1990">
    <title>Cake</title>
    <artist>The Trash Can Sinatras</artist>
    <track>Obscurity Knocks</track>
    <track>Maybe I Should Drive</track>
    <track>Thrupenny Tears</track>
    <track>Even the Odd</track>
```

```
      <track>The Best Man's Fall</track>
      <track>Circling the Circumference</track>
      <track>Funny</track>
      <track>Only Tongue Can Tell</track>
      <track>You Made Me Feel</track>
      <track>January's Little Joke</track>
      <comments>Brilliant first release from the most underrated
      band in existence.</comments>
   </audio>

   <!-- This is the Jazz section of the collection. -->
   <audio type="jazz" review="5" year="1993">
      <title>Criss-Cross</title>
      <artist>Thelonious Monk</artist>
      <track>Hackensack</track>
      <track>Tea for Two</track>
      <track>Criss-Cross</track>
      <track>Eronel</track>
      <track>Rhythm-A-Ning</track>
      <track>Don't Blame Me</track>
      <track>Think of One</track>
      <track>Crepuscule with Nellie</track>
      <track>Pannonica</track>
      <comments>Excellent collection of Monk across five
      different sessions.</comments>
   </audio>

   <!-- This is the Hip Hop section of the collection. -->
   <audio type="hiphop" review="5" year="1987">
      <title>Paid In Full</title>
      <artist>Eric B. &amp; Rakim</artist>
      <track>I Ain't No Joke</track>
      <track>Eric B. Is on The Cut</track>
      <track>My Melody</track>
      <track>I Know You Got Soul</track>
      <track>Move the Crowd</track>
      <track>Paid in Full</track>
      <track>As the Rhyme Goes On</track>
      <track>Chinese Arithmetic</track>
      <track>Eric B. Is President</track>
      <track>Extended Beat</track>
      <comments>Possibly the best rap recording of all
      time.</comments>
   </audio>
</audiocollection>
```

Even though I haven't formally introduced you to the details of the XML language, you can probably study this document for a few moments and make out most of its meaning. This is because XML tags tend to be pretty descriptive. By the way, Internet Explorer allows you to view XML documents and interact with them to some degree. Figure 17-1 shows the audio collection XML document as viewed in Internet Explorer 5.5.

Figure 17-1.
Although Internet Explorer doesn't attempt to interpret the meaning of XML documents, it does allow you to view them.

XML documents don't necessarily include any information about how they are to be displayed, and Internet Explorer doesn't try to interpret the meaning of the audio collection document. Instead, it focuses on highlighting the different structural parts. If you look carefully you'll see a hyphen (-) to the left of some of the elements. Clicking this hyphen allows you to close the element, thereby hiding the information contained within it. This could be helpful in large XML documents. When you close an element, the hyphen turns into a plus sign (+), which can be used to reopen the element. Figure 17-2 shows the audio collection document with all the audio elements closed.

Figure 17-2.
Closing elements in an XML document can help you to see the higher level of the document's structure.

Now that you've seen the audio collection document from different angles, let's use it to learn about the primary XML components.

Understanding Elements and Tags

As you might have guessed, tags form the basis of all XML documents, and are used to mark up elements. This is evident in the example of the audio collection by the artist element. It's marked up using the <artist> and </artist> tags. The distinction between elements and tags is admittedly subtle; think of elements as logical pieces of markup, and tags as specific text strings used to represent elements in XML documents.

Earlier in the chapter I mentioned that elements can have both start and end tags, in which case they contain character data. Or they can be empty. Empty elements must be closed with a forward slash (/). A good example of an empty element in HTML is the br element, which is used to create a line break on a page. The br element doesn't contain any character data and according to XML standards must be coded as `<br/>`. Throughout the book I've deliberately avoided using the forward slash to close empty HTML elements because most HTML code does not adhere to XML rules. But from here on we'll work on getting you into the habit of doing so.

Note

Web browsers are flexible and don't care about the XML empty-element forward-slash rule, but this may change as the Web becomes more structured. Even if browsers don't tighten up regarding Web page structure, you may find it important to validate your HTML documents in the future. You will learn more about document validation later in the chapter.

Note that the forward slash used in empty tags is a carryover of the forward slash used with end tags. For example, consider that all end tags begin with a forward slash: `</html>`, `</body>`, `</p>`, and so on. Using a forward slash at the end of an empty tag is like combining a pair of start and end tags into a single tag. As evidence that this is the motivation behind the forward slash, I must point out that it's possible in XML to code an empty tag as a pair of tags, like this:

```
<br></br>
```

In this example, a line break is coded as a pair of tags, instead of the empty `<br/>` tag. Although the two-tag variation is valid XML, the empty tag approach is preferable because it's more concise.

Referencing Entities

Because of the rigid structure of XML, there are some pieces of information that must be specially encoded in order to include them as content. For example, the apostrophe character (') serves a special purpose in XML and must be specially coded if you intend to use an apostrophe as part of document content. To understand, consider the following XML content:

```
Last summer we visited Pike's Peak.
```

Because XML interprets apostrophes as markup, you must use a special technique to identify the apostrophe in Pike's Peak as content. An *entity reference* is a way of referring to a piece of a data by using a special name. It's basically a unique name that identifies a piece of XML data. You use an entity reference by enclosing the reference between an ampersand (&) and a semicolon (;). The standard entity reference for an apostrophe character is ', which means the previous XML content would be coded like this:

```
Last summer we visited Pike&apos;s Peak.
```

I realize this code isn't easy to read, but the ' entity reference clarifies that the apostrophe is XML content, and not markup. Entity references are also utilized in the audio collection XML document in the name of the artist Eric B. & Rakim. Because the ampersand character is used to identify entity references, you must use the entity reference & for an ampersand that is content. Following is the line of the code in the audio collection document that uses the ampersand entity reference:

```
<artist>Eric B. &amp; Rakim</artist>
```

Entity references are usually unique to the specific document in which they appear. However, there are several built-in entity references. Table 17-1 shows the built-in entity references that are available for use in all XML documents:

Table 17-1. **Built-In Entity References in XML**

Entity Reference	Description
&amp;	Ampersand character (&)
&quot;	Double-quote character (")
&apos;	Apostrophe character (')
&lt;	Less-than character (<)
&gt;	Greater-than character (>)

Using Comments

Like HTML, XML allows you to create comments that aren't interpreted as document markup or content. Comments are useful for adding notes that explain a certain part of a document, or maybe mentioning an aspect of the document that you intend to improve on later. Document markup and content is designed for interpretation by your computer; it's either processed or displayed, but comments are there solely for your benefit as the XML author. Put another way, comments are ignored when an XML document is processed or displayed.

You can place comments in a document anywhere content appears, which makes it possible to add comments throughout a document if you so desire. Comments are unique because they are enclosed by special symbols. More specifically, you start a comment with `<!--` and end it with `-->`. Following is an example of a simple comment:

```
<!-- Copyright (c) 2001 Gas Hound Games -->
```

This code shows how you could add a copyright notice to your XML documents with a comment. Comments are used a few times in the audio collection document, as the following code reveals:

```
<!-- This is the Rock section of the collection. -->
<!-- This is the Jazz section of the collection. -->
<!-- This is the Hip Hop section of the collection. -->
```

Note

The only significant limitation on comments is that you can't use double-hyphens (`--`) in the text of a comment, a good reason not to rely on them in your Web pages!

Using Processing Instructions

Contrary to what I've led you to believe so far, XML documents don't consist of only markup, content, and comments. In fact, a couple of other pieces of information commonly show up in XML documents. One is *processing instructions*, special commands passed along to the program that process or view the XML document. Processing instructions are easily distinguished from other XML components because they always start with `<?` and end with `?>`. For example, following is a processing instruction that you will see in virtually every XML document:

```
<?xml version="1.0"?>
```

Notice in this code that the processing instruction begins with `<?` and ends with `?>`. Inside of the instruction, you may notice that the structure is similar to tags. This is because processing instructions typically include a name followed by an attribute/value pair. The previous processing instruction example is used to identify an XML document as adhering to version 1.0 of the XML standard. This processing instruction was used at the beginning of the audio collection document and is an important part of all XML documents.

Note

The latest version of XML as of this writing is 1.0, the only version of XML.

Declaring the Document Type

The last XML component you need to understand is document type declarations, which are extremely important because they describe the structure of an XML document. A *document type declaration* appears near the top of an XML document just below the xml processing instruction, and identifies the document's root element and document type definition. The document type definition (DTD) is responsible for describing the tags and attributes capable of being used in the document, along with the relationships between them. The document type declaration is responsible for performing three primary tasks:

- Specifying the document's root element (for example, html is the root element of HTML documents)

- Defining elements, attributes, and entities specific to the document

- Identifying an external DTD for the document

This document type declaration stuff is confusing, so let me clarify its purpose. One of the principle features of XML is the ability to validate documents based on whether or not they adhere to the strict XML rules. In addition to making sure that a document follows the fundamental language rules of XML, it's also important to see that they adhere to the specific language rules of the markup language they are based on. For example, it's possible for a Web page to completely adhere to XML language rules yet completely violate HTML rules. A simple example of how this is possible is if you use the <joke> tag I mentioned earlier on a Web page. You can code the <joke> tag so that it's perfectly legal in XML, but HTML has no <joke> tag.

The point is that XML documents have two different levels of *correctness*. The first level is determined by whether a document meets the strict language requirements of XML. If it does follow these rules, it's described as a *well-formed document*. The second level of correctness is determined by whether a document adheres to a DTD for a particular markup language such as HTML.

If the document passes this test as well, then it's referred to as a *valid document*. It's considered an accolade of the highest order for an XML document to be valid. Ideally, all XML documents—and ultimately all Web pages—would be valid documents. It goes without saying that a valid document is also a well-formed document, but the reverse is not always true.

Let's circle back to the document type declaration for a document, whose main purpose is to identify the root element of the document as well as the DTD, usually contained in an external file. The DTD is essential for creating valid documents, and the audio collection document includes its document type declaration on a single line of code:

```
<!DOCTYPE audiocollection SYSTEM "AudioCollection.dtd">
```

In this code, the root element of the document is identified as `audiocollection`, and the external DTD as the external file AudioCollection.dtd. This DTD can be used to validate the document, which you will learn about in Chapter 19, "XHTML: XML Meets HTML." The main point to understand now is the structure of the document type declaration and how it identifies the root element and external DTD.

In case it isn't obvious, the root element of a document is the element that contains all other elements. In HTML documents, the root element is `html`. In the audio collection document, it's `audiocollection`.

Modeling XML Data

By now you're probably thoroughly confused by document type declarations and how they are used to describe XML documents. This section will help clarify the role of both document type declarations and DTDs so that you can fully understand why they are an important part of XML.

In case it's not abundantly clear yet, XML is all about the structuring of information. Almost every facet of XML is directly aimed at accomplishing this task so people can better understand information. To do this, it's necessary to model the data. An XML document model serves as a template that determines what kind of information can appear in the document, as well as how it's structured.

The XML document models are sometimes referred to as *schemas*, and are used to describe a class of data. For example, the information contained within the audio collection document you saw earlier in the chapter could be considered a class of data: audio data. Once you've established a class of data by using a schema, you can create highly structured documents that can be tested for validity. The benefit of having valid documents is that they can be processed with automated programs such as search engines.

An XML schema describes the arrangement of markup and content within a valid XML document; it must strictly adhere to a schema to be considered a valid document. Knowing this, you can think of a schema as an agreement between an XML document (perhaps a Web page) and the XML vocabulary (HTML) in which it's written.

Consider a simplified, real world analogy. If you meet people and they give you their phone numbers, you expect the number to be in a certain format. If the person gives you an 8-digit number, you immediately know something is wrong. Domestic phone numbers adhere to a ten-digit format. This format is the schema that you use to determine that the 8-digit number is invalid. Although this example is simplified, it nonetheless shows how we employ schemas in many areas other than Web development.

Note

It's perfectly legitimate to create XML documents without schemas, in which case the documents can be well-formed, but not valid.

The specific role of a schema is to describe an XML vocabulary, naming every tag and attribute and their relationships with each other. Of course, a document without a schema can use any custom tag or attribute. This is fine, but it precludes the document from being considered valid. And as you now know, validity is the ultimate goal of all XML documents. If documents without schemas can use any tags or attributes, then it's fair to say that schemas impose constraints on how a document of a certain type can be structured. More specifically, schemas constrain the structure of documents in two ways:

1. They define the data model, which determines the specific order and nesting of elements

2. They establish the data types of document data

The first function is the most important, because it determines which elements can be used in a document and how they relate to one another. DTDs rely primarily on this approach for describing document structure, and are weak in establishing data types for document data. DTDs represent the standard approach for describing document structure, but are at risk of being replaced by an alternative called XML Schema.

XML Schema is a newer approach, promoted by Microsoft, that includes rich support for describing document data. DTDs do a great job detailing what tags and attributes can be used in a document, as well as how they can be nested. But XML Schema goes a step further; you can nail down the data types of document content. The next two sections introduce you to both DTDs and XML Schema, and show you how to use each of them to establish the structure of the audio collection document.

Working with DTDs

Document type definitions serve as the standard schema approach for describing the structure of XML documents. Although DTDs represent the first schema approach for XML, they aren't without flaws. One complaint is that they use a specialized language for describing the structure of XML vocabularies. Although this language is simple, it's cryptic and seemingly unnecessary when you consider that XML itself could be used to describe document structure. The only upside to the special language used in DTDs is that it's compact, making most DTDs relatively small. The DTD language describes the structure of documents, using individual characters such as question marks, asterisks, and plus signs; hence, its cryptic look.

Even so, DTDs are easy to follow once you understand what the different characters mean. For proof, take a look at the following DTD, which describes the structure of the audio collection XML document:

```
<!ELEMENT audiocollection (audio)+>

<!ELEMENT audio (title, artist+, track+, comments?)>
<!ATTLIST audio
  type (rock | pop | jazz | classical | country | soul |
```

```
     hiphop | comedy | other) "rock"
     review (1 | 2 | 3 | 4 | 5) "3"
     year CDATA #IMPLIED>
```

```
<!ELEMENT title (#PCDATA)>
```

```
<!ELEMENT artist (#PCDATA)>
```

```
<!ELEMENT track (#PCDATA)>
```

```
<!ELEMENT comments (#PCDATA)>
```

As you can see, there isn't a whole lot to this DTD. The main thing to understand is the relationship between the elements. Notice that the root `audiocollection` element is listed first. The word `audio` in parentheses next to the `audiocollection` element indicates that the `audiocollection` element contains the `audio` element as a child element. The plus sign (+) next to `audio` indicates that the `audio` element can appear multiple times within the `audiocollection` element.

You'll also see that the `audio` element contains several child elements of its own: `title`, `artist`, `track`, and `comments`. The plus sign next to `artist` and `track` indicate that there can be multiple elements of each. The question mark (?) next to `comments` dictates that the `comments` element is optional but can only be used once. This is the cryptic mumbo-jumbo DTD language I was talking about earlier. It's easy to understand but not necessarily intuitive.

Back to the `audio` element. It has three attributes, as noted by the `ATTLIST` notation in the DTD: `type`, `review`, and `year`. The `type` and `review` attributes are interesting because they specify a list of possible values, along with a default value for each. This is an important part of the DTD because you must adhere to the attribute lists for the `type` and `review` attributes when you create audio collection documents. In other words, the values for these attributes must be one of the values appearing in the lists. The `year` attribute is a text attribute that can contain any kind of text data; the `CDATA` notation indicates that the attribute can contain Character DATA.

You may notice that the remaining elements in the DTD contain #PCDATA, or Parsed Character DATA. This is a fancy way of saying that the elements contain text content.

There are certainly more subtleties to DTD design than I've mentioned in this brief explanation of the audio collection DTD, but I think I've given you an idea how a DTD lays the ground rules of XML vocabularies. More importantly, DTDs provide the guidelines to which XML documents can be compared to determine validity.

Working with XML Schema

I mentioned earlier that Microsoft offers a more powerful alternative to DTDs. This method uses XML as the language describing document structure and also allows you to use specific data types. The Microsoft alternative to DTD is known as XML Schema, and it's quite interesting because it uses a custom XML vocabulary to describe XML documents. This might seem strange at first, but all it means is that you create an XML Schema as an XML document using tags and attributes, much like you create an HTML document. The only thing necessary for you to do differently is learn how to use the XML Schema tags and attributes.

Rather than spending time studying the details of the XML Schema vocabulary, let's look at an example. Following is the code for an XML Schema that describes the structure of the familiar audio collection document:

```xml
<?xml version="1.0"?>

<Schema name="AudioCollectionSchema"
  xmlns="urn:schemas-microsoft-com:xml-data"
  xmlns:dt="urn:schemas-microsoft-com:datatypes">
  <ElementType name="title" content="textOnly"/>

  <ElementType name="artist" content="textOnly"/>

  <ElementType name="track" content="textOnly"/>

  <ElementType name="comments" content="textOnly"/>

  <AttributeType name="type" dt:type="enumeration"
    dt:values="rock pop jazz classical country soul hiphop
    comedy other" default="rock"/>

  <AttributeType name="review" dt:type="enumeration"
    dt:values="1 2 3 4 5" default="3"/>

  <AttributeType name="year" dt:type="int"/>

  <ElementType name="audio" content="eltOnly">
    <element type="title" minOccurs="1" maxOccurs="1"/>
    <element type="artist" minOccurs="1" maxOccurs="*"/>
    <element type="track" minOccurs="1" maxOccurs="*"/>
    <element type="comments" minOccurs="0" maxOccurs="1"/>
    <attribute type="type"/>
    <attribute type="review"/>
    <attribute type="year"/>
  </ElementType>

  <ElementType name="audiocollection" content="eltOnly">
    <element type="audio" minOccurs="1" maxOccurs="*"/>
  </ElementType>
</Schema>
```

Although it isn't nearly as compact (or as cryptic), this XML Schema is roughly the equivalent of the DTD for the audio collection document that you saw in the previous section. Unlike the DTD version, XML Schema is fairly easy to understand because it uses XML tags and attributes. For example, the minOccurs and maxOccurs attributes of the

`<element>` tag are used to determine how many times an element may appear as a child, as opposed to the strange character codes used to carry out the same chore in the DTD.

Additionally, the content of each element is specified clearly in the `content` attribute, set to `eltOnly` (elements only), `textOnly` (text only), `mixed` (elements and text), or `empty`. Perhaps the most significant improvement of XML Schema over DTDs is the usage of specific data types. For example, the `year` attribute is specified as type `int`, which means that it's an integer number.

Knowing how XML Schema improves on its DTD equivalent, you might think that all XML vocabularies use XML Schema to describe their structure. However, this currently isn't the case. The reality is that DTDs were around before XML and are widely used in large information management programs. This means that they aren't going anywhere in a hurry. The other compelling reason not to throw away DTDs is they work. XML Schema might work better, but such changes take time to catch on. For now you may find yourself creating both a DTD and an XML Schema for any XML vocabularies that you dream up.

The Practical Side of XML

So far this chapter has spent a great deal of time delving into the theory of XML and how it works as an organizational technology for information. What I haven't spent much time doing is assessing the role of XML in your life as a Web page creator. Sure, your new XML knowledge can be put to great use impressing your geeky friends the next time document structure becomes the hot topic at a lunch meeting. But exactly how does XML benefit you in terms of your Web pages?

The relevance of XML to Web pages is twofold. First and foremost, the Web is evolving toward a more structured information repository, so you might as well jump on the bandwagon early. Chapter 19, "XHTML: XML Meets HTML," goes much further into this topic. For now, just take my word that XML is dictating the future of HTML. The second aspect of XML that relates heavily to Web pages is the use of specialized XML vocabularies to mark up special types of information. Custom XML vocabularies will allow you to create documents containing information that can be tied into your Web pages.

The discussion of DTDs and XML Schema in this chapter assumed to some degree that you're interested in creating your own XML vocabulary. For example, the audio collection document uses a custom XML vocabulary with its own set of tags and attributes. Although this is a powerful use of XML and quite liberating, you probably won't be creating your own XML vocabularies often, if ever. But you will use vocabularies created by others. A wide variety of XML vocabularies exist today for marking up all kinds of interesting data in XML documents. Here are examples, along with the types of data they model:

- MathML: mathematical equations
- VML: two-dimensional vector graphics
- 3DML: three-dimensional virtual worlds
- VoxML: interactive speech
- SMIL: multimedia integration
- RELML: real estate listings
- HRMML: human resource management
- XMLNews: news articles
- P3P: personal privacy

As you can see, XML vocabularies vary greatly in the kinds of data they model. If you include any of these kinds of data in your Web pages, you should consider using an XML vocabulary to mark up the data.

Conclusion

I sincerely hope you can forgive me for blindsiding you with an enormous amount of XML theory in this chapter. Trust me, I would have loved nothing more than to explain XML by means of a bunch of memorable example pages, but XML is not that kind of animal. In truth, XML is too vague and difficult a technology to explain in a few words.

It's hard to get the point across that XML is an enabling technology, allowing you to do cool things—but it doesn't do much by itself. In order to be fully appreciated, it must be applied, which is why HTML is so much easier to understand than XML. I hope this chapter served as a good introduction to XML, and has given you the courage to press onward.

The chapter began by explaining what XML is, along with how it relates to HTML. You then learned about the major components of XML documents, thanks to the audio collection XML document. From there, you found out that data modeling is an extremely important part of XML; it determines whether XML documents are valid. You finished up the chapter with a quick look at the practical side of XML, and why it is an important technology for Web page designers.

Chapter 18

Styling XML with XSL

Web fact for the day

Sixty-eight percent of Americans who watch television commercials for computer processors—such as the Intel Pentium 3 or 4—actually believe processors speed up Internet connections.

But you know better, right? In fact, it's your modem that determines how fast a connection you have to the Internet. Sure, a faster processor will help your Web browser process and display Web information a little more quickly, but the modem is the limiting factor when it comes to connection speeds. I mention this not to make fun of people's misconceptions about computers, but to point out that computers and the Internet have infiltrated mainstream advertising. Dotcom ads have even come to dominate the biggest advertising event of the year: the Super Bowl!

The significance of advertising with respect to this chapter is that ads are typically all about style. In particular, most television ads attempt to make their products look stylish in order to convince us that we'll be hip if we own them or use them. Although we all understand and appreciate style to different degrees, I think it's safe to say that we are style-conscious animals.

As you might have gathered in the previous chapter, XML is pretty much devoid of style. XML is a calculated, supremely logical markup language that doesn't leave any room for style—and that's a good thing. XML is about rigidly structuring information so that it can be consistently processed and understood without question. However, there comes a time when even the most uptight, unstylish person has to dress up for a special occasion. And the same thing applies to XML. Fortunately, there are several technologies that make it possible to stylize XML documents so that they can be displayed attractively. If you are a style junkie yourself, then you can think of styling an XML document as the XML equivalent of a personal makeover.

Style Sheets and XML

Styling an XML document means creating a description of how you want the information in the document to appear visually. As the information typically doesn't include special cues for how it should appear, it's entirely up to you to determine by applying a set of styles to the document.

This set of styles is specified in a *style sheet*, a special document containing a list of styles that apply to the information when using an XML document. It's used to determine how to display the XML information in a program such as a Web browser. Again, style sheets are needed because many, if not most, XML documents aren't designed to be viewed directly.

This separation of content from formatting is one of the design goals of XML; it encourages the distinction between pure information and the manner in which it's to appear. For example, consider the weather report on local television. On the screen, you see a colorful map with neat graphics showing rain, wind, sun, and other weather elements as they sweep across the country.

However, the information driving that map is really just a bunch of numbers that indicate the temperature, wind speed, relative humidity, and barometric pressure at given points on the map. Weather software takes the data and uses it to generate the colorful map. Or to put it another way, the weather software stylizes the data so that it's easier to view and understand. For all you know, the weather data could be stored in an XML document. If that were the case, then a style sheet would dictate the appearance of the weather map.

More specifically, a style sheet defines presentation rules describing the display of an XML document's parts. These rules are used to convert the information in an XML document into a form suitable for presentation. In the case of a Web browser, a style sheet converts an XML document into a suitable HTML document that can be viewed in the browser.

Hold on there—how did HTML suddenly enter the picture? HTML is a markup language used primarily to display information on a Web page, viewable in a Web browser. One way to obtain a graphical/stylized version of an XML document is to intelligently convert it to an HTML document. I use the word "intelligently," because you may not want every piece of information in an XML document to be displayed. Fortunately, style sheets give you exacting control over this conversion.

In Chapter 11, "Style Sheet Basics," you learned how to use cascading style sheets (CSS) to add style to HTML documents. CSS can certainly be used with XML documents, but they aren't as powerful as another style sheet technology known as eXtensible Style Language (XSL). XSL is a powerful XML vocabulary used to stylize XML documents.

Understanding XSL

XSL is a style sheet technology used to convert XML documents into other formats. This conversion process is often referred to as *transforming* an XML document. The idea is that by transforming a document, you can reformat it to be suitable for viewing in an existing program, such as a Web browser. Keep in mind, however, that XSL is not targeted simply at transforming XML documents into HTML documents. XSL is very general and can be used to transform XML documents into virtually any other markup language.

This is significant because Web browsers aren't necessarily the only applications to which XML is relevant. What if your favorite fast-food restaurant wanted to code their menu in XML? A computer inside the restaurant would need to transform this XML code into a form that could be displayed on a screen at the drive-through window, and possibly even be read aloud to the customer. This might seem like a bit of a stretch, but XML and XSL are that broad in their goals.

Moving away from fried foods, let's clarify exactly what it is that XSL brings to the XML table:

- XSL transforms XML documents into other document formats
- XSL adds styles to XML documents, by using special formatting rules

These two facets of XSL are carried out by two different parts of XSL technology: XSL Transformation (XSLT) and XSL Formatting Objects. With XSLT, you can transform XML documents into other document formats, such as HTML. XSL Formatting Objects is a newer XSL technology that provides many of the same styling features as CSS, plus many new ones. Both XSLT and XSL Formatting Objects are XML vocabularies; you use them by creating XML documents with elements and attributes that describe how to carry out each portion of the transformation or styling process.

Note

As of this writing, XSL Formatting Objects is so new that it isn't yet supported in any Web browsers. However, XSLT is supported in Internet Explorer 5.5, so you can use it today. Since XSLT is the only part of XSL that is currently supported in Web browsers, the remainder of the chapter focuses solely on it. This means that you'll be learning how to use XSLT to transform XML documents for viewing in Web browsers.

Applying XSL to XML Documents

Similar to an HTML document, an XSL style sheet must be processed to be of any use. Although they can be processed in any type of XML program, they will be processed primarily by Web browsers, at least in the immediate future. It's important to understand this process because it reveals the connection between the style sheet and XML documents—and how those documents are transformed by applying the style sheet.

Envision XML documents as an upside-down, tree-like structure of elements—like the directory tree for your hard disk—with a sole root element at the top of the tree. Any elements appearing beneath the root element are considered branches of the tree. This XML tree continues to grow as additional elements are nested within each other. As examples, the `html` element is the root element of HTML documents; the `audiocollection` element is the root element of the audio collection document you saw in the previous chapter. The root element is significant because it represents the starting point for an XSL processor.

Note

An XSL processor is an application that processes an XSL style sheet and uses that style sheet to transform XML data in an HTML document. In most cases, you will rely on an XSL processor that is built into a Web browser such as Internet Explorer.

When an XSL processor processes a style sheet, it looks for templates that describe special patterns in an XML document. Trust me, this isn't as tricky as it sounds. A *template* in an XSL style sheet simply describes *how* the XML information is to be transformed whenever it is encountered. The XSL processor determines *which* XML information to transform by searching for information that matches a certain *pattern*.

A pattern could be something as simple as an element name. Whenever the XSL processor encounters an element named `artist`, for example, it applies a certain template to transform the data. This pattern-matching scheme requires an XSL processor to have an intimate connection with the XML document being styled. The pattern-matching process begins with the root element of the document and continues throughout the entire document.

When the XSL processor finishes working through an entire XML document, matching patterns and applying templates, you have a complete transformation of the original XML document. If you transform an XML document into an HTML document, it can be displayed in a Web browser.

The beauty of this is that the processing work happens behind the scenes. In other words, if you open an XML document in Internet Explorer, its style sheet will automatically be processed and applied to the document to generate an HTML document that can be displayed in the browser window. Someone viewing the resulting Web page would never know what was going on behind the scenes to give the XML data a visual appearance.

Peeking Inside a Style Sheet

So far I've done my best to bore you with abstract theory surrounding XSL style sheets and how useful they are. Now it's time to move beyond theory and dig into the guts of XSL style sheets and how they are structured. As you begin to learn the coding specifics of XSL style sheets, understand that this is only an introduction. XSL is a broad, often complex technology, so I've distilled the basics and will give you enough fundamental knowledge to start using XSL style sheets today.

The basic structure of XSL style sheets is surprisingly straightforward. As we've discussed, XSL style sheets basically consist of two types of information: patterns and templates.

The next two sections explore how patterns and templates are used to transform XML documents for display purposes. First, let's look at the overall structure of XSL style sheets, specifically the `stylesheet` element, required as the root element of all XSL style sheets. This element, along with several other XSL elements and attributes, is part of the XSLT vocabulary. To use elements and attributes in this vocabulary, you first declare the namespace where they're contained. A *namespace* is an identifier for XML documents, and in this case serves to identify the XSL vocabulary. Following is an example of how to use the `stylesheet` element to declare the XSL namespace:

```
<xsl:stylesheet xmlns:xsl="http://www.w3.org/TR/xsl/">
```

This code makes available all the elements and attributes in the XSL namespace, and assigns them the prefix `xsl`. This is standard practice in all XSL style sheets. The implication of this code is that you must precede all XSL element and attribute names with the prefix `xsl`. This will make much more sense in the next two sections as you begin to see how patterns and templates are coded in XSL.

Drilling for Data with Patterns

You learned earlier in the chapter that when an XSL style sheet is processed, patterns are the basis for finding XML data to transform. Patterns are simply a means of performing matches for XML data. More specifically, a pattern identifies an element or attribute, in an XML document, that corresponds to a branch of the XML "tree."

Although this may sound abstract, patterns are identified in a familiar manner. Patterns look much like paths in a file system such as your hard drive, except that patterns specify elements and attributes, while paths specify folders and files. As an example, consider the `head` element that appears within the `html` element of an HTML document. To identify the `head` element using a pattern, you simply refer to it as `html/head`. Patterns really are this simple.

Don't forget that the significance of patterns is to identify a portion of an XML document for transformation. When the XSL processor matches up a chunk of XML data by using a pattern, it shuttles the data to a template to be transformed. (More on templates in the next section.) If you want to process an entire XML document using a single pattern, specify the pattern as a single forward slash (/); this identifies the root element of the document. When specifying other patterns, the pattern for the root element is assumed; this pattern for the root element is known as the *root pattern*. That's why the `html/head` pattern you just learned didn't begin with a forward slash. This means that all patterns are referenced with respect to the root pattern (/).

This explanation is simplistic because patterns can be used to perform complex matching operations. In fact, patterns represent a scaled-down query language that can be used to carefully control the portions of XML documents that are transformed. Going any deeper into patterns is beyond the scope of our needs for this book, so let's move on to templates.

Transforming Information with Templates

Templates are used in XSL to carry out the transformation of XML data. When an XSL processor matches a pattern in a style sheet, the XML data associated with the pattern is routed through a template and transformed. There's nothing magical or tricky about templates—they simply accept a chunk of XML data and transform it into another format, such as HTML code to be displayed in a Web browser. An XSL style sheet can contain as many templates as necessary to carry out a transformation, or as few as one. When multiple templates are used in a style sheet, each corresponds to a different section of an XML document. Think of templates as little workers that take on the task of transforming different sections of an XML document.

Keep in mind that XSL is itself an XML vocabulary, meaning that XSL style sheets are coded using XML. The element used to define a template in a style sheet is `xsl:template`. A pattern is associated with a template by the `match` attribute of the `xsl:template` element. As an example, the following code shows how to start a template matched to the root element of a document:

```
<xsl:template match="/">
```

This code means that the template will transform the document beginning with the root element, which means the entire document will be processed by the template. You will typically create templates that match elements beneath the root element. Here's another example of a more complete template that matches the `artist` element of the audio collection document:

```
<xsl:template match="audiocollection/audio/artist">
...
</xsl:template>
```

As you can see, the `artist` element is specified by listing its parent elements. Notice the closing `</xsl:template>` tag, which is necessary for all templates. Of course, this template still doesn't do anything, as is evident by the ellipsis (. . .) between the `<xsl:template>` tags. The ellipsis doesn't actually appear in the code—it is used to show you where code for the template would normally appear. To carry out a transformation on data within the `artist` element, you must use the `<xsl:value-of/>` tag, as the following code demonstrates:

```
<xsl:template match="audiocollection/audio/artist">
  <b>Artist: </b><xsl:value-of/>
</xsl:template>
```

This code shows that the data stored in the `artist` element can be formatted for display purposes by placing the bold text "Artist:" in front of it. If you recall, the `<b>` tag is used in HTML to apply a bold font to text. In this code the `xsl:value-of` element serves as a placeholder for the content in the `artist` element. This meaning and the code's usefulness will be more apparent in the following paragraph, which explains the details of the `xsl:value-of` element.

The `xsl:value-of` element is one of several used to create templates and help transform XML documents. Following are perhaps the most commonly used of these elements, all of which are included in the standard XSL namespace you learned about earlier in this chapter:

- `xsl:value-of`—inserts the value (content) of an XML element or attribute
- `xsl:if`—performs a conditional match for a template
- `xsl:for-each`—loops through the elements in an XML document
- `xsl:apply-templates`—applies a template to an XML document

These elements are explained in more detail in the next few sections. Later in the chapter, you create a style sheet that formats and displays the audio collection document.

The `xsl:value-of` Element

The `xsl:value-of` element is used to insert the value of an element or attribute into a transformed document. You have the ability to place HTML code around the `xsl:value-of` element, which affects how the value is displayed in the resulting Web page. This allows you to include HTML code in a style sheet, with placeholders for XML data inserted via the `xsl:value-of` element. Following is an example of a template that uses the `xsl:value-of` element to display the `title` element of the audio collection as a large heading:

```
<xsl:template match="title">
  <h1><xsl:value-of/></h1>
</xsl:template>
```

Note the absence of the parent elements (`audiocollection/audio`) from the `match` attribute in this code. This is because you will use the `xsl:for-each` element to cycle through the elements in an XML document, alleviating the need to specify the full pattern for the `title` element. This will make more sense in the section where you learn about the `xsl:for-each` element.

The `xsl:if` Element

Similar to an `if` statement in a programming language such as Java or BASIC, the `xsl:if` element is used to conditionally match an element or attribute in a template. To establish the condition that's matched, the `xsl:if` element uses the same `match` attribute that you learned about earlier with the `xsl:template` element. The most common use of the `match` attribute is to check for a specific value in an element or attribute. Following is an example of how you might use the `xsl:if` element to match only jazz entries in the audio collection:

```
<xsl:if match="@type=jazz">

  <xsl:apply-templates select="audio"/>

</xsl:if>
```

In this example, the `type` attribute of the `audio` element is used as the basis for the conditional match. More specifically, the value of the `type` attribute must be *jazz* for the match to occur. If it does, the template for the `audio` element is applied and the audio data is transformed. The net effect of this code is that the audio collection data is filtered so that only jazz entries are transformed and displayed. It's important to note that the @ symbol in the code is used to signify that `type` is an attribute, not an element.

The `xsl:for-each` Element

Perhaps the most powerful of the XSL template elements is the `xsl:for-each` element. It's used to create a loop that steps through all the elements in an XML document to match patterns and apply templates. The `select` attribute of the `xsl:for-each` element determines which elements of the document are included in the looping process. It's also possible to alter the order of the looping by setting the `order-by` attribute of the `xsl:for-each` element. The best way to understand how the `xsl:for-each` element works is to look at a quick example:

```
<table>
<xsl:for-each order-by="+ review"
  select="audiocollection/audio">
  <tr>
    <td><xsl:value-of select="artist"/></td>
    <td><xsl:value-of select="title"/></td>
    <td><xsl:value-of select="@review"/></td>
  </tr>
</xsl:for-each>
</table>
```

This example begins to show the power of XSL. The `xsl:for-each` element is used in this code to step through all the `audio` elements in the audio collection document. The order in which the elements are processed is determined by the `order-by` attribute, which states that the elements should be ordered according to their review, and in increasing order ("+ review"). Within the `xsl:for-each` element the artist, title, and review values for each `audio` element are formatted together as a row of table data. This code takes the audio collection document and formats it as an HTML table so that it can be viewed in a Web page.

The `xsl:apply-templates` **Element**

The `xsl:apply-templates` element is used to apply a template to a portion of an XML document. Templates improve the organization of style sheets by isolating the transformation code associated with each part of an XML document. Before applying a template with the `xsl:apply-templates` element, you must first use the `match` attribute of the `xsl:template` element to specify the element or attribute that's transformed by the template. Following is an example of how the `match` attribute is used with the `xsl:template` element to identify the `comments` element of the audio collection document:

```
<xsl:template match="comments">
  <b>Comments:</b><br/><xsl:value-of/><br/><br/>
</xsl:template>
```

Notice that the `match` attribute is set to `"comments"`, which means that the template applies only to `comments` elements within the document. The code within the template then uses the `<xsl:value-of/>` tag to insert the value of the `comments` element and transform it for display purposes with the help of some HTML code.

Once you've defined a template with the `match` attribute of the `xsl:template` element, you can then use the `xsl:apply-templates` element to apply the template to the style sheet. Following is an example of how to use the `xsl:apply-templates` element to apply the "comments" template:

```
<xsl:apply-templates select="audiocollection/audio/comments"/>
```

This code causes the style sheet to associate `comments` elements with the "comments" template. The end result is that `comments` elements appearing in an XML document are transformed according to the "comments" template of the style sheet.

Constructing Your Own XSL Style Sheet

Before you officially begin this section, take a moment to recover from what you've learned so far in this chapter. Admittedly, XSL style sheets aren't the easiest things in the world to comprehend at first. Don't worry if this chapter has been overwhelming. XSL style sheets go several steps beyond HTML and even XML, and can almost be considered a type of programming. In fact, you were somewhat equipped for this chapter thanks to what you learned back in Chapter 14, "Dynamic HTML." In many ways, you can think of XSL as a type of scripting language, even though it's completely focused on processing XML documents.

Now that you've had a breather and are ready to proceed, I have good news: the remainder of this chapter is focused on creating an XSL style sheet that will transform the previous chapter's audio collection document into an HTML document to be viewed in a Web browser. Not only is this a good example of an XSL style sheet, but it opens up the possibility for you to create your own audio collection documents in XML, and then integrate them into your Web site by using an XSL style sheet.

Before getting into the details of the style sheet, it's worth revisiting the audio collection XML document to make sure you remember how it's structured. Here's the code:

```
<?xml version="1.0"?>
<?xml-stylesheet href="AudioCollection.xsl" type="text/xsl"?>
<!DOCTYPE audiocollection SYSTEM "AudioCollection.dtd">

<audiocollection>
  <!-- This is the Rock section of the collection. -->
  <audio type="rock" review="5" year="1990">
    <title>Cake</title>
    <artist>The Trash Can Sinatras</artist>
    <track>Obscurity Knocks</track>
    <track>Maybe I Should Drive</track>
    <track>Thrupenny Tears</track>
    <track>Even the Odd</track>
    <track>The Best Man's Fall</track>
    <track>Circling the Circumference</track>
    <track>Funny</track>
    <track>Only Tongue Can Tell</track>
    <track>You Made Me Feel</track>
    <track>January's Little Joke</track>
    <comments>Brilliant first release from the most underrated
    band in existence.</comments>
  </audio>

  <!-- This is the Jazz section of the collection. -->
  <audio type="jazz" review="5" year="1993">
    <title>Criss-Cross</title>
    <artist>Thelonious Monk</artist>
    <track>Hackensack</track>
    <track>Tea for Two</track>
    <track>Criss-Cross</track>
    <track>Eronel</track>
    <track>Rhythm-A-Ning</track>
    <track>Don't Blame Me</track>
    <track>Think of One</track>
    <track>Crepuscule with Nellie</track>
    <track>Pannonica</track>
    <comments>Excellent collection of Monk across five
    different sessions.</comments>
  </audio>

  <!-- This is the Hip Hop section of the collection. -->
  <audio type="hiphop" review="5" year="1987">
    <title>Paid In Full</title>
    <artist>Eric B. &amp; Rakim</artist>
    <track>I Ain't No Joke</track>
    <track>Eric B. Is on The Cut</track>
    <track>My Melody</track>
    <track>I Know You Got Soul</track>
    <track>Move the Crowd</track>
    <track>Paid in Full</track>
```

```
    <track>As the Rhyme Goes On</track>
    <track>Chinese Arithmetic</track>
    <track>Eric B. Is President</track>
    <track>Extended Beat</track>
    <comments>Possibly the best rap recording of all
    time.</comments>
  </audio>
</audiocollection>
```

As you can see, the audio collection document starts with an audiocollection element as its root element. Beneath this root element are several audio elements that are used to mark up individual entries in the audio collection. Each audio element then contains several other child elements (title, artist, track, comments), along with a few attributes (type, review, year). With this document structure in mind, it makes sense that an XSL style sheet for the document would need to step through the individual audio elements and format each one for display. If you recall, the xsl:for-each element allows you to step through elements in an XML document. Following is the beginning of the xsl:for-each element that makes this possible for the audio collection document:

```
<xsl:for-each select="audiocollection/audio">
```

As each audio element is processed within this loop, you will want to apply templates to transform different parts of the document. Following is the complete xsl:for-each element, which applies templates for the most important parts of the audio collection document:

```
<xsl:for-each select="audiocollection/audio">
  <xsl:apply-templates select="title"/>
  <xsl:apply-templates select="@year"/>
  <xsl:apply-templates select="artist"/>
  <xsl:apply-templates select="track"/>
  <xsl:apply-templates select="comments"/>
</xsl:for-each>
```

A loop is established that steps through each audio element in the XML document and applies templates for the title element, year attribute, artist element, track element, and comments element. Now it's time to put these templates together in order to transform each of the elements and attributes. Following are the templates for this style sheet:

```
<xsl:template match="title">
  <b>Title: </b><i><xsl:value-of/></i>
</xsl:template>

<xsl:template match="@year">
  (<xsl:value-of/>)<br/>
</xsl:template>

<xsl:template match="artist">
  <b>Artist: </b><xsl:value-of/><br/>
  <b>Tracks:</b><br/>
</xsl:template>
```

```
<xsl:template match="track">
  <xsl:value-of/><br/>
</xsl:template>

<xsl:template match="comments">
  <b>Comments:</b><br/><xsl:value-of/><br/><br/>
</xsl:template>
```

Although this template code looks somewhat messy on the surface, if you look closely at how each element and attribute is transformed, you'll realize that it's quite simple. For example, look closely at the template for the title element. All it does is display the text "Title:" in bold, followed by the value of the title element in italics. The template for the year attribute continues by placing the year value in parentheses, followed by a line break. We'll look at the results of this code in just a moment. But first, it's important to examine the entire audio collection style sheet (AudioCollection.xsl), which follows:

```
<?xml version="1.0"?>
<xsl:stylesheet xmlns:xsl="http://www.w3.org/TR/WD-xsl">
  <xsl:template match="/">
    <html><head><title>Audio Collection XML Example</title></head>
      <body bgcolor="#FFFFFF">
        <h2>My Audio Collection</h2>
        <xsl:for-each select="audiocollection/audio">
          <xsl:apply-templates select="title"/>
          <xsl:apply-templates select="@year"/>
          <xsl:apply-templates select="artist"/>
          <xsl:apply-templates select="track"/>
          <xsl:apply-templates select="comments"/>
        </xsl:for-each>
      </body>
    </html>
  </xsl:template>

<xsl:template match="title">
  <b>Title: </b><i><xsl:value-of/></i>
</xsl:template>

<xsl:template match="@year">
  (<xsl:value-of/>)<br/>
</xsl:template>

<xsl:template match="artist">
  <b>Artist: </b><xsl:value-of/><br/>
  <b>Tracks:</b><br/>
</xsl:template>

<xsl:template match="track">
  <xsl:value-of/><br/>
</xsl:template>
```

```
<xsl:template match="comments">
  <b>Comments:</b><br/><xsl:value-of/><br/><br/>
</xsl:template>
```

```
</xsl:stylesheet>
```

The most interesting aspect of this style sheet is that it includes a considerable amount of familiar HTML code. This is because the document created by the transformation of the audio collection is an HTML document; it must conform to the structure of a complete HTML document. That's why you see the `<html>`, `<head>`, and `<body>` tags in the code. Also important is how the main section of the style sheet is the template for the root element (`/`), which contains the loop that steps through the audio elements and applies the remaining templates in the style sheet.

The code for the audio collection style sheet is interesting in terms of its organization, but it wouldn't mean much if you couldn't use it. Fortunately, you can use it to transform the audio collection document and view the results in Internet Explorer. Figure 18-1 shows the audio collection XML document as it's styled for display by the audio collection XSL style sheet.

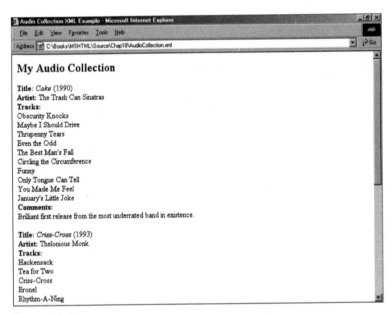

Figure 18-1.
The audio collection XSL style sheet allows you to view a neatly formatted version of the audio collection XML document.

If you noticed that the actual document opened in Internet Explorer is the AudioCollection.xml document, you may be curious as to how Internet Explorer knows that there's a style sheet for the document. You must use a special processing instruction (xml-stylesheet) in the XML document to indicate that it has an XSL style sheet. The following code shows how this processing instruction appears in the audio collection XML document:

```
<?xml-stylesheet href="AudioCollection.xsl" type="text/xsl"?>
```

Mainly notice in this code that the file name of the XSL style sheet is specified in the href attribute. This makes it possible to create different style sheets that provide different ways of viewing an XML document. To use a different style sheet, you just change the value of the href attribute in the processing instruction.

Conclusion

This concludes one of the most ambitious chapters of the book. Even if you found XSL style sheets to be difficult to grasp, hopefully you can appreciate the power they offer in terms of adding style to XML documents so that they can be displayed attractively. As you've probably surmised throughout this chapter, XSL is a "deep" technology, and this chapter only scratched the surface of it. Does this mean you need to go into seclusion and become an XSL wizard in order to be a good Web designer? Absolutely not. What it does mean is that you are now much more informed about how, thanks to XSL, XML documents can be used within existing Web pages. And if you should decide you want to learn more about XSL, there are plenty of good books to help.

This chapter began by introducing the concept of style sheets as they relate to XML. You then found out about XSL and the unique approach it takes to providing a means of styling XML documents. From there you learned how XSL style sheets are processed, and how this processing affects the transformation of XML documents. You dove headfirst into the specifics of XSL style sheets and how they are structured by patterns and templates. The chapter concluded by guiding you through the development of a complete XSL style sheet—which I hope helped to put all that you've learned into perspective.

Chapter 19

XHTML: XML Meets HTML

Okay, I admit that this fact has nothing to do with the World Wide Web or HTML. But it's interesting and highlights that significant oversights occur even on a popular news show. Fortunately, the globe on the NBC Nightly News has no direct bearing on the real world, so the oversight had no serious impact.

In the Web world, HTML has a few problems that can't be treated as mere oversights. One is the loose structure of the HTML language in coding Web pages. Like the NBC globe, this lack of structure isn't noticeable to most Web surfers. But it does have ramifications that affect the future of the Web, its overall power, and its usefulness. XHTML, or eXtensible HTML, is a technology developed to add structure to HTML code and establish ground rules for a better, more powerful Web.

XHTML is the application of XML to HTML; in other words, the rigid rules of XML are applied to familiar HTML elements and attributes. This added structure takes HTML to a new level of consistency and compatibility. Browsers and other Web-based programs will ultimately have the ability to perform advanced processing of HTML documents. This chapter explores XHTML and how it came to be. You will examine the differences between XHTML and HTML, and learn why XHTML offers the possibility for a brighter future with a more structured Web. Along with learning XHTML background and theory, you will find out how to create and validate XHTML documents—as well as convert HTML documents to XHTML.

The Significance of XHTML

It would be easy for me to say that XML is an interesting technology, so it's a great idea to blend it with HTML. This might be a true statement, but busy Web developers need a much better reason to tinker with anything but the familiar HTML. You might not realize that much of what's on the Web looks good because Web browsers do an impressive job of displaying pages built from butchered HTML code that violates fundamental rules of the HTML language. It's a good thing browsers don't pop up error messages every time a Web page is coded improperly.

The Problem with HTML

If you ask your average Web surfers, they would say that the Web works just fine. But if you ask an experienced Web page designer about the difficulties with HTML structure, you would likely hear something I can't print. It's not that it's a flawed technology; it's that HTML has been forced to solve a problem it was never intended to solve. HTML was originally designed to share technical notes among scientific researchers, which required little in the way of formatting for display.

However, the HTML language changed dramatically when the first Web browser appeared. HTML was the most convenient approach at hand for creating Web pages. New features that were added quickly to HTML only twisted the language into doing unsupported things such as laying out graphical information. To make things worse, browser vendors scrambled to add new features that only worked on their browsers.

Of course, the leniency of browsers shielded users from the coding inconsistencies of Web developers, but at what cost? Complicated HTML processors in Web browsers, not to mention Web pages that don't work reliably across different browsers.

The XHTML Solution

So how does XML solve the problems of HTML? As you know, XML can give structure to virtually any kind of information; XHTML is a specific XML vocabulary you use to create highly structured Web pages. XHTML enforces the structure of XML within the HTML language, which is quite beneficial for Web designers and users alike. One huge benefit is that XHTML documents can be validated, which means they can be analyzed for correctness. Don't worry, I'm not talking about political correctness. In this case, correctness means that an XHTML document meets all the coding requirements of the XML language, as well as adhering to the rules of an XHTML schema (document type definition or DTD).

Validated XHTML code is extremely important because it alleviates the need for browsers to perform tricky analysis of documents to determine how they should be displayed. It also puts an end to the coding tricks that some Web designers use to make Web browsers do things for which they weren't intended. For example, there have been some known discrepancies between the manner in which different browsers process certain HTML tags. By taking advantage of such discrepancies, Web designers have sometimes been able to get interesting effects on one browser at the expense of other browsers.

Note

To refresh your memory, schemas are used to describe the structure of an XML document. The DTD is the default schema technique used with XML documents.

One solution to the HTML formatting problem is the now-popular style sheet. But style sheets don't address the fundamental structure problem of HTML. Only by enforcing the rules of XML can you tie up the loose ends of HTML. This is where XHTML comes in. Yet, even it won't have an overnight impact on the Web; unstructured HTML will likely be around for a long time.

Additionally, XHTML and style sheets involve a steeper learning curve, so Web developers will likely take their time switching over. XHTML also requires planning, which isn't something all Web designers take the time to do. So, browsers will continue supporting unstructured Web pages, but developers will phase in the structured XHTML code as its benefits become more visible. Visual Web design tools will likely play an important role in this goal because many Web designers already use them. They automatically generate code for Web pages, an ideal way to transition.

The Leap from HTML to XHTML

At this point, you're probably thinking that XHTML is a complicated technology that requires you to learn a completely new approach to creating Web pages. As much as I love practical jokes, I wouldn't spring that on you in the last chapter of a book primarily about HTML. The truth is that XHTML isn't all that different than HTML. The latest version of HTML, 4.0, has solved many of the problems in earlier versions. It's a short leap from HTML 4.0 to XHTML. Throughout the remainder of this chapter, we'll assume that sample documents are based upon HTML 4.0.

Note

HTML isn't installed like new versions of software programs. You can't upgrade from HTML 3.0 to HTML 4.0, because HTML is built into Web browsers. You upgrade to a new version of HTML by upgrading your Web browser.

The process of converting an HTML document to XHTML primarily involves making subtle coding changes. Although this can be tedious, you don't need to make sweeping changes to the overall design and layout of an HTML document. It's helpful to run through a checklist that highlights the primary differences between the two markup languages. Following are the main requirements of XHTML documents that should be taken into account when you consider bringing HTML documents up to XHTML standards:

- Place a document type declaration at the top of the page.
- Declare an XHTML DTD in the document declaration.
- Declare an XHTML namespace in the `html` element.
- Ensure that the `head` and `body` are present.
- Make the `title` element the first element in the `head` element.
- Make element and attribute names lowercase.
- Ensure that non-empty elements have end tags.
- Ensure that empty elements consist of an empty tag or a start-tag and end-tag pair.
- Assign values to attributes.
- Enclose attribute values in quotation marks.

Note

Because valid XML documents must be well-formed, you must ensure that an HTML document is well formed when you convert it to XHTML. You may recall that a well-formed XML document is a document that meets the rigid language requirements of XML.

You'll notice that most of these requirements highlight the greater degree of structure inherent in XHTML. Fortunately, you can modify most HTML documents according to these requirements without too much pain and suffering. Later in the chapter you will work through the steps for converting an HTML document to XHTML.

The Need to Accept XHTML

At various times during our formative years, most of us yearn for acceptance. If you agree that the need for human acceptance reaches a peak during the teenage years, then it's safe to say that XHTML is an adolescent technology. XHTML documents need approval, which means that they are deemed accurate and correct in the eyes of others. *Others* in this case are software programs such as Web browsers. Add to that the Web-based programs that process XHTML code. These might be e-commerce programs that handle orders for an online store or they might be search engines.

The Three XHTML DTDs

The standard XHTML DTDs target certain kinds of XHTML documents. Specifically, three XHTML DTDs provide varying levels of detail for XHTML, resulting in three different classifications of XHTML documents.

Note

The XHTML DTDs were created by the World Wide Web Consortium, or W3C, which oversees most Web-related technologies. You can learn a great deal about HTML and XHTML by visiting the W3C Web site at *http://www.w3.org/*.

The three XHTML DTDs provide flexibility in using different XHTML features. They are divided according to the number of XHTML features they include. So, if you create an XHTML Web page that doesn't require advanced features such as frames, you can use a minimal DTD. Smaller DTDs result in faster validation, which is a significant benefit to using an XHTML DTD that includes only the support you need.

This matters, because at some point in the future, XHTML documents will be verified as they are being displayed. Obviously, the faster the validation process the better. Use the full-featured XHTML DTD if you require its functionality. Remember that your choice of DTD could speed up the validation of your documents.

Examine the three XHTML DTDs, listed in order of increasing XHTML features:

- Strict: No HTML presentation elements are available (`font`, `table`, and others)
- Transitional: Adds HTML presentation elements to the strict DTD
- Frameset: Adds support for frames to the transitional DTD

The strict DTD is the most streamlined of the three, and provides a minimal XHTML language for creating documents without any presentation elements. This might sound limiting when you consider that XHTML documents are typically designed for viewing in Web browsers. The idea is that you format such documents for display using style sheets instead of presentation elements. As you might guess, style sheets are the preferred approach for formatting XHTML documents for display, which is what the strict DTD encourages. Not surprisingly, the strict DTD is the most efficient and enables the fastest validation of XHTML documents.

The transitional DTD picks up where the strict DTD leaves off, adding support for presentation elements. You already know that one of the main purposes of XML is to separate presentation code from content, which the transitional DTD violates. Although this may be true, Web designers won't be giving up presentation elements for style sheets anytime soon.

So, the transitional DTD provides validation of XHTML documents that contain presentation elements. It's useful when converting HTML documents to XHTML, because it includes most of the HTML features found in Web pages. But, it doesn't include support for frames, which display multiple Web pages in a single browser window.

The most full-featured XHTML DTD is the frameset DTD, which takes the transitional DTD a step further by adding support for frames. Frames are coded using presentation elements, so the same rules governing the separation of content and formatting apply to the frameset DTD. It's the most complex DTD, and the slowest of the three to validate documents.

Document Validation Requirements

The validation of an XHTML document requires one of the three XHTML DTDs and fulfillment of the following:

- A document type declaration (DOCTYPE) must appear in the document prior to the root element.
- The root element of the document must be html.
- The root element of the document (html) must designate an XHTML namespace using the xmlns attribute.

The first requirement shouldn't come as a surprise given that XHTML DTDs are required to validate XHTML documents. But the last two requirements are unrelated to the DTD. The root element of all XHTML documents must be html, which indicates that the document is in fact an HTML document. This is an interesting requirement, indicating that XHTML is simply a structured version of HTML—not a new language. In other words, XHTML doesn't change the root element to xhtml; the idea is to require minimal changes to HTML documents to be able to validate them as XHTML documents.

The last validation requirement for XHTML documents enforces the use of the XHTML namespace. The xmlns attribute of the root element used to stipulate this namespace is a standard XHTML namespace, as specified by the W3C. The next section describes the code required to specify the DTD and namespace for a valid XHTML document.

Declaring an XHTML DTD and Namespace

Declaring an XHTML DTD and namespace within an XHTML document is straightforward, and requires entering only a few standard lines of code. The DTD is declared at the top of a document before the html root element. The following code shows how the strict DTD is declared:

```
<!DOCTYPE html PUBLIC "-//W3C//DTD XHTML 1.0 Strict//EN"
  "DTD/xhtml1-strict.dtd">
```

This document type declaration identifies the strict DTD as a public resource hosted by the W3C (World Wide Web Consortium). Don't worry about the specifics, because this code is always entered exactly as you see it here. It appears in any XHTML document based on the strict DTD. Transitional and frameset DTDs also have standard document type declarations. Next is the document type declaration for the transitional DTD:

```
<!DOCTYPE html PUBLIC "-//W3C//DTD XHTML 1.0 Transitional//EN"
  "DTD/xhtml1-transitional.dtd">
```

The document type declaration for the frameset DTD is similar:

```
<!DOCTYPE html PUBLIC "-//W3C//DTD XHTML 1.0 Frameset//EN"
  "DTD/xhtml1-frameset.dtd">
```

It's important to include one of these document type declarations in every XHTML document, because every valid XHTML document must specify a DTD. Just be sure to use the appropriate DTD for the required level of XHTML support. Never mind that document type declarations are messy, as long as you understand when to use them.

To ensure that a document is valid, you must also declare an XHTML namespace in the root html element. This namespace is a standard XML namespace that must appear in every XHTML document. Following is the code used to declare the XHTML namespace in the root html element:

```
<html xmlns="http://www.w3.org/1999/xhtml">
</html>
```

As the code shows, the xmlns attribute of the html tag is used to specify the standard XHTML namespace. Like the declaration of the DTD in the document type declaration, the declaration of the XHTML namespace in the html element is required for all valid XHTML documents. Also like DTDs, this code is standard code that will be the same in all of your XHTML documents.

Validating an XHTML Document

Just as human social validation requires other people to affirm your acceptance into a social group, XHTML documents require a special software tool that carries out the validation process. It can be a stand-alone tool or one that's incorporated into a Web program such as a Web browser. Either way, the tool's job is to validate an XHTML document to make sure that it adheres to one of the three XHTML DTDs.

Document validation is extremely valuable for XHTML Web page design because it detects errors in XHTML code, helping to ensure that documents are properly displayed in Web browsers. I'm sure you'll want to get in the habit of validating all XHTML documents that you create. Ideally, Web browsers would support XHTML validation so that you could test XHTML Web pages. Until then, it makes sense to validate XHTML documents some other way.

The W3C has a tool called the W3C Validator that is quite useful in validating XHTML documents. The interesting thing about the W3C Validator is that it's an online tool; you don't have to download or install anything to use it. It validates both HTML and XHTML documents and is available on the Web at *http://validator.w3.org*.

To validate a document using the W3C Validator, enter the URL of the document into the Address box and click Validate This Page. Figure 19-1 shows the results of validating an HTML document using the W3C Validator. The document wasn't coded according to the rigid rules of XHTML for a transitional DTD, and several errors were found.

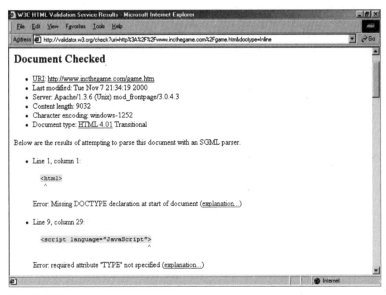

Figure 19-1.
Not surprisingly, the W3C Validator finds lots of errors when attempting to validate a conventional HTML document.

Granted, you can validate XHTML documents that you create yourself, but many documents on the Web are automatically generated by Web programs. With the W3C supporting XHTML as the future of the Web, we can expect browsers to support XHTML validation in the near future.

Creating an XHTML Document

This is the last chapter in the book, and I hope you're comfortable creating HTML documents by now. Creating XHTML documents is similar to creating HTML documents. The important thing to remember is to observe the rigid rules of the XML language and XHTML vocabulary. It's also important to include the standard XHTML DTD and namespace declarations. Following is code for a basic XHTML document that includes a heading and a paragraph, along with a link to a Web page:

```
<!DOCTYPE html PUBLIC "-//W3C//DTD XHTML 1.0 Transitional//EN"
  "DTD/xhtml1-transitional.dtd"   >
```

```
<html xmlns="http://www.w3.org/1999/xhtml">
<head>
  <title>Inc. The Game of Business Link</title>
</head>

<body>
<h1>Inc. The Game of Business
</h1>
<p>
Click <a href = "http://www.incthegame.com">here</a> to go to the Inc. Web
site.
</p>
</body>
</html>
```

This simple XHTML Web page reveals the basic structure of a valid XHTML document. It includes the all-important document type declaration with the transitional XHTML DTD specified. The XHTML namespace is also declared with the xmlns attribute of the <html> tag. The remainder of the document follows the familiar structure of an HTML Web page, containing both head and body sections. Notice the small coding differences, such as all attributes are enclosed in quotation marks and all start tags are accompanied by end tags. You might find this document useful as a template for creating XHTML documents of your own. Figure 19-2 shows the document as viewed in Internet Explorer.

Figure 19-2.
XHTML documents are easily opened and viewed in Internet Explorer.

Creating more complex XHTML documents is no different than the creation of this simple document, except that you include a wider range of tags. Keep in mind that I used a simple text editor, Windows Notepad, to enter the code for this XHTML document. Unfortunately, no visual Web design tools currently generate XHTML code, so you have to code XHTML by hand for the time being.

Another option is to first create an HTML document in a Web design tool such as Microsoft FrontPage and then convert it to XHTML. This saves time if you find it easier to build Web pages visually.

Converting to XHTML

The future belongs to XHTML, but today the Web is built on conventional HTML code that violates most XHTML rules. You can use XHTML for new documents but it's likely that you will convert existing HTML documents to XHTML at some point. If you create Web pages with a visual Web design tool, then you'll need to convert generated code to XHTML. None of the major Web authoring tools currently does so.

XHTML Conversion Guidelines

The good news is that you can follow simple guidelines to convert HTML to XHTML code. These guidelines flow directly from the differences between HTML and XHTML. You can take either of two main approaches to converting HTML to an XHTML document: manual conversion or automated conversion.

Manual conversion means that you make the changes by hand to bring the code up to XHTML standards. The automated approach uses a special tool to analyze and automatically make changes to the code. Hand coding is more accurate but tedious; the automated approach is, well, automated. The downside to the automated approach is that it isn't perfect, so you will probably have to make a few more changes by hand after running the conversion tool.

You learned earlier that the differences between HTML and XHTML are primarily picky language details and therefore don't involve significant changes to HTML documents when you convert them. Use this checklist of syntax differences between HTML and XHTML to make changes in the HTML code:

1. Add a document type declaration that indicates the appropriate standard XHTML DTD. Note that the transitional DTD usually works best for most HTML documents.

2. Declare the XHTML namespace in the `html` element.

3. Ensure that all elements and attributes are defined in the XHTML DTD.

4. Convert all element and attribute names to lowercase.

5. Match every start-tag with an end-tag.

6. At the end of all empty tags, replace `>` with `/>`.

7. Enclose attribute values in quotes (`""`).

8. Assign values to attributes even if they are empty quotation marks.

9. Set the values of required attributes.

You will have a valid XHTML document if you carefully apply this list. Although it might be tedious, it's relatively painless once you're in the habit of eliminating the offending HTML syntax. You will grow to appreciate the structure and consistency of XHTML as you sift through more and more conventional HTML code.

Converting an HTML Document to XHTML

Take a look at the following HTML code for a Top Ten Movies page on the Web to see how simple it is to convert to XHTML:

```
<html>
<body bgcolor=silver text=navy>
<h1>Sparky's Top Ten Movies Page</h1>
Hello, this is the Top Ten Movies page for me, Sparky
the Clown.
The following list of movies are my all-time favorites,
and hopefully you'll like some of them too. If you have
any questions or movie recommendations, please feel free to
<a href=mailto:sparky@sillyclowns.com>send me e-mail</a>.

<p>

<table>
<tr>
  <td>
    <img src=Movie.gif align=left>
  </td>

  <td valign=top>
    Here are the movies:
    <ol>
    <li>Quick Change</li>
    <li>Shakes the Clown</li>
    <li>Killer Klowns from Outer Space</li>
    <li>Funny Bones</li>
    <li>Dumbo</li>
    <li>Big Top Pee-Wee</li>
    <li>The Greatest Show on Earth</li>
    <li>He Who Gets Slapped</li>
    <li>Freaks</li>
    <li>It</li>
    </ol>
  </td>
</tr>
</table>
</body>
</html>
```

This HTML document contains a Web page that might be included on the Web site for Sparky the Clown, whose personal Web page you first created back in Chapter 1. Even though this code contains several coding inconsistencies, it can be viewed with no problems in a Web browser. Figure 19-3 shows the Sparky's Top Ten Movies Web page as viewed in Internet Explorer.

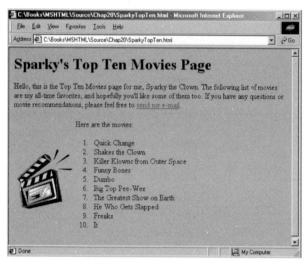

Figure 19-3.
The Sparky's Top Ten Movies Web page displays fine in a Web browser, even though it contains some problematic HTML code.

If you carefully applied the conversion checklist to the Top Ten Movies Web page, you would find several problems that need to be addressed. To get an informed opinion of the *validity* of this document, I suggest running it through the W3C Validator at *http://validator.w3.org/*. To do so, click the *upload files* link on the W3C Validator home page, then browse your hard disk to locate the file to be validated. Figure 19-4 on the next page shows the result of this attempt to validate the Top Ten Movies HTML document.

In addition to validating documents, W3C Validator tracks down problematic code. By working through the code's problems, you'll gain a better understanding of how to convert HTML documents to XHTML. So, let's work on this Web page and bring it up to XHTML standards.

The first step in converting the Top Ten Movies document from HTML is to add the standard document type declaration and namespace declaration for the document. The following code shows how:

```
<!DOCTYPE html PUBLIC "-//W3C//DTD XHTML 1.0 Transitional//EN"
  "DTD/xhtml1-transitional.dtd"   >
<html xmlns="http://www.w3.org/1999/xhtml">
```

These three lines of code should appear at the beginning of the document; note that the third line of code replaces the existing `<html>` tag.

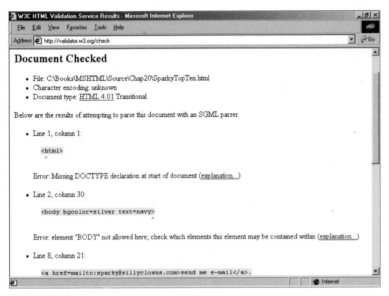

Figure 19-4.
The W3C Validator reveals the problems with the Sparky's Top Ten Movies Web page that prevent it from being considered a valid XHTML document.

A quick look at the previous HTML code reveals that there is no head section. A headless XHTML document is not only gruesome, but also just not allowed. So, the following code adds a suitable head to the document:

```
<head>
  <title>Sparky's Top Ten Movies Page</title>
</head>
```

Now, let's move on to the other problems with this Web page, keeping the conversion checklist in mind. A start-tag and end-tag problem occurs with the `<p>` tag, which is missing a matching `</p>` end tag. This is a common error in Web pages because many Web designers think of the `<p>` tag as a divider between paragraphs—simply not correct. As you know, the `<p>` and `</p>` tags enclose paragraphs, not divide them.

The empty tag problem applies to the `<img>` tag, which should end with `/>`. This coding detail was introduced by XML, so it doesn't appear on many Web pages. You'll need it for any empty elements in the Web pages that you convert to XHTML. Also, little HTML code uses quotation marks for attribute values unless a multiple-word value is necessary. So, you'll need to add quotation marks around most attribute values when you convert to XHTML.

Setting the values of any required attributes is the last problem on the Top Ten Movies Web page. It requires a subtle fix, but it's necessary for XHTML document validation. Although you probably didn't realize it, `alt` is a required attribute of the `<img>` tag. You must give it a value, even if it's just a pair of empty quote marks (""). However, you might as well give the attribute a meaningful value if you're going to the trouble of setting it.

Applying these simple conversion rules is sufficient to convert the Top Ten Movies document to XHTML. This is the successfully converted code for the new XHTML version of the Web page:

```
<!DOCTYPE html PUBLIC "-//W3C//DTD XHTML 1.0 Transitional//EN"
   "DTD/xhtml1-transitional.dtd"    >
<html xmlns="http://www.w3.org/1999/xhtml">
<head>
  <title>Sparky's Top Ten Movie Pages</title>
</head>

<body bgcolor="silver" text="navy">
<h1>Sparky's Top Ten Movies Page</h1>
<p>
Hello, this is the Top Ten Movies page for me, Sparky the Clown.
The following list of movies are my all-time favorites, and
hopefully you'll like some of them too. If you have any questions or movie
recommendations, please feel free to
<a href="mailto:sparky@sillyclowns.com">send me e-mail</a>.
</p>

<table>
<tr>
  <td>
    <img src="Movie.gif" alt="Movie icon" align="left"/>
  </td>

  <td valign="top">
    Here are the movies:
    <ol>
    <li>Quick Change</li>
    <li>Shakes the Clown</li>
    <li>Killer Klowns from Outer Space</li>
    <li>Funny Bones</li>
    <li>Dumbo</li>
    <li>Big Top Pee-Wee</li>
    <li>The Greatest Show on Earth</li>
    <li>He Who Gets Slapped</li>
    <li>Freaks</li>
    <li>It</li>
    </ol>
  </td>
</tr>
</table>
</body>
</html>
```

You might want to run the XHTML document through the W3C Validator at *http://validator.w3.org/* to double-check this conversion. Figure 19-5 shows the results of validating the newly converted XHTML document using the W3C Validator.

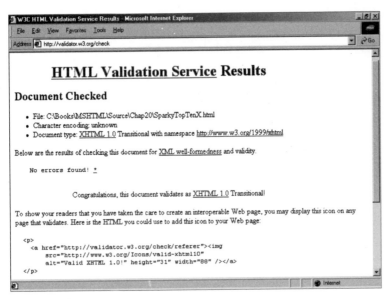

Figure 19-5.
The newly converted Sparky's Top Ten Movies Web page passes the W3C Validator with flying colors.

An Alternative HTML Conversion Option

Admittedly, converting HTML code by hand isn't for everyone. If you don't relish the idea of sifting through HTML code and analyzing syntax, you might consider using an automated tool to carry out the conversion. One such tool that I've used with reasonable success is HTML Tidy, developed by Dave Raggett, an engineer at Hewlett Packard Laboratories in the United Kingdom.

HTML Tidy was originally designed to clean up sloppy HTML code, but it also converts HTML to XHTML. In truth, I might add, the process of translating HTML code to XHTML does boil down to cleaning up sloppy code. The HTML Tidy tool is a command-line tool and is freely available for download from the HTML Tidy Web site at *http://www.w3.org/People/Raggett/tidy/*.

Conclusion

Although XHTML might not strike you as the most fascinating aspect of Web design, it certainly is one of the most important. The very fact that the future of the Web is being described in terms of XHTML is encouragement enough for all Web designers to get up to speed. By learning XHTML alongside HTML, you have a unique perspective on the relationship between the two languages.

Perhaps the most significant benefit of learning XHTML so early in your Web design career is that you won't have to unlearn the HTML coding techniques that are no longer allowed in XHTML. In many ways this puts you ahead of the seasoned HTML gurus who've spent years perfecting coding techniques that are now being phased out by XHTML.

This chapter began by introducing you to XHTML and delineating its relationship to HTML. You learned that XHTML presents a solution to several problems inherent in HTML. You also explored some of the specific coding differences between HTML and XHTML documents, which are important as you move from HTML-based Web pages to XHTML-based Web pages.

You learned about validation next, which is extremely important in XHTML because it determines whether or not an XHTML document is coded properly. After working through the creation of a simple XHTML document, the chapter concluded by guiding you through the conversion of an HTML document to XHTML. You now have the skills to face the future of the Web head-on by creating your Web pages as XHTML documents.

Part 6

Appendixes

Appendix A

HTML Quick Reference

This appendix serves as a quick reference for the most commonly used tags in HTML. This reference doesn't go into painstaking detail about each tag; instead it focuses on the start and end tags and their meanings.

Structural Tags

Structural tags are used in HTML to describe the overall structure of a Web page. Table A-1 lists the HTML structural tags you'll see most often.

Table A-1.   The Most Commonly Used HTML Structural Tags

Start Tag	End Tag	Meaning
`<html>`	`</html>`	Encloses HTML codes
`<head>`	`</head>`	The head of the page
`<title>`	`</title>`	The title of the page
`<body>`	`</body>`	The body of the page
`<!--`	`-->`	A comment that won't be displayed

Text Tags

Text tags are used a great deal in Web pages to lay out and format text content. Table A-2 lists the most commonly used HTML text tags.

Table A-2. The Most Commonly Used HTML Text Tags

Start Tag	End Tag	Meaning
`<p>`	`</p>`	A paragraph of text
`<div>`	`</div>`	A block of content
`<span>`	`</span>`	Inline content
` `	Empty tag*	A line break, which initiates a new line
`<hr>`	Empty tag*	A horizontal line, often called a rule
`<font>`	`</font>`	The font used for text
`<b>`	`</b>`	Bold text
`<i>`	`</i>`	Italic text
`<h1-6>`	`</h1-6>`	Headings
`<tt>`	`</tt>`	Typewriter text

List Tags

List tags make it possible to organize Web content into unordered lists, ordered lists, and even definition lists. Table A-3 shows the most commonly used HTML list tags.

Table A-3. The Most Commonly Used HTML List Tags

Start Tag	End Tag	Meaning
`<ul>`	`</ul>`	An unordered (bulleted) list
`<ol>`	`</ol>`	An ordered (numbered) list
`<li>`	`</li>`	An item in a list
`<dl>`	`</dl>`	A definition list
`<dt>`	`</dt>`	A term in a definition list
`<dd>`	`</dd>`	A definition in a definition list

* Empty tags don't have text content and therefore don't require closing tags such as `</p>` or `</b>`. Instead, empty tags consist of only a starting tag and any appropriate attributes.

Table Tags

Table tags make it possible to create tables that can organize tabular data or control the layout of a Web page. Table A-4 lists the most commonly used HTML table tags.

Table A-4.   The Most Commonly Used HTML Table Tags

Start Tag	End Tag	Meaning
`<table>`	`</table>`	A table
`<tr>`	`</tr>`	A row in a table
`<td>`	`</td>`	A cell of data within a table row
`<th>`	`</th>`	A table heading
`<caption>`	`</caption>`	A table caption

Form Tags

Form tags allow you to create data entry forms that you can use to obtain information from visitors to your Web pages. Table A-5 shows the most commonly used HTML form tags.

Table A-5.   The Most Commonly Used HTML Form Tags

Start Tag	End Tag	Meaning
`<form>`	`</form>`	A form
`<input>`	`</input>`	An input field in a form
`<select>`	`</select>`	A selection list in a form
`<option>`	`</option>`	An option in a form
`<textarea>`	`</textarea>`	A scrolling multi-line text field in a form

Miscellaneous Tags

In addition to the tags shown in Tables A-1 through A-5, some popular HTML tags don't fit the standard categories. These miscellaneous tags are listed in Table A-6.

Table A-6.   **The Other Most Commonly Used HTML Tags**

Start Tag	End Tag	Meaning
`<img>`	Empty tag*	An image
`<a>`	`</a>`	An anchor hyperlink
`<map>`	`</map>`	An image map
`<area>`	`</area>`	An area within an image map
`<meta>`	`</meta>`	Additional information for a Web page
`<style>`	`</style>`	A style sheet
`<link>`	Empty tag*	A link to an external file
`<frameset>`	`</frameset>`	A set of frames
`<frame>`	`</frame>`	A frame within a set

* Empty tags don't have text content and therefore don't require closing tags such as `</p>` or `</b>`. Instead, empty tags consist of only a starting tag and any appropriate attributes.

Appendix B
HTML Resources on the Web

I hope this book serves your every HTML need, but that probably isn't realistic. You'll need additional information about HTML at some point in the future. For more information or even a second opinion, numerous online resources are available to fill you in on the complexities of HTML and other Web technologies. This appendix highlights some of the Web sites I've found most useful as a Web designer.

Microsoft's Web Workshop

http://msdn.microsoft.com/workshop/
Microsoft's Web Workshop site contains a dizzying amount of information on every facet of Web design. Huge sections of the site are devoted to HTML, CSS, and DHTML, not to mention other related sections on security and streaming media, to name but a few of the topics. I encourage you to visit this site and have a look around.

Webmonkey

http://www.webmonkey.com/
Webmonkey is an excellent resource for learning about the practical side of Web design. One of the strong appeals of the Webmonkey site is its numerous short tutorials on virtually all aspects of HTML and Web page design.

HTML Goodies

http://www.htmlgoodies.com/
Like Webmonkey, HTML Goodies is a Web site that's rich in tutorials. It's organized into the primary areas of Web design, and includes articles and discussions related to almost any facet of HTML you can imagine.

HTML Help

http://www.htmlhelp.com/

HTML Help is a Web site that promotes the creation of Web pages that function smoothly across all Web browsers. Emphasis is on developing HTML code that's highly browser-independent. Even if you're okay with supporting a single browser, this is still a good resource to learn about how browser inconsistencies affect HTML code.

The HTML Writer's Guild

http://www.hwg.org/

If you're one of those people who have always dreamed of being part of a guild, now is your chance. The HTML Writer's Guild is an organization of Web designers consisting of over 120,000 members. The HTML Writer's Guild Web site includes resources for designers and is priced reasonably if you feel the need to belong. If nothing else, the HTML Writer's Guild T-shirts are pretty cool.

World Wide Web Consortium

http://www.w3.org/

If you want the absolute bottom line on an issue related to HTML, XML, or CSS, the World Wide Web Consortium (W3C) Web site is the place for you. The W3C oversees HTML specifications and is the governing body for most Web standards. Although much of the documentation is technically arcane, it's nonetheless the last word on the structure of the Web.

Network Solutions

http://www.networksolutions.com/

At some point you may decide to register a domain name and have your very own dot com. When the time comes, drop by the Network Solutions Web site and run a search. If the name you want is available, you can lock it in for a reasonable fee. You might even want to set up a Web hosting service.

Electronic Frontier Foundation

http://www.eff.org/

The Electronic Frontier Foundation (EFF) is a site that doesn't directly have anything to do with HTML or Web page design. It relates to the entire Internet and its continued availability to all of us. Every Web user should have a basic knowledge of their civil rights with respect to the Internet; the EFF Web site is a great place to learn about them.

Appendix C
Using Custom Colors

Color plays an important role in Web pages, entering the HTML code picture in a variety of ways. You will typically need to specify a color as the value of an attribute or style property. For example, the bgcolor attribute for the <body> tag allows you to specify the background color of a Web page. Likewise, the color style property allows you to set the color of text. Both approaches allow you to use standard colors. However, you may want a higher degree of flexibility in your use of color. Consider creating a custom color.

Each color on a Web page is described by a combination of three primary colors: red, green, and blue. A color described using this system is known as an *RGB color;* R for red, G for green, and B for blue. Just as you mix different colors of Play-Doh to come up with different colors, you vary the amount of the red, green, and blue to create custom colors in HTML.

Each of the color components range in value from 0 to 255, but you don't specify the color components as ordinary base 10 numbers. Instead, you must use the hexadecimal number system that computers rely on internally. The primary advantage to the hexadecimal approach is that it allows you to describe a complete color in six digits. The downside is that hexadecimal numbers are tricky to work with if you aren't a binary math whiz.

Following is an example of a hexadecimal number that identifies a simple color:

#FF00FF

Note

Unlike decimal numbers, hexadecimal numbers are described using a strange-looking combination of letters and numbers. Instead of numbering from 0 to 10, the hexadecimal system consists of numbers from 0 to F. Think of the letters A through F as continuing on from 9, in that A is 10, B is 11, and so on. So, if you're working with two-digit hexadecimal numbers, the lowest is 00, and the highest is FF.

Note that six digits follow the number symbol (#). The first two digits (FF) specify the hexadecimal value of the red component of the color, the second two digits (00) specify the value of the green color component. The final two digits (FF) identify the value of the blue color component. The actual color described by this number is fuchsia. Because the hexadecimal value 00 represents the lowest value a two-digit hexadecimal number can have, and FF represents the highest value, you can learn a great deal about HTML colors by examining the RGB values of the standard HTML colors:

Table C-1.   RGB Values of Standard HTML Colors

Color	Value
white	#FFFFFF
black	#000000
red	#FF0000
lime	#00FF00
blue	#0000FF
yellow	#FFFF00
aqua	#00FFFF
fuchsia	#FF00FF
green	#008000
silver	#C0C0C0
gray	#808080
maroon	#800000
olive	#808000
navy	#000080
purple	#800080
teal	#008080

The first colors in this list are easy to figure out, because you can see how the maximum and minimum hexadecimal values are used for each color component. As the list goes on, it's tougher to visualize the colors. But, this is still a good way to learn how to create custom colors of your own. Start with a known color in the list and experiment by tweaking the hexadecimal values for each of its color components.

To specify a custom color on a Web page, use the hexadecimal value preceded by the number symbol:

```
<body bgcolor="#1100FF">
```

Similarly, the following code shows a custom color used in a style property:

```
<p style="color:#1100FF">
```

You now know how to move beyond the standard HTML colors and create custom colors for your own Web pages.

Index

<> (angle brackets), 7
3DML, 146

Absolute paths
  of image URLs, 40–41
  relative path distinguished from, 40
absolute positioning, 210–213, 240
accesskey attribute, 121
action attribute, <form> tag, 99–100, 102,
  112–113
active, as hyperlink state, 187
Adobe Acrobat files, 124
Adobe GoLive, 154
Adobe Photoshop, 152
align attribute
  <embed> tag, 133
  <img> tag, 44–46
    values for, 45
  <p> tag, 9, 25–26
  <table> tag, 86
alignment
  of tables, 86–88
  of text, 202–204
    aligning images with surrounding text,
    44
Alignment Styles Web page example, 204
Allaire HomeSite, 155, 156
alt attribute
  <area> tag, 73
  <img> tag, 41–42, 326–327
alternate text, 41–42
America Online (AOL), 18
anchor hyperlinks, 59–62

anchor tag. *See* <a> tag
<!-- and --> (comment delimiters), 35
angle brackets (<>), 7
animated ad banner (example Web page),
  242–244
animated images, 50
  GIF, 39
animation, definition of, 39
AOL (America Online), 18
<area> tag, image maps and, 72–73
.asx metafiles, 145
<a> tag, 11, 14, 47, 56–62
  hyperlink states and, 187
  linking to other resources with, 57
  linking to Web pages with, 57
attributes, 10–11
  converting to XHTML and, 323, 326–
  327
  definition of, 9
  event, 232–233
  lowercase for, 10
  required, 11
autostart attribute, <embed> tag, 132,
  138–139

Background attribute, 48, 49, 92
background-color property, 198, 199
background-image property, 198, 199
background images, 48–50
  for a paragraph of text, 198–199
  for tables, 92
background property, 199
background-repeat property, 198–199

Michael Morrison

is a writer, developer, toy inventor, and author of a variety of computer technology books and interactive Web-based courses. In addition to his primary profession as a writer and technical consultant, Michael is the creative lead at Gas Hound Games, a game company he co-founded with his wife and two close friends. Gas Hound's first commercial debut is *Inc. The Game of Business*, a fast-paced financial board game based on starting and growing businesses. When not glued to his computer, playing hockey, skateboarding, mountain bike racing, or watching movies with his wife, Masheed, Michael enjoys hanging out by his koi pond.

The manuscript for this book was prepared and galleyed using Microsoft Word 2000. Pages were composed by Helios Productions using Adobe PageMaker 6.52 for Windows, with text in AGaramond and display type in Garamond Condensed. Composed pages were delivered to the printer as electronic prepress files.

Cover Designer:	Tom Draper Design
Interior Graphic Designer:	James D. Kramer
Principal Compositor:	Sybil Ihrig, Helios Productions
Principal Proofreaders:	Deborah O. Stockton, J. Scott Strayer
Indexer:	Maro Riofrancos, Riofrancos & Co. Indexes

Your *fast-facts*
guide
to **digital imaging**
and your PC

U.S.A. **$12.99**
U.K. £9.99
Canada $18.99
ISBN: 0-7356-1012-6

Picture yourself creating amazing digital images for print, e-mail, and the Web with DIGITAL SCANNING AND PHOTOGRAPHY. Best-selling author Dan Gookin makes it easy to get started with the tools and how-tos for digital imaging on your home computer. Dan offers friendly, expert advice for matching the right scanner, digital camera, and software to your needs. And he shows you—with fun tips and easy-to-follow steps—how to take, scan, photo-edit, print, and e-mail digital pictures right now!

Microsoft®

mspress.microsoft.com

If you can plug *in a* PC, *you can* build *your own* home network!

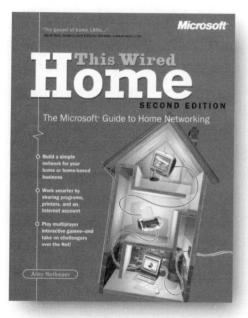